THE DREAM

MESSENGER

How Dreams of the Departed
Bring Healing Gifts

Patricia Garfield, Ph.D.

SIMON & SCHUSTER

SIMON & SCHUSTER
Rockefeller Center
1230 Avenue of the Americas
New York, NY 10020

Designed by Richard Oriolo

Manufactured in the United States of America

10   9   8   7   6   5   4   3   2   1

Library of Congress Cataloging-in-Publication Data

Garfield, Patricia
The dream messenger : how dreams of the departed bring healing
gifts / Patricia Garfield.
p.   cm.
Includes bibliographical references.
1. Death in dreams.   I. Title.
BF1099.D4G   1997
154.6'32—dc21   96-43396
CIP
ISBN 0-684-81359-9

Acknowledgments

Two women in particular have my special thanks for their contributions to this book. Friend and colleague Marcia Hilton first supplied the idea for it years ago. Her work as a grief support counselor at Sacred Heart Hospital in Eugene, Oregon, led her to realize how much a book on dreams and grief was needed. Marcia's helpfulness and access to her groups showed me first hand the importance of grief support and the role of dreams in bereavement.

Patricia Keelin, another colleague and friend, also made a journey of a few years to Oregon, as I did. Inspired by her reaction to the death of her brother, Keelin (as she's called) wanted to write an anthology of dreams about people who had died. Independent of each other, we gathered material on the same topic. When she learned that I was in the area and working on the identical issue, Keelin contacted me and offered her material.

Keelin and Marcia, I'm most grateful for your generosity and friendship. Thanks, too, to Campbell Senior Center, in Eugene, for providing an interview room for volunteers to the study, as well as for hosting a lively folk dance group that helped sustain my energy.

Several members of the Association for the Study of Dreams opened their dream journals to locate records of their dreams after a loss. Special appreciation to Joanne Rochon, Ernest Hartmann, and Claire Sylvia; also to Alan Siegel and Kelly Bulkeley, whose books, in unfinished or final form, added unique examples.

Katinka Matson, my agent at John Brockman, upheld and encouraged the project. My editor at Simon & Schuster, Sydny Miner, who "inherited" the manuscript from a predecessor, faithfully carried it forward to completion. I value you both.

Dreamers everywhere shed a tear and shared a dream. Each gave so abundantly that I was able to use only a fraction of the wonderful material. It's proved impossible to thank you all. To those who were missed, or unwillingly became anonymous in the text, thank you wherever you are. Your dreams will help others.

Family and friends have been unstinting in their support. Many in my inner circle told their stories of loved ones lost, and their return in dreams. Longtime friend Thomasine Kushner came up with the term "dream messenger" as we discussed my still-forming ideas; she also suggested the classic image of Mercury—the messenger of the gods—for the cover.

New friends emerged in the process of writing this book. Isabel Allende, in a perfect example of synchronicity, sat down beside me in an airport the very week I was studying her dreams about her deceased daughter Paula. We discovered our mutual joy in dreamlife and have continued the exchange ever since. Mary Winslow, who was referred to me as a person with an extraordinary dream about her deceased son Greg, became a firm friend whose help with the tedious job of galley reading I welcomed.

All lives of all ages are touched by death, whether it is my ten-year-old grandson Nick, who recalled the death of his orange and white cat, Casey, or three-year-old grandson Ryan, who, after a playmate's father had died from cancer, reported a dream that his own father died and he "couldn't talk with him anymore." Daughter Cheryl, step-daughters Wendy and Linda, stepson Steve, their mates and children, my mother Evelyn, my brother Fred, my godmother Kathryn Lee, my Aunt Twila—each had tales of grief to tell.

As Zal, my dear husband and best friend, accompanies me on life's journey, we witness the falling away of lives around us. Inevitably, we will join those who are gone.

Yet my life has been enriched with the writing of this book. I discovered that, truly, no one is without loss, but if we are lucky, our love lives on. Perhaps, too, our creations will endure. I hope the words in this book will bring you some of the nourishment that flowed into its creation. May the dreams recorded here inspire your own, and fill your nights with a balm that brightens your days. May you be blessed.

P.G.

August 31, 1996
San Francisco

To our lost loved ones,
whose shining presence
still speaks to us
when they visit our dreams

Contents

Introduction

M ost of us already have lost one or more loved persons. Survival leaves us facing the deaths of more family and friends around us. It's a lonely reality. No wonder we yearn to find a way to stay in touch.

Is death the end of communication with the person who died? The subject is on my mind because my husband turns seventy-seven this year, and I will soon be sixty-two, the same age at which my father suddenly died. My mother is eighty-seven and my dear godmother is ninety-one. Yet you don't have to be older to be dealing with loss. Must we lose these ancestral voices permanently?

The solution may be as near as our pillows. The pages that follow chart my voyage of exploration among dreams about the dead. You will find in them the pattern I uncovered that exists—a pattern I call the "universal dream about the dead," which is described for the first time in this book.

My lifelong work has been with dreams, as those of you who are familiar with it know. From my early adolescence, dinner table discussions initiated by my mother, who was then reading Sigmund Freud and Carl Jung, led to fledgling efforts to decipher the images in my always vivid dreams. When I was about fourteen, I began a dream journal that lasts to this day. Entries in 1948 were scattered, but by 1949, when I turned fifteen, they became consistent. For the forty-eight years since my fourteenth birthday, my dream journal has been constantly at bedside—almost a half-century of knocking at the door of dreams.

Through a first marriage, birthing a daughter, graduating from a Ph.D. program in clinical psychology, getting remarried, undertaking world travel, and professional work, my dream journals supported me in troublesome times and opened new vistas in glad ones.

Today the dream diaries fill six three-foot shelves in my bookcases, with over forty binders, and still more boxes of untranscribed notes. I can understand why Freud destroyed his dream journals, and why Jung kept records only from a four-year period of intense concentration on them. Yet, despite their massive nature, these volumes are a great resource for me, a kind of encyclopedia of my dream and waking lives through which I can recall any period of time by referring to the relevant yearbook. And so *your* dream records can be a resource for you.

In attempting to make sense of this mass of material, and to better understand the themes and motifs emerging in it, I began to write.

My first book was *Creative Dreaming,* published in 1974, a "best-seller" in print steadily since, and updated for a new edition in 1995. At the time it first appeared, the prevailing idea was that dreams could only be worked with by professionals. The average person might use their dreams for lottery numbers, but unless one was in psychotherapy, little attention was paid to dreaming. Yet my own experience said otherwise. I had seen how my dreams changed with changes in my life circumstances, and when I was exposed to diverse cultures and styles of working with dreams. I knew it was possible to plan one's dreams, and to become active within them, as well as to work with the images afterward. In *Creative Dreaming* I told how to do these things. The book became a rapid best-seller throughout the country, and on the *Los Angeles Times* list. It has been published in more than nine foreign languages, including Japanese. Many people still tell me it altered their lives for the better. People appreciated being given access to their own dreams.

The public response was almost overwhelming. I went from being a relatively obscure college teacher of psychology, and classes on dreams, to appearing on national television shows, eventually including *To Tell the Truth;* ABC's *20/20* three times; *Good Morning America;* shows with Hugh Downs, Merv Griffin, Mike Douglas, Tom Snyder, and Lou Gordon; *The Home Show* with Gary Collins; Cable News Network; NBC's *The Other Side;* and several special network productions on dreams. I made foreign appearances with the BBC, and on Scottish, Canadian, French, and German television and radio shows. Local TV, magazine articles, and newspaper articles were too numerous to count. This semicelebrity status seemed almost a dreamlike experience itself.

Perhaps this is why my second book, *Pathway to Ecstasy: The Way of the Dream Mandala,* in 1979, was more introspective. I needed a retreat to the world of dreams and soul that nourishes me. In it, I wrote about lucid dreaming and meditation, and I made fifty Chinese brush paintings illustrating dream images. This book found a narrower, but devoted, audience, and was republished in 1989.

Three other books followed: *Your Child's Dreams,* in 1984, summarized the most common nightmares and the happy themes I found in the dreams of children, along with their probable meanings, and guidance for coping with bad dreams. *Women's Bodies, Women's Dreams,* in 1988, examined the patterns in normal women's dreams throughout the life cycle. Then, *The Healing Power of Dreams,* in 1991, tracked how dreams warn us when our health is at risk, diagnose incipient physical problems, support us during physical crisis, forecast our recuperation, suggest treatment, help heal us, and signal return to wellness.

That concise history of my work brings us to the current *The Dream Messenger.* From illness to death can be a short step. We turn, in this book, from what happens when health is recovered to what happens after a person dies.

You will see revealed here the types of dreams people have about the dead; the "messages" that are conveyed in them; suggestions for possible responses you may wish to make; the typical symbolism in dreams about the dead; how your dreams assist you to accomplish the tasks of grief; and how they may nurture your waking life. I have found it so.

Before reading about how you might best benefit from the book, you may be interested in the sources of the material it is based upon.

Subjects for This Study

You will find that the main part of the book deals with dreams in which the image of the dead person directly appears. I drew from five sources of bereavement dreams:

1. *In-depth interviews with fourteen bereaved women.*
   This group of women, between the ages of twenty-two and sixty-four, lived in a medium-sized town in Oregon. They volunteered in response to a newspaper article about me that mentioned I was studying dreams about the dead. The average interview lasted two hours, plus numerous follow-up dream reports by letter. One subject contributed over fifty dreams, but I set a limit to those used for tabulation of six dreams per subject. With this limit, forty-nine dreams about the dead were collected, plus seven symbolic dreams about them, over the course of one year.
2. *Participants in bereavement support groups in Oregon, principally those run by Marcia Hilton.*
   Hilton kindly invited me to attend her bereavement support groups held at Sacred Heart Hospital in Eugene, Oregon. Participants there, along with those from other organizations, as well as individuals who heard that I was working with this material, informally volunteered their dreams about the dead.
3. *A collection of dreams about the dead from Patricia Keelin.*
   Keelin, who also had planned to write in this area, advertised in various journals for contributors to an anthology. She obtained answers from over one hundred people. Ulti-

mately, Keelin was unable to proceed with her planned work and generously offered the material to me so that it might not languish. I am grateful for her bountiful gesture and to those who shared their dreams with her and, eventually, me. When premonition dreams, dreams about the death of a pet, and incomplete or secondhand dream accounts were eliminated, there remained one hundred subjects (eighty-two female and eighteen male), with 186 bereavement dreams. Most were from women (159 dreams); a few were from men (27 dreams).

4. *My personal dream journal.*
   Dreams from the first two years after my father's death were extracted from the forty-eight-year record. This sample consisted of twenty-six dreams in which his image was present, and eighteen dreams in which he was mentioned, for a total of forty-four bereavement dreams. Additionally, several symbolic dreams about his death from this same period were examined.

5. *Published accounts of dreams about the dead.*
   Several contemporary writers tell their own dreams following a death. Writers through the ages have traced their own struggles with mourning. In classical literature, too, I found descriptions of the dreams of Roman emperors and Greek heroes. Sacred literature in various cultures likewise contains dreams about the dead. These varied reports enriched those I had collected, underscoring certain themes and adding others.

Combining the dreams in the first four units yielded a group of about four hundred dreams. Since I gathered these samples, I've been invited to speak on the topic to the Association for the Study of Dreams, at meetings in Leiden, the Netherlands, and in New York, leading to an avalanche of further contributions. The present collection is approximately one thousand dreams about the dead.

My investigation into this hefty collection will help you understand your dreams about the dead. The vast volume of dreams during grief suggests the importance of this mysterious territory to us all.

How to Use This Book

If you have been recently bereaved, you may not feel up to reading this entire book at the moment. In such a case, turning to the last chapter, "Your Personal Dream Journey," is a good way to begin. There you will find activities and visualizations related to dreams that will help guide you through the grief process. Reading the first chapter, "The Journey of the Dream Messenger," will give you a good orientation to the pattern of dream messages you are likely to encounter. If you wish, you can postpone the chapters in between the first and last until you feel ready, or until you have a dream that is explicitly explored.

If you already have begun to dream about the person who died, you may wish to turn directly to the chapter that deals with the closest approximation to one of your dreams. Dipping into the book to see what messages match your dreams may give you the most immediate guidance.

You may be a person whose loss occurred some time ago but whose wounds from it remain raw and aching. A good approach is to read a chapter at a time, in order, and then, as you finish each chapter, to turn to the last chapter and do the related exercises.

Perhaps you have lost a person and found great consolation in a dream about them. You may prefer to look for confirmation of the types of dreams you have had. Reassuring yourself that others have had similar experiences can bring further solace. Reading the book straight through might be for you.

If you have not yet had a significant death among your family or friends but know it is inevitable, reading this book and seeing how I classify dream messages will help prepare you to cope more effectively with the future.

In all cases, you should find the definitions given for individual dream messages useful. In order to make these easy to locate, I have placed them within bordered boxes. Each definition follows a specific form: the class of dream message is given; the dream about the dead is briefly described; its frequency or importance is commented upon; and finally, the reaction the dreamer usually has after awakening is identified.

No classification of dream messages can be complete. I have defined and described the most frequent and the most essential to know about. You may dream up others. Even so, you will probably find dream messages in this book that are similar enough to your own to assist you.

The next-to-the-last chapter, "Nine Major Symbols in Dreams About the Dead," sets forth the images every dreamer should be familiar with in dreams during mourning. For each symbol, meanings are explained. You will learn to recognize and comprehend the implications of these images.

You will probably want to record your dreams—if you do not do so already—while reading this book. I hope you will carry out the suggested activities and visualizations, not just read about them. You may well make personal discoveries, and come to new understandings, as a result of doing them. Many people have.

A personal confession: I had a superstitious fear about writing this book. Perhaps someone close to me would die, or I myself. It's strange to recollect, now that the book is done. Death has been a taboo topic for ages. What I came to realize—odd as this may sound—is that we all die. Every single person living today will die. Indeed, there have been many deaths during the years I wrote, among my more distant family and friends. Like the woman in the Buddhist tale who was grieving over her son's death and was sent by a saint to collect a mustard seed from each home where there had never been a death, I learned something. She returned empty-handed, but full of an understanding heart. Death touches us all.

What is crucial is maintaining the connection. Those we love live on so long as we remember them, so long as we say their names, so long as we see their faces in our dreams. Is this not a kind of immortality?

The dead have something to say to us in dreams. And we have responses to give. We need to hear these ancestral voices, to remember them, to honor them, to bless them . . . and allow their blessing to flow into our lives. In our turn, we may well inhabit the dreams of those generations that follow us.

1

The Journey of the Dream Messenger

The people we love—or hate—will eventually die, and so will we. Whichever comes first, our death or theirs, the direct contact is broken. Most of us have already lost loved ones, as I did with my father, who died suddenly at the age of sixty-two. Sooner or later, all of us will have to endure the trauma of the death of a significant person in our lives.

Is death the end of communication with the deceased? Folk traditions hold that our ancestors and lost loved ones speak to us through dreams. Some cultures and religions that assert an afterlife say the dead become guardian angels, even gods; still others think of the deceased as lost souls gradually working their way toward a higher level of existence; yet others claim there is nothing beyond—dead is dead and that's the end of it.

Regardless of your beliefs about whether there is an afterlife or not, one thing is certain: you will dream about the person who has recently died.

Are these dream images of the dead simply memories of them, infused by our imagination, to help us cope with grief during bereavement? Are they part of an internal process we employ to adjust to loss and assist us in solving daily problems? Or are dream images of the dead actual encounters with the spirit of the deceased? Elisabeth Kübler-Ross thinks they are, calling dreams about the dead "true contacts on a spiritual plane."[1]

There is no way yet known to prove either position: that dreams about the dead are "real" contacts, or that they are images conjured by the dreamer to meet psychological needs. Regardless of what may be the facts, we know that bereaved people dream about the lost person, that their dreams are exceptionally vivid, emotionally packed, and may dramatically alter the life and belief system of the dreamer.

Our relationship with the dead is eternal. In our dreams, the dead have messages for the living. The living also have messages for the dead that can be delivered in dreams. Conflicts left pending when the death occurred can sometimes find resolution in the meeting place of the dream world.

This book will help you understand the nature of these dream exchanges with images of the dead. You will learn what are the most typical dreams about the dead, which dreams are rare, and how all of them influence your life. You will find guidance for enriching the relationship that still exists between you and the person who has died. You will learn the meaning of the most common symbols occurring in dreams about death, and you will get practical techniques for benefiting from your dreams about the dead in such a way as to nourish your waking life.

First, however, it is essential to have some sense of the usual phases of grief. If this topic is familiar to you, you may wish to skip the next section and move directly to the section captioned "The Universal Dream about the Dead."

The Seasons of Grief

If you have been recently bereaved, you don't need a grief expert to tell you that your sleep is likely to be disturbed for some period of time and that you may well suffer from nightmares. This is a normal response reported by most researchers in the area of grief.[2]

Despite the fact that grief experts know disturbed sleep and dreaming is probable, only a very few of them describe the nature of these distressing dreams, offer guidance in coping with them, or demonstrate how dreams change throughout the course of mourning.[3]

Let's look briefly at the phases of grief.[4] Although they are given different labels and various numbers of stages by assorted investigators, there is an overall agreement that bereavement consists of at least three basic parts:

- Numbness

- Disorganization

- Reorganization

Numbness

The first phase of grief, numbness, is characterized by shock or even outright denial of the death. Many survivors have almost no recall of the funeral or who was present following a death. Other survivors see everything vividly, but as though they were observing things from a distance. Some refuse to believe that the death has taken place. Survivors almost always feel dazed and exhausted. Everything around them seems unreal.

Don't be surprised if you seem to feel nothing at first. This numbness and "distancing" is actually a natural protective mechanism to allow survivors time to absorb the reality of what has happened before descending into the depths of their reactions to it.

Disorganization

In the second phase of grief, disorganization, there is emotional chaos. The survivor usually feels anxious, afraid, grieved, angry, depressed, and/or anguished. Other common feelings include guilt, relief, restlessness, or behavior that suggests searching for the deceased. In cases of sudden death, the response of shock may last for a long time. In violent deaths, survivors may experience hatred, horror, revulsion, or obsessive desire for revenge.

Feelings swing wildly during this time, periods of normality alternating with depths of agony or depression. Many survivors suffer physical pain or fear that they are going crazy. Yet all these reactions are part of the necessary process.

Those people who repress their emotional responses at this stage, who seem to be handling things so well, are setting themselves up for "freezing" all their feelings for years to come. A delayed response to grief can be even more extreme when it hits. Meanwhile, the survivor may have lost years of living.

Painful as your feelings about a death may be, allowing yourself to experience them and express them is the route to healing. Some grief counselors advise "leaning into the pain." It's the quickest way through.

Reorganization

In the third phase of grief, reorganization, survivors develop new roles, skills, and relationships, or resume former ones. New possibilities are glimpsed, new behaviors tested. Eventually, survivors find out how to readjust, treasuring memories of the deceased, while becoming able to emotionally reinvest in life.

These three phases are not discrete. Survivors move back and forth between them for as long as they need, like waves flowing forward and ebbing backward. Gradually, a new life emerges.

Your Tasks in Grief

You can help yourself emerge from the swamp of grief by fulfilling four "tasks," according to one of the leading grief experts.[5] J. William Worden believes that the person in mourning needs to encourage himself or herself to play a more active role in bereavement, rather than passively moving through phases of grief. He has evolved four tasks for the person who is grieving:

1. You need to accept the reality of your loss.
2. You need to work through the pain of your grief.
3. You need to adjust to an environment in which the deceased person is missing.
4. You need to emotionally "relocate" the deceased and move ahead with your life.

Obviously, a person requires time to accomplish these tasks, but you will see how it is here that our dreams about the dead are especially helpful.

Let's turn then to what dreams about the dead are like.

The Universal Dream About the Dead

By now, I have examined approximately one thousand dreams about the dead. (The sources of these dreams were described in the Introduction.) As I synthesized material from these hundreds of dreams, I discovered that they have a pattern. I realized that, like near-death experiences, dreams about the dead have several elements in common that take a particular form. These nine basic elements are described here for the first time.

I call the image of the deceased person the "dream messenger." The composite dream depicts the "journey of the dream messenger." Not every dream about the dead contains all nine elements, but most dreams about the dead have several of them. In brief, they are: (1) the announcement, (2) the arrival, (3) the appearance, age, condition, and clothing of the dream messenger, (4) the attendants, (5) the message, (6) the gift, (7) the farewell embrace, (8) the departure, and (9) the aftermath. What follows is an ideal or complete model of a dream about the dead.

This universal dream about the dead will help you understand your own dreams about them. The dead live on in our dreams long after they die. We see them, yearn for them, talk with them, love them, fear them, hate them, or hold them. Sooner or later, you will have some of these dreams. Perhaps you have already. Here's how it may transpire.

1. The Announcement

First of all, you are likely to sense that something unusual is coming. Dreamers describe feeling an anticipation, an odd awareness just prior to the signal predicting the imminent arrival of the dream messenger. (All the examples given throughout the book are from actual dreams about the dead.)

The announcement that the dream messenger is here occurs in a number of ways. You may hear:

- the front doorbell ringing

- a knock at the door

- the telephone jangle

- the screen door bang

- a shuffle in the hall

- a familiar cough

- someone calling out, "Your father is here!"

Other dreamers report seeing something first. You might observe:

- a door swinging open

- a beam of yellow light emerging from the ground

- a light at the end of a tunnel

- dappled sunlight against a white wall

Your presentiment might arrive through the sense of smell, as it did for some dreamers:

- catching a whiff of his cigarette

- sniffing the scent of his aftershave

Perhaps, like other dreamers, you will notice a cosmic event:

- the full moon rising above the "tree line"

- the earth moving out of orbit

- a new planet rising

By these various signs and sensations, an announcement is made that the border between the living and the dead is about to be temporarily suspended. In a way, these dream images parallel what mythologist Joseph Campbell has labeled "the call to adventure."[6] You—the hero or heroine of your dream—are about to have an adventure.

2. The Arrival at the Meeting Place

The announcement having been made, the dream messenger arrives in the dream. You may see the deceased:

- stepping through an open door into your living room

- entering an unlit hallway

- walking in an illuminated passage in a mall

- climbing a staircase

- riding an elevator or escalator up

- getting out of a car

- strolling down the street

Or you may observe the deceased at home, performing normal activities:

- sitting at the kitchen table talking with relatives

- playing cards with friends

- having a celebration feast with friends

- reading in a window seat

- lying in bed

You are just as likely to meet the deceased in an outdoor dream setting:

- walking in a grassy, green meadow
- in a garden filled with flowers or vegetables
- on the beach
- in a river
- at a fair
- in a valley, on a footpath going home

The encounter with the dream messenger often takes place in settings that involve transportation. You may bump into the deceased:

- in an airport in the waiting area
- riding a train
- on a bus
- in a boat on a foggy lake
- in a spaceship in space
- inside a cart in a "haunted house" ride

These transportation settings are places of transition that underscore the journey that is being undertaken by both the deceased and yourself.

Often the place where the dreamer meets the dream messenger has some barrier between the living and the dead. It may be a simple garden gate, a barrier at the airport, a glass partition, or some other boundary marker.

For a moment—through a door or a gate, in a hallway or a tunnel, in a room, a garden, a meadow, a station, or in outer space—the dreamer meets the dream messenger. You will find this element of a meeting place present in almost all of your dreams about the dead.

3. The Dream Messenger

Who is this dream messenger? The deceased, of course, but often the dead do not look exactly like themselves in dreams. Their appearance depends upon your feelings—your hopes and your fears—about the dead person, and upon the message that follows. Don't be surprised if the deceased has a different appearance.

Appearance: Ill or Transfigured

Do the dead look like themselves, or as you last saw them? Sometimes. But more often, you are likely to find the deceased looking much worse than they did, or completely changed for the better.

You can expect the dead in your dreams, especially if they died after a long or debilitating illness, to sometimes look much worse than they did while dying. Some dreamers reported seeing:

- my grandmother suffering terribly from cancer, with tumors popping up like mushrooms all over her body

- my mother lying in a bed, very weak, her face to the wall

- my dead father's face melting

- my dead friend looking like a skeleton, grotesque

- my husband very far off and thin like a soda cracker

- my husband's face in a mirror scribbled on and erased

Distasteful as these images are, they do help the dreamer accept that the death occurred. If you experience such images of the dead, don't be alarmed. It's quite common. They express your feelings of distress about the death. Later on, you are likely to see the person who has died in a much improved condition.

For example, several dreamers reported the dream messenger appearing radiantly transformed:

- My lover looks so beautiful, his eyes sparkling, smiling, all the pain and sadness gone.

- My brother has the most healthy, beautiful tan, looking really good.

- My grandmother wears a light lavender gown, her hair is up, white and glowing, she's just beautiful.

- My grandfather's eyes are radiant with peace and love.

- My mother is sitting in the grave in her favorite rocking chair, knitting, rocking, and humming.

- My dad is healthy and young, vibrant like I've never seen him before, except in old sepia photos, smiling, his face alight.

- My mom is revitalized and youthful—she talks with joy and wonder and peace.

These positive dream images of the dead make the dreamer very happy. They seem to convey a spirit at peace, and give hope to the dreamer for a joyful afterlife.

You will be most likely to dream of meeting the dream messenger looking radiantly transformed when you are beginning to recover from loss. Eventually these glowing images emerge.

Age: Younger or Older

When the dream messenger appears in resplendent guise in your dreams, he or she is frequently depicted as younger and healthier than when death occurred. Those people who died in their older years shift their dream shapes into the prime of life. We have seen a few examples of this and will come across several more.

If the person who has died is immature, dreamers often meet the messenger looking older. For instance, some dreamers reported:

- My stillborn daughter looks two years old, wearing a pretty green dress with ruffled petticoat, her chubby legs showing.

- My little boy [miscarried at six months] is running happily, playing baseball in a golden field with his father.

Dreamers found these poignant images comforting. Believing that the lost child was continuing to exist on some plane gave great solace. You, too, may find it so.

Infirmities: Present or Vanished

Another element numerous dreamers find consoling is that the dead often appear without their infirmities. One dreamer, for instance, said:

- My dead father's voice on the telephone sounds clear and normal (he had had his larynx removed and spoke in guttural tones); he says, "I'm whole again, they gave me back my voice."

Many dreamers mentioned seeing the dead who were wheelchair-bound or walked with a cane now able to move about normally. The blind were able to see, the lame to walk. Whatever limitations had been present due to illness or old age had evaporated. This aspect, too, brought inspiration. Watch for it in your dreams.

Clothing: Shabby or Shining

You are almost certain to notice changes in the dream messenger's face, hair, or clothing. This aspect arose consistently. You might see, as several dreamers did:

- my mom wearing a shimmering white gown, her long black hair flowing around her face and down her shoulders

- my dead friend wearing a graceful white satin nightgown

- my father in a white robe surrounded by brilliant white light expanding to purple mist

- my murdered friend wearing a beautiful wreath of flowers, looking radiant

"Radiant" is the adjective most frequently used by dreamers to describe the dead in dreams about them during the latter phases of mourning. Luminosity often emanates from sparkling eyes, shining hair, light-colored clothing, gleaming jewelry, and brilliant lights. This illumination seems to represent a transfigured condition in the deceased, and when present, invariably indicates positive emotions about the dream. You can anticipate glorious light in your later dreams about the dead.

4. The Attendants of the Dream Messenger

Most of your dreams about the dead will contain the deceased and yourself. However, some dreamers see the dead accompanied by deceased family members or other deceased people known to the dreamer.

Only a very few dreamers reported images of strangers in their dreams who seemed to represent death personified:

- A tall man in a black three-piece suit follows my friend.

- A shadowy figure goes down the dark hall.

- A hideous old woman, small, skinny, dressed in a tattered black dress, enters the sickroom.

- I catch a glimpse of Death, a gaunt man in a carriage, waiting.

What is one to make of these "attendants"? Are they part of the "death party," as one might be part of a wedding party? Joseph Campbell might say they are some kind of border guardians. In any case, if they appear in your dreams about the dead, they need give you no cause for alarm. They are pictures of your feelings about death and the threat it represents.

When you meet your dream messenger, with or without attendants, the threshold between the living and the dead has been crossed.

Look carefully at the dead, their facial expressions, their ages, conditions, and clothing—each aspect conveys clues to the messages they bring to you.

5. The Dream Message Delivered

Here we come to the heart of dreams about the dead. What messages do they bring the living, and in what form are they brought? The bulk of the remainder of this book will set forth these messages in detail. For now, we'll take a quick overview.

Forms of the Dream Message

First of all, you need to be aware that dream messages may be delivered in a variety of forms. You might get yours:

- by telephone
- by letter
- on a bulletin board
- on an answering machine
- by fax
- on a computer screen
- in person

The majority of dream messengers deliver their message in person—we might better say "in spirit," if that is our persuasion. If you prefer a psychological explanation, you might say that the dreamer delivers a message to himself or herself in the image of the deceased person.

Some of these messages are spoken in the dream; others are conveyed "mentally." Without words, the dreamer understands what the dream messenger intends to communicate. Still other messages are understood by the actions within the dream, the mood expressed in it, and the "aftertaste" that lingers when you awake. Stay open to all these routes of communication.

Even if you do dream directly about the person who died, you may also dream of getting a telephone call from that person. When dream messages are not delivered by the image of the deceased, the next most common method is the receipt of a telephone call from the dead.

Dreams of telephone calls are more common in bereavement dreams than in general dreams (three percent).[7] In my dreams in which my dead father appeared, twelve percent of them contained telephone calls. Dream researcher Deirdre Barrett reported that fifty-three precent of the category she called "state-of-death" dreams involved telephone calls from the deceased, while telephone calls in her other categories appeared in twenty-four percent of the dreams about the dead. Accounts of apparitions of the dead often involve telephone calls, too.[8]

Modern equipment—answering and facsimile machines, computers—takes its place in dream messages from the dead, as it did for the man who dreamed his deceased father left a garbled message on his answering machine. He commented, "I never did understand that man."

Receiving a telephone call from the deceased, making a call, getting a letter, or finding a message on a bulletin board or on an answering machine—these appear to be metaphors for communication with the spirit of the dead person. These dream motifs may help you accept the reality of the death, may give you confidence that communication with the dead person is intact, and may reassure you that your person is at peace.

Negative Dream Messages

Turning to the contents of the message, I'll summarize here a few of the most frequent. You will find these categories and others expanded throughout the book. All of them are ones I have observed and designated with original labels.

"I'm Suffering"

Don't be startled if you experience some extremely unpleasant dreams about the dead at first. It is very common to see the deceased once again suffering the symptoms that caused death, either as they were in actuality, somewhat exaggerated, or grossly distorted.

Especially if you were present at the death, or if the circumstances were sudden or violent, you are likely to "replay" the death scene. This type of nightmare is characteristic of the post-traumatic nightmares that follow violence or personal injury.[9] Among the dreams I had about my deceased father, who died suddenly, fifteen percent involved his suffering or dying again.

At times, the replay of the event is far worse than the original, as we saw in the dreams where the dream messenger was severely disfigured in appearance.

This frequent dream message may take other forms, including the dead person appearing and complaining of hunger, searching for his or her grave, or struggling to get into heaven. In these, the deceased becomes like the "hungry ghosts" in some cultures who are said to wander about in need of food or resting places.

If the dream messenger should deliver to you the message "I'm Suffering," you are being helped in the first task of grief, accepting the reality of the death, and in the second task, expressing the painful emotions of grief. These objectives must be accomplished in what Freud called "the work of mourning."[10]

When grief is not resolved, "I'm Suffering" nightmares may continue for a long time. As with other post-traumatic nightmares, replaying the event helps desensitize the survivor to it, eventually allowing him or her to bear the unbearable.

"I'm Not Really Dead"

Another very common dream message you may receive is "I'm Not Really Dead," in which you see the person who has died, but the death is explained away as a mistake. You may not realize during the dream that the person is actually dead, or you may be startled, even shocked, to see them. This dream motif is characteristic of the early stages of loss.[11]

You may find yourself dumbfounded to see the person again, or just plain puzzled, as some dreamers were:

- Suddenly my husband walks into the kitchen looking just as he always did. I am astonished. I run to him, hug him, and am ecstatic that he is alive.

- I am very surprised to see my mother alive. I ask, "But didn't we hold a funeral for you?" She replies, "Yes, but I don't want anyone to know, so don't tell."

- I am astounded to see my dead uncle again, singing, laughing, and making jokes; I say, "My God, what are you doing here? You're dead!" He smiles and replies, "Honey, when you die, you lose your body, not your sense of humor."

The amount of humor in these dreams surprised me. It seemed to arise especially when it was typical of the deceased.

You may find yourself angered by the appearance of the deceased in a dream, as some dreamers were:

- I see my wife playing cards with her cronies. I am furious with her and want to berate her for "all the trouble you put me through when you were actually out having a good time."

- I see my husband walking down the street in another part of town, moving into an apartment. He's dyed his hair to disguise his appearance. He only pretended to die. I am very angry.

The dreamer seems to be saying, in such dreams of aggravation, that it would be better to have the death be a trick than to have it be a reality. One of the unexpected but usual reactions during mourning is an anger at the deceased for "deserting me." This feeling finds expression in dreams of being deceived into thinking the person was dead when they were not. In waking up, of course, one has to face the loss all over again.

If your person died violently, you may find his or her appearance in early dreams about the person agonizing. A young widow, whose husband had recently died after having his chest crushed in an industrial accident, told me her nightmare about seeing him wearing a navy coat and moving stiffly toward her, "almost not alive." In another disturbing dream she saw him "very far off, and thin, like a soda cracker," and in yet another she saw his face "in a mirror, scribbled on and erased." These nightmares about her husband were so unsettling that she ceased dreaming about him directly and began to substitute the image of a fish caught on a hook, and other negative scenarios that were more tolerable.

Such dreams evoking terror in the survivor echo the fear of ghosts common in past times. They also reflect the sense of distortion and unreality that follow traumatic deaths.

In general, if you receive a dream message that "I'm Not Really Dead," you are probably wishing that were the case. With brutal deaths, you may fear that the dead person's spirit is still suffering. Excruciating as these dreams may be, they do help you accept the reality of the person's loss. Be assured that these dreams are common ones, and, although they may temporarily enhance your grief, they are still part of the recovery process.

Other negative dream messages include: "You Fool!"; "You'll Be Sorry!"; "Join Me!"; "Your Turn Is Coming"; and "Avenge My Murder." We'll explore their meanings throughout this book.

Positive Dream Messages

Turning to some of the satisfying and uplifting dreams you may have about the dead, there are two that are most frequent.

"I'm O.K."

By far, the most prevalent positive dream message you are likely to receive is "I'm O.K." In these dreams, you will meet the dead looking or acting as they did when young or healthy. This message is where the clothing of the dead is often flowing or shimmering, their hair glowing, their eyes sparkly and faces bright. If the individual who died was a fetus or infant, the dream image will be a few years older, looking outstandingly well.

This message has a number of variations in precise form, such as "Everything's All Right," "I'm Fine," "Don't Worry About Me," and so forth. You may not get the message delivered in so many words. Rather, you might sense from the jubilant content of the dream action, or the emotions evoked in you by the dream messenger, that "so-and-so came to let me know he or she was all right."

"Goodbye"

Another exceedingly typical dream message you might get is "Goodbye." In this instance, you will see the dead person specifically take leave of you, saying in words or by mental communication, "Goodbye," "Farewell," or "I have to leave now."

Again, exact words may not be specified, but you will "know" during the dream or after you awaken that "so-and-so came to say goodbye to me."

These dreams often include physical contact, and the exchange of loving comments, as well as an affectionate goodbye.

The dream message "Goodbye" is a classic. It has been reported over and over again in literature, usually when a death has taken place at a distance from the dreamer, or is sudden or vicious.

You can also expect a "Goodbye" dream message to be delivered when you have been deprived of a chance to say goodbye in person. Sometimes people claim this message arrives in a waking state, with the deceased appearing at the foot, head, or side of the survivor's bed. This dream message is often thought to involve extrasensory perception, as the dream may occur simultaneously with the death. In parapsychological writings, it is the most commonly reported telepathic experience and is referred to as a "crisis apparition."

Other positive dream messages include: "Here's a Gift"; "Congratulations"; "Stop!"; "Go Ahead!"; "Please Forgive Me"; "I Forgive You"; "I'm Evolving"; "I'm Being Reborn"; and "I Give You Life." We explore several examples of these, as well as "Goodbye" and "I'm O.K." in the pages to come.

Neutral Dream Messages

"Hi! How Are You?"

As you enter the latter stages of bereavement, and perhaps sporadically throughout the remainder of your life, you may find yourself receiving a friendly visit from the dream messenger. At this point, your dreams about the dead are no longer likely to be filled with negative images or even illuminated with brilliant ones. The meetings with the dead seem less like a direct encounter and more like a casual visit, with the dream action centered elsewhere.

One dreamer, for instance, made an introduction at a party, saying, "This is my brother who died six months ago (it was actually three years). He comes for a visit every once in a while." The dreamer felt her brother was just trying to tell her he was around, checking on how she was doing.

You can expect that your later dreams about the deceased will show him or her performing routine actions, such as shopping, fishing, riding in a car, cooking, or other activities typical of the person. Or the dead may simply be present as part of the background. There is not a strong emotional charge to these dreams, but you may feel pleased to have seen the person.

This category of dreams about the dead is typically found when you have fulfilled the tasks of grieving and you return to your more usual dream style.

6. The Gift of the Dream Messenger

"Here's a Gift"

You may receive a concrete gift from the dream messenger in one of your dreams about the dead. Here's a sample of assorted "dream gifts" received from the hands of the deceased person:

- a white embossed covered plate, a Chinese urn and dragon
- a small bowl with a Mexican design (the next day the dreamer received an unexpected actual gift of a large amount of money from the deceased)
- a white Buddha brooch of beautiful translucent jade
- a cross on a necklace that belonged to the friend
- a corsage of greenery and delicate purple flowers
- a row of pink rosebushes

Most of these gifts represented love to the dreamer; one specifically symbolized artistic talent handed on from the deceased; another stood for forgiveness for the murder of the deceased. Several other extremely meaningful gifts to the dreamer were received from the dead, as you will see in Chapter 5. Gifts of love in words or images are especially comforting to the grieving dreamer.

If you should dream of getting a present from a dead person, and it is something desirable to you, honor it. If its meaning is not clear at the moment, study the image. Find something in your waking life that is a reasonable facsimile and ponder it until its meaning for you emerges. These gifts from the dead can be precious beyond all riches.

You may receive a unique dream message, especially designed for you.

7. The Farewell Embrace

Do the dreamer and the dead touch? This seems to depend upon your beliefs about "physical" contact with the deceased. You, like many dreamers, may find the embrace of the dream messenger the most important part of the meeting. Those who engaged in "one last hug" remembered it with joy for years afterward.

Or perhaps, like some dreamers, you may feel touching is an essential taboo because of the deceased's fragile state:

- He asked me not to touch him, since he was in a delicate condition and could fall apart easily; he was in a period of transition.

- She says not to touch her, that it's too soon, it would feel like a burn.

- The other person with him said, "You can't hug him because it will bring him back to this side," so we just stood there and smiled at each other.

Those dreamers that did embrace the dream messenger with hugs and kisses seemed to be especially consoled by the dream meeting, so unless you have real reservations about it, you may wish to open your arms and savor the departed person before saying goodbye.

8. The Departure of the Dream Messenger

After you have received your dream message, accepted the gift if one was bestowed, embraced the messenger or not, you will probably know the visit is over. The time for departure may be explicitly stated, as with:

- I have to go now!

- I can't stay long; I've only come to tell you that I'm O.K.

You may simply understand that the dead person's time is short. Or the dream action makes the end of the meeting apparent:

- He turned pale as a corpse and began to fade.

- The spaceship soared into space.

At times, the dream messenger orders the dreamer to return:

- You have to go back right now!

- You must get off the airplane at this stop!

The implication of being told to return seems to be that if the dreamer lingers longer, he or she will die too, or some other danger will ensue.

Whether the dream messenger departs or the dreamer awakens, the border between life and death is erected again. Folk beliefs, such as the idea that the ghost must return to the grave by midnight, underlie the concept that the encounter between the dreamer and the deceased occurs under specific conditions, for a limited time, and has a precise ending.

9. *The Aftermath of the Visit*

Your feelings after the departure of the dream messenger may vary widely, depending upon the nature of the message. Vast emotions may be unleashed. Numerous dreamers report awakening in tears. Here's a sampling:

- I felt so wonderful and happy; the pain in my heart had been kissed away, my suffering gone; I know I'll see him again; he came to say goodbye and it healed me . . . I've been blessed.

- The dream left me shaken for days afterward; his embrace communicated great love, acceptance, understanding, and appreciation; he was happy with my values and just loved me.

- I awoke in wonder; he tried to tell me that his death was O.K.; I was able to get on with my life.

- I no longer felt resentment; I was able to see him as a human being, not a tyrant.

- The dream helped me realize that we will all die; the time is not for us to know; that even though she was murdered, she was all right and there was an opportunity for spiritual growth in this.

· I felt he knew I loved him, that he loved me still, and we'd said goodbye, and he was peaceful.

· The dream of her served as an inspiration and a guide; by the questions she asked, she pointed me in the right direction.

You may not only find yourself solaced by your dream about the dead, but also feel deeply loved. You may find inspiration and new confidence in the reality of an afterlife. Perhaps you, like so many before you, will find your life transformed by a visit from the dream messenger. Then the journey of the dream messenger is finished.

Awaiting Your Visit from the Dream Messenger

What can you do to encourage a dream meeting with your missing person? Some primitive tribes still practice using the skull of an ancestor as a pillow, intending to hear their counsel in dreams. In ancient times, people literally slept upon the gravestone of the person who died, in hopes of dreaming about them. Edgar Allan Poe, who wrote,

> For the moon never beams without bringing me dreams
> Of the beautiful Annabel Lee;
> And the stars never rise but I feel the bright eyes
> Of the beautiful Annabel Lee;
> And so, all the night-tide, I lie down by the side
> Of my darling, my darling, my life and my bride,
> In the sepulcher there by the sea—
> In her tomb by the sounding sea,[12]

actually spent many nights sleeping upon the grave of his child bride, whom he called Annabel Lee in his poetry.[13] Other, less morbid practices include sleeping with a photograph of the dead person under the dreamer's pillow.

Deliberately evoking meetings—in dreams or otherwise—with the dead is regarded by some groups as dabbling with the occult and bordering on necromancy.

Perhaps the best policy is to remain open to the dreams about the dead that come to you. Welcome even the painful ones. Remember that they are ultimately healing. Engaging in certain rituals on special anniversaries is part of mourning practices in almost every religion. You may find some suggestions in the last chapter of this book useful for planning a rite of remembrance that honors the person who died. Many dreams about the dead arise spontaneously on an anniversary or another special date, so you can anticipate this happening for you.

When you do receive a positive message from the dead, it can become the basis for healing visualizations. Some dream messages from the dead also become the foundation of creative works that benefit society at large, as well as the dreamer.

Having received a dream message, you will want to ask yourself, "What is my response?" It may be:

- I love you too.

- Help me!

- Don't worry, I'll take care of so-and-so.

- Be at peace.

- I'll never forget you.

Visualizing the dream again, including your response, may pacify and pleasure you. In answering the dream messenger, we complete the cycle. Ideas for working with your dream messages appear in the last chapter.

The purpose of these activities and visualizations is to integrate the dream message into your waking life. By doing so, you preserve something from the life that was lost to give something to the lives to come. The wheel turns.

As we dreamers accompany our lost loved ones on the rite of passage through life's great mystery, dreams are our guiding star.

"I'm Suffering" and "I'm O.K."

Our most common dreams about the dead involve our fears and hopes for lost loved ones. The two most frequent dream messages from the dead I found were what I call "I'm Suffering" and "I'm O.K." You are almost certain to have dreams about one or the other or both of these messages. "I'm Suffering" depicts our fears that deceased spirits are in pain; "I'm O.K." portrays the hopeful assurance that they are well and at peace. We'll examine the more disturbing of these dreams first, but keep in mind that the second type nearly always eventually emerges.

"I'm Suffering"

Don't be alarmed if several of your early dreams about a deceased loved one involve images of that person suffering. These are quite normal in the survivor.

If you have watched your loved person undergo severe physical

> ## Dream Message: "I'm Suffering"
>
> Deceased is once again experiencing the symptoms that caused death: fairly realistic, exaggerated, or profoundly distorted.
>
> ## Frequency: Extremely common.
>
> Response after Awake: Dreamer feels distressed, even agonized, and may reexperience the anguish of loss.

deterioration prior to death, the emaciated body, flushed or swollen face, or other conditions you observed might be present in your dreams about the person soon after he or she dies.

If you witnessed a sudden or violent death, or a person you loved died tragically, the fatal scene may "rerun" in nightmares for some time. As with all traumatic experiences (such as a severe accident, a mugging, or a rape), a violent death characteristically shows up in nightmares, flashbacks, and other symptoms of post-traumatic stress. Even if you were not there when it happened, a brutal, unexpected death is likely to torment the dreamer in nightmares for a long time.

Agonizing, even excruciating as these nightmares may be, their dream images serve a positive purpose. Psychologists think that nightmares replaying a violent death are an attempt by the dreamer to cope with the trauma; it is healthier to dream about it than to cease dreaming altogether. (If you have witnessed a cruel death or lost a person close to you through violence, and have no dreams whatsoever, it's a good idea to seek professional help. It's far more typical to have repetitive bad dreams about the death. These, too, may require professional assistance to dispel.) Nightmares about a violent death help desensitize the survivor to it, eventually allowing him or her to bear the unbearable.

When the dream messenger delivers the message "I'm Suffering," unsettling as it may be, you are forced to accept—yet again—

the reality of the death. Expressing your painful emotions in dreams gradually helps resolve your grief.

If you have bad dreams about the suffering of a deceased person you love, remember that such dreams do gradually lessen and finally cease. You are likely to find that comforting and healing dreams about the person emerge in time.

Dream Replay of the Death Scene

Reenactment of the death scene is the most common form of the dream message "I'm Suffering." Many widows described to me disturbing dreams about their husband's dying, their desperate attempts to prevent it, and the futility of their efforts.

Man's Murdered Daughter Suffers Again

A psychiatrist in Seattle, Edward Rynearson, interviewed fifteen people in a local support group who had lost a person to homicide at least three years earlier.[1] One man, whose daughter had been murdered, reviewed the gruesome details in his nightmares. Although he had not witnessed the events, he knew what had taken place:

> Night after night in his dreams, he saw his daughter walking from the bus-stop to school. Powerless to cry out and protect her, he watched in agony as a man grabbed her and dragged her into a car. He saw the assailant tie her up, gag her, and drive her to an isolated house, where he raped her, beat her, and branded her with cigarettes . . . he would awaken gasping and screaming.[2]

Grief following the murder of a close family member or friend is far more intense than after deaths of older relatives that seem to be part of the normal course of life. Everyone in this bereavement support group reported violent, recurring nightmares. They frequently tried to save the victim in these dreams. They were tormented with waking fantasies, as well as nightmares, about killing the murderer.

Rynearson was able to help the man whose daughter was murdered to recall positive experiences with his child. Gradually the father's horrific nightmares diminished in frequency and intensity. He was finally able to dream of a reunion with his daughter. This kind of dream emerges as one begins to come to resolution with loss.

If you have suffered the devastating loss of a child, you know how torturous it can be. A parent may never fully recover from such an event, as in the case of the mother whose fifteen-year-old son was raped, tortured, and killed by a serial murderer. She still has nightmares about the death nearly two decades later. In her recurrent horror dream, she is sitting at home when there is a knock at the door; she opens it to find the murderer smiling at her. "He just stands there and says, 'I can get your son when I want him, and you can't hide him from me.'"[3] The distraught woman wakes up screaming, helpless. She hopes the killer's scheduled execution at San Quentin for the murders of her son and thirteen other young men and boys will end her nightmares.

For most parents of murdered children, the misery decreases and some consolation is eventually found. Support groups can help.[4]

Losing a spouse to violence can be almost as shattering as losing a child. A case that took place in San Francisco will show you how these dreadful nightmares can change for the better, even when the death was traumatic.

Michelle's Husband Dies in Murderous Rampage

Michelle and her husband, John, a young attorney, had been married less than a year when tragedy struck.

On the afternoon of July 1, 1993, John was at his law office at 101 California Street in San Francisco, when Michelle stopped by to visit him.[5] At that moment, a crazed gunman, who had briefly been a client of the firm, went on a rampage in the building. Armed with semiautomatic assault weapons, he raced through the thirty-second, thirty-third, and thirty-fourth floors shooting wildly. In fifteen minutes, he killed eight people—including John—and wounded six others before shooting himself to death.

Catastrophic for all concerned, the event left Michelle with tormenting guilt. Twenty-nine-year-old John had been in the part of the building where he was killed because he had accompanied her there. Furthermore, John had courageously thrust his wife behind him to shield her from the bloody slaughter. John died and Michelle lived. She was wounded in the right arm but her emotional wounds were worse.

At night Michelle relived the horror of that day:

For weeks, I had dreams of him lying on the ground after he was shot, the blood pouring from his mouth and nose.[6]

After months of treatment to regain use of her arm, psychotherapy, and consultation with a priest, Michelle's guilt and grief began to ease. About three months after the disaster, Michelle reported in a newspaper interview:

I'm getting better. In my last vision, he was holding me and we were kissing.[7]

Overcoming such a loss is a long, hard struggle. Michelle's initial dreams were typical replays of a trauma as the mind struggles to tolerate the intolerable. Being able to feel her husband's love and express her own in a dream of kissing him was an important step in her healing process. Eventually, Michelle became an advocate for nonviolence and handgun control.

Actively working on behalf of others who have suffered what you have or striving to prevent such suffering is a productive way to cope with personal grief.

Dream Distortion of the Death Scene

At times the replay of the traumatic event is worse than the original, weaving distortions into the dream image of the dead, as in the following cases.

Ruth's Father Turns into a Monster

When Ruth's eighty-year-old father was dying, he was weak, and "his mind started to go." She remembers one day trying to play chess with him—a game he always enjoyed—when suddenly he said, "Interesting . . . I can't remember the rules."

After his death, Ruth scarcely dreamed at all. She wrote a touching poem three weeks after her father's death that concludes:

> I put his picture
> by my pillow. I asked him
> to answer me, tonight, in dreams.
> I tucked myself, a little frightened,
> into bed, but all night
> no dreams came and I woke
> empty as ever.
>
> I still haven't cried
> for my father.[8]

When Ruth did begin to dream again, the first dreams about her father were "ghoulish." In them, his face would melt away and he resembled a monster. These images might have reflected Ruth's uncomfortable reaction to the changes in her father's mental capacity, as well as his physical deterioration. This dream reaction is not uncommon, as with another dreamer who reported watching her dead father turn into a monster after his slow, painful death from cancer. Yet another dreamer described seeing the howling face of a friend who had committed suicide. Distressing dreams of distortion like these are most common when the dying process is prolonged and the dreamer witnesses physical changes.

Luckily, like Michelle's, Ruth's later dreams of her lost loved person improved. Finally she had comforting and fulfilling dreams about him. You will see that these changes in dream content are the normal healing pattern.

Alice's Grandmother Grows Mushrooms

When Alice's grandmother underwent a drawn-out dying process from cancer of the abdomen, she was literally producing tumors in this area. For many months, Alice's mother helped care for the sick woman, whose body seemed to shrink as her abdomen swelled. After the grandmother's death, Alice had a most distressing dream in which she saw poisonous mushrooms popping up all over the grandmother's body.

Alice felt very connected to her grandmother, and the dreams about her dying replayed for a long time without reaching resolution. In a poem expressing her reactions to losing her grandmother, Alice concluded:

> *Grandmother, for nine years*
> *you have visited my dreams.*
> *I have watched you die*
> *over and again.*
>
> *Release me, I cannot let go*
> *this grief I failed to recognize*
> *your dying took so long.*[9]

Alice feels she still has work to do to sort out her grandmother's values from what are hers and what are not, to find her real identity. Her dream-based poetry assists her in the exploration.

New Suffering for the Deceased

"I'm Suffering" dreams sometimes take the form not only of replaying the death or distorting its symptoms, but also of inventing new pitfalls for the dead person. One woman reported this dream:

> *My husband rolls out from under the bed, tells me he hasn't eaten in a long time and is very hungry. I'm terribly distressed because I've no money for food.*

Her imagery involved a literal "hungry ghost."

In another case, the dreamer had made arrangements to have a tombstone erected over her mother's grave, yet the woman dreamed:

> *My mother is walking down a country road looking for a place to "hang her shingle."*

The dream amused yet puzzled her with the image of her mother's spirit in search of her resting place.

In yet another case, a man seemed to struggle with his uncertainty about an afterlife, resulting in an unusual kind of dream about his recently dead mother:

> *My mother (or I, probably she) has just died and is trying to get up into the sky on a sort of bouncing ball—hippity hop. And I think if there is a God, he'll notice and take her into heaven. If not, we'll just fall back and so what.*

These forms of new suffering seem relatively innocuous, but dreams can take horrific shapes, especially if the death has been brutal. New circumstances can aggravate an old wound.

Robert Samuel's Twin Brother Loses His Head

Robert Samuel's identical twin, Richard Daniel, hanged himself when he was a teenager. Some twenty years later, Robert has never fully recovered from the ghastly experience of finding his twin in a place known only to the two of them. Especially when he is happiest, the agony of that loss can reemerge.

A couple of evenings before his wedding, Robert Samuel told me the previous night's fearsome dream:

> *My fiancée and I were making a barbed wire enclosure around a group of unknown people. As we completed the circle, I saw Richard Daniel holding the end of the wire. He wrapped it around his neck and decapitated himself. Then the cut-off head said to me, "Now are you sorry?" I woke up distressed.*

Such literally "barbarous" imagery is more than a message of "I'm Suffering," although that is certainly part of the picture. Robert Samuel said, "I think I'm probably feeling guilty about being happy." Survivor guilt can be stifling. Death of an identical twin has maximum impact because of the bonding that makes the other seem like an extension of oneself.

Aside from the issue of twinness, how does one reconcile the right to happiness when a loved person has died in misery? It is a problem too many men and women are forced to face. Sometimes our dreams supply the solution, as you will see in the section "I'm O.K."

Fear of the Dead

There is more than sadness, sense of loss, and fears for our lost loved ones behind the nightmares after their deaths. Today, we seldom think of the dead as trying to harm us, unless we somehow caused the death, or feel responsible for it. We are not generally afraid of the dead cursing or injuring us. Yet people in olden times often regarded the dead as dangerous to the living. I suspect some of these ancient fears linger in contemporary dreamers' minds.

The expression "Rest in peace" (or the Latin words *Requiescat in pace*) is not a simple wish for the dead; it is also a heartfelt hope.

As long ago as Neanderthal times, seventy thousand years ago, the dead were buried with food—to keep their spirits happy—and with their bodies bound tightly by leather thongs—to keep their spirits in the tomb. The road from the graveyard was sometimes strewn with thorns to prevent the ghost walking home to the village. Worldly goods of the deceased were sometimes burned or buried to prevent the spirit of the dead from returning for desired belongings, thus haunting the vicinity.

Lost Souls by the Riverside

The ancient Greeks and Romans, too, thought it was necessary to provide for the souls of the dead. In their mythology, when the dead arrived in the underworld, the first thing they had to do was cross a swampy river in a ferryboat rowed by a sinister old man, Charon (his name means "fierce brightness").[10] In some accounts it is the river of woe or pain (Acheron) that must be traversed to reach Hades; in others it is the hateful river (Styx). The underworld region was described as a vast marsh crossed by several rivers with ominous names; in addition to the two mentioned, there was the river of groans (Cocytus), the river of fire (Phlegethon), and the river of forgetfulness (Lethe). Those who crossed over and reached Hades were judged by a tribunal, the guilty being sent to hell (Tartarus) and the elect to the Elysian fields.

The catch was that Charon charged a fee of a coin (penny, farthing, half-dollar, according to country and local custom) to carry the dead across the river. For this purpose, the dead person's relatives placed a coin underneath the corpse's tongue, between the teeth, or upon the eyelids, for the ferryman's toll.

Those poor souls who did not possess the fare to cross the river were abandoned to languish along the riverbank. The unburied dead also shared this dismal fate, stuck wandering on the shore, eternally lost. Some cultures say these lost souls suffer hunger and thirst that is never satisfied. These ideas spread and are still followed in certain areas of the world.

Ancient Greeks also believed it was important to "slake the thirst" of a ghost by pouring a cupful of wine over his or her gravestone. In India, folk traditions say that the goldfish is the favorite food of ghosts. Many cultures today still harbor beliefs that the ghost is hungry or thirsty and needs "spirit food," which is provided by relatives or religious officials at certain times and festivals for the dead.

The Vampire Myths

As anyone who reads the movie page of today's newspaper knows, the myth of the vampire is alive and well in twentieth-century America. Originating in European ideas of vengeful spirits, the notions of vampirism traveled with immigrants to the New World. In the case of vampires, the dead are thought to be hungry for blood. A recent examination of bodies in graveyards from the eighteenth and nineteenth centuries in New England showed that bodies of the dead were sometimes mutilated to prevent what was believed to be attacks from beyond the grave.

The basic idea behind all these practices was that the dead could come back and harm their families if their spirits were hungry, restless, or unhappy. This concept has led to the development of certain burial customs and rites, as well as to death festivals.

It is also the basis of dozens of horror movies about "revenants" (from the French word *revenir,* meaning "to come back") or "the undead." We can't help but be exposed to these ideas in films, books, and theater, and feel their emotional impact even if we intellectually reject them. Jung would say they are already a part of our collective unconscious. You need to be aware of these ideas and their origins because they sometimes arise in our dreams about the dead. They are not as alien as you might first think.

Folk Traditions About Revenants

According to folk traditions, a spirit may return from the grave:

- to complete unfinished business

- to warn or inform

- to punish or protect

- to impart information that couldn't be given before death

- to reenact its death

Violent deaths are said to produce vengeful ghosts. Victims of murder, suicides, those killed in accidents, those who die young or in childbirth, and those who remain unburied are said to return most frequently. The more unhappy the dying person, the more dangerous his or her spirit. Recently departed spirits are thought to envy the living. Correct burial rites are said to exorcise the spirit and protect the survivors. Mourning clothes may have originated as a warning to others that the person wearing them had been contaminated by contact with the dead. The shrouded and unattractive garb of mourners was also thought to make the survivors less appealing, so that the departed spirit would not become jealous of the living, and as a result, trouble them.

Various techniques have been used to put ghosts to rest, such as burning a haunted building. The building of funeral pyres in some parts of the world is believed to release the spirit directly, forcing it away from the body. Our word "bonfire" comes from Middle English words for a fire built to consume bones—a bone-fire—that would thwart dangerous returns. Perhaps the ghost may be satisfied when the unfinished business is complete, or when certain kindnesses have been done that put the spirit to rest.

A few of the folklore traditions depict the spirit of the deceased as kindly. The motif of "the grateful dead" refers to tales in which the hero encounters people mistreating a corpse. His compassion leads him to pay the deceased's debts or in some other way stop the mistreatment. Later in the tale, the hero is joined by a traveling companion who assists him on his journey. The unknown fellow traveler turns out to be the grateful ghost of the corpse he defended.

Odd as it may seem, many of these ancient ideas about unhappy or dangerous spirits, and elements from folk traditions, appear in modern-day dreams about the dead.

We can be thankful that beliefs from olden times about dead ancestors who guide, advise, and protect us also surface in our dreams, as you will see next.

"I'm O.K."

Dream Message: "I'm O.K."

Deceased appears looking younger and healthier, even radiant. If the individual died as a fetus, infant, or child, he or she may appear older than at the time of death.
Deceased reassures dreamer that all is well.
Physical flaws have frequently vanished. Clothing, hair, or face is often described as shimmering, flowing, or luminous.

Frequency: Extremely common.

Response after Awake: Dreamer feels joyous, uplifted. May be inspired to believe in life eternal.

Physical Restoration

In addition to appearing younger and healthier—or in the case of an infant's death, older and healthier—the dream messenger often seems to be cured of any physical problems. One woman dreamed that her deceased aunt told her she was so happy where she was because she no longer had to smoke. Another woman's father had been confined to a wheelchair her whole nine years of life. After his death, her father walked in her dreams and assured her that he no longer needed a wheelchair, that he was well and they would be together someday. You will know that you have begun to heal when the deceased appears in normal health in your dreams, as in the next case.

Gayle's Father's Voice Restored

Some time before his death, Gayle's father had had his larynx removed. He spoke using esophageal speech, which has a unique sound. After his death, in Gayle's early dreams about him, her father still spoke in the same distorted manner. Then about five months later, Gayle had a dream about him that gave her peace:

> I am asleep in my bed. The telephone rings, so I get up to answer. On the other end of the line is my dad. As I answer the phone, the voice returning is clear and normal. It is the voice I remember as his "real" voice. He says to me, "Hi, Gayle, it's me. I need to talk to you." I tell him how glad I am that he called because I was worried about him. He says, "I know how you worry, so I wanted to let you know everything is all right. I'm whole again. They gave me back my voice." "I know," I reply. "No, you don't understand, Gayle, it's me. I'm talking. I'm well again. Everything is going to be all right." "I know, Daddy, I really do know." He wants me to tell my mom that he is O.K., that we should never be afraid of dying, being dead isn't a terrible thing. It is such a good place to be. I tell him he should tell her, but he says, "She won't believe me. You understand such things." I agree I will tell my mom.

Gayle awoke from this dream astonished. She marveled, "I know I was dreaming, but it seemed so real." She felt she had really had a visit from her father. When she called her mother four days later to tell her the dream, her mother announced, "I had the strangest dream about your father." She proceeded to describe a dream almost identical to her daughter's. It seems the dream messenger delivered his message to both, to make sure it got through. Some dream experiences are hard to explain other than by accepting that communication is possible between the living person and the spirit of the deceased. Whatever the explanation, such dreams bring profound reassurance to the dreamer. Watch for such changes in your own dreams.

Soul Finds Peace

If you have undergone the death of a child, you know the torments of deep sorrow. Difficult under any circumstances, a child's death is particularly hard to bear when it was catastrophic.

Connie's Son Reappears Whole

Connie, a mother whose nineteen-year-old son died in a fire, was tortured by the remembrance. "All of my waking hours were filled with thoughts of him burning. It was truly hell."

Connie did not dream about her son at all. Some tragedies are too excruciating to be relived even in dreams. This refusal of the mind to dream is a protective reaction. When the shock and horror diminish, dreams return with their healing consolation.

With therapy, it was about a year and a half before Connie's life began to seem even moderately normal. Then she longed to dream about her son. Prayers and wishes did not produce the desired dreams. Three years after the tragedy, when Connie had accepted the reality of his death as best she could, and hoped to meet her boy again in the afterlife, she suddenly dreamed of him four times.

At first, Connie dreamed about her son as a child of about six playing Little League baseball as she watched from the stands. He turned to look at her, smiled, waved, and was gone. Then she dreamed her son was playing with her brother, to whom he was very close, laughing and acting silly as they lay on the floor of his room. Connie was impressed at how her son had grown taller. He smiled and hugged her for a long time. In the third dream, Connie saw her son at a local store. He felt cold and borrowed a flannel shirt from a friend. She called to him to come get in the car. Finally, Connie dreamed of her son younger again, at nine or ten; she had found him after he'd been gone a long time. Again they embraced. Connie felt calmed by these dreams. She thought her son's spirit was communicating that he loved her and was all right. Dream smiles and dream hugs can bring waking-life comfort.

Rosalind Cartwright's Daughter Reappears

Psychologist and dream researcher Rosalind Cartwright lost her daughter, Christine, in an automobile accident when she was struck by a speeding driver. Twenty-eight years old, a new Ph.D., the young woman had been walking across a poorly lit rural road when she was hit. She died instantly.

Cartwright, who was awakened by a late-night telephone call from the police to report that her daughter was dead, says that seven years later, she still feels frightened when the telephone rings late at night.

At first, Cartwright could not dream about her daughter at all. A few weeks after her daughter's death, she began to dream about her child as a toddler in trouble; she would hear her cry and rush to rescue her. In one dream, the child had fallen down a toilet and she pulled her out. In another, she was struck by the car, but her padded snowsuit protected her from injury; Cartwright lifted and comforted her. In each dream, the daughter grew a little older. Finally, she dreamed:

> I was at a big convention, waiting for an elevator with a crowd of people. Now an adult, Chris joined me there. "Christine!" I said. "I'm so glad to see you. I thought you were dead." "I am," she said. "I only came to be with you until you are used to the idea."[11]

Cartwright says that she found this dream very comforting, it was so like her daughter. She finally accepted that she could not save her child, but that "she could stay with me in a way that gave me some peace."[12] It was the last dream she had during the mourning period. The dreams of threat and rescue turned into dreams of appreciation.

Many parents find their dreams taking the same form.

Marian's Son Laughs Again

When he was in his late thirties, Marian's son was stabbed in the abdomen in a fight following a traffic accident. Although he survived for a few years afterward, the internal injuries he sustained eventually killed him. Marian cared for her dying son during his final months. His death left her drained and desolate, despite the presence of her husband and other grown children.

About two months after her son died, Marian had a "very comforting" dream:

> We are at our old house (in a lovely wooded suburb where the boy grew up). He is about nine or ten years old, sitting on the grass. Laughing, he looks up at me and says, "It's all right, Mom."

All of us yearn to hear those words from loved ones who have died. We want them to be well—not just surviving, not still suffering, but joyful. Happily, many bereaved people find that very reassurance when the message "I'm O.K." is delivered in a dream. May it be so for you, too.

Stacy's Fiancé Recognizes Her

Stacy was only eighteen when she became engaged to twenty-three-year-old Ned. Very much in love, they were enjoying a carefree holiday whitewater-rafting on an Oregon river. As they idled in a calm area on the warm day, they removed their life jackets. Unfortunately, when they ducked under some low-hanging branches, the raft capsized. Stacy was caught by a fierce undertow and whirled downstream over some falls. The last she saw of Ned, he was standing waist-high in water, grappling to hold on to the raft. Eventually, Stacy was able to scramble ashore beyond the falls. Ned never reappeared.

Hysterical, Stacy searched everywhere. Finally she clambered to a road, where she flagged a car and got to a telephone. The rescue crew and divers who responded found Ned three hours after the accident, trapped underwater by some rocks, drowned. The crew prevented Stacy from viewing Ned's body; she was taken by ambulance to a hospital for treatment of her cuts and bruises.

During the next few days, Ned's family also refused to let Stacy see her fiancé's body, trying to protect her from the battered and bloated sight. "You wouldn't want to remember him that way," they said. The funeral service was held with a closed casket. Stacy has always regretted that she didn't insist on seeing Ned's body. She feels it would have helped her accept what had happened. Her instinct is endorsed by most grief experts. Agonizing as it may be, viewing the body of a person who died in a trauma enables the griever to accept the reality of the death.

Like so many people whose loved ones have tragic deaths, Stacy was tormented by nightmares for months afterward. In her case, there was no depiction of Ned's suffering. Instead, she dreamed that he had amnesia. "Don't you remember me?" she would implore. The reply was always, "No." In one of these nightmares, "Ned was living in a house with a bunch of guys. He didn't recognize me." Stacy woke up sobbing from these frightful dreams.

After two months of these miserable scenarios, Stacy finally dreamed:

> Ned and I are rolling around on the beach. He looks at me tenderly and says, "Don't worry about me. I'm O.K." At last he knows who I am.

This dream brought Stacy some degree of reassurance.

More than three years after Ned's death, Stacy still has occasional distressing dreams about him. Married now, she dreamed of having to choose between Ned and her husband, was unable to do so, and woke in anxiety. This dream motif often arises in people who lose one partner and later choose another. They seem to feel they are being unfaithful to the deceased person by committing to a living one. Stacy's husband is supportive and understanding, but some people in her situation may require professional help before being able to invest in a new relationship, or even take pleasure in life again.

Nina's Mother's Soul in a Treetop

People who are grieving need confirmation that the spirits of their loved ones are at ease after death. Nina was forty when her much-beloved sixty-four-year-old mother died. Nina was brokenhearted and mourned continuously for over a year. Her friends in Europe, where her mother had lived, told Nina she must "release" her mother, as though her excessive sadness kept her mother's spirit bound. But Nina's grief could not be assuaged.

About fifteen months after her mother's death, Nina finally had a dream that made it possible to cease obsessing about her loss. She had taken a trip to the American South to visit some relatives she had not met before, ones her mother had always wanted her to contact. Nina arrived in the dark and did not see much of the setting. That night she dreamed:

> My mother's soul comes out from my heart and flies to the top of a very tall tree with a beautiful crown. I watch, feeling no fear, only great wonder and peace.

The next morning, Nina drew open the drapes of the bedroom and there outside the window was the identical tree she had seen in her dream, very tall, with smooth bark, no flowers, but lovely leaves and a beautiful crown. Nina was amazed.

Later that day, Nina reluctantly attended an exhibition on the life of cowboys. Imagine her surprise when the guide spoke of the Cherokee belief that, after death, the souls of their ancestors went to live in the tops of trees.

For the first time since her mother's death, Nina felt that her mother's soul—and her own—were at peace. Symbolically, it was as though the deceased mother had taken up her spirit home in the heights of the tree on her relatives' land. You will see, in the material on symbolism in dreams of death, how trees play a major role. Wherever and however the resting place is found for the spirit of the deceased, the grieving dreamer finds respite too.

Nancy's Mother Grants Her Heart's Desire[13]

You saw how "I'm Suffering" dreams usually change over time. They may evolve not only into "I'm O.K." dream messages, but also into ones that are profoundly helpful to the dreamer's future life, as they did in the following case.

Nancy was a twenty-six-year-old single mother with two young children when her mother died unexpectedly of a massive heart attack. Although Nancy had had a forewarning dream (in which her mother died) a week before the actual death, and a strong premonition when she was with her mother the day before, she was stunned when it happened. "It was as if someone had shot a cannonball through me," she said. She felt alone, abandoned, afraid, and angry that she had been deprived of her mother's emotional support.

About two weeks after her mother's funeral, Nancy began to have horrifying, recurrent dreams:

> I would find my mother in the middle of the heart attack and not be able to save her. She would die in my arms.

These nightmares were the typical replays of a death scene, yet Nancy had not been present, so the dreams were adding an element that seemed to say, "Even if you'd been there you couldn't have prevented it."

On other nights, Nancy would dream that she was with her mother in their old farm kitchen, chatting in their usual manner:

> I'd become aware that Mom was dead and mention it. She would say, "Yes, but because you are so sad, they let me come to visit you. I am here to help you get over your grief and get on with your life."

The dream theme "Go Ahead!" as you will see, is one that arises as grievers begin to recover.

After two months of dreams in which her mother was dying again, or trying to soothe her daughter, Nancy had a life-changing dream about her mother:

> I am kneeling in our potato garden. It is dark and the full moon has just risen over the trees of the east forty. Mom walks up to me wearing a shimmering white gown. Her long black hair flows around her face and down her shoulders. She says, "This is the last time I will be able to visit you. I have to go to another place now. But they have said that I may grant your heart's desire. Do you know what that is?" Without a heartbeat of hesitation, I reply, "A good education."

Two weeks after she had this dream, Nancy enrolled at a community college, received a grant, and eventually completed an Associate of Arts degree with many awards, including a fellowship to a four-year college. At the graduation ceremony, she at first felt sorrowful that her mother wasn't there to see her receive her degree; then she sensed her mother's presence in the empty chair beside her.

Nancy managed to attend the four-year college full-time, work three part-time jobs, and maintain her family. Again she graduated with honors and afterward had a full-time job waiting for her.

Obviously Nancy worked hard to fulfill her heart's desire, but she feels it was her mother's final dream visit that served as an inspiration and guide. "By asking the question (Do you know what your heart's desire is?), she forced me to see what I wanted and pointed me in the right direction. I took it from there," Nancy said. When we have dreams of this sort, the ancestor is taking a protective and guiding role for the dreamer. We can all use such help.

Brenda's Father Transforms

You have seen how dream messages of "I'm Suffering" are gradually replaced by messages of "I'm O.K." Sometimes you may experience the transition within a single dream. Poet Brenda Shaw gives a dramatic account of this in a poem based on the most comforting dream she had after her father's death:

> *I watch you walk away from me up the road,*
> *an old man—lame, sad,*
> *gaunt with illness,*
> *rough work clothes heavy on your frame.*
>
> *As I watch, the concrete road before you*
> *turns to tar, then dirt,*
> *then rough track through forest,*
> *then pristine wood.*
>
> *Naked, young again, you leap,*
> *fling up your arms in joy toward the sun,*
> *and disappear, running,*
> *through the trees.*[14]

As with Brenda, some dreamers find that the image of the deceased changes within the same dream, as it did for the woman who saw her aged father climbing a staircase, and when he turned to smile at her, he was transformed to a vital and youthful young man, before climbing out of sight. For most of us, the metamorphosis from "I'm Suffering" to "I'm O.K." takes place slowly over time.

Don't be despondent if you dream of your loved one suffering. This reaction is a normal part of the healing process. As in Nancy's case, "I'm Suffering" dream messages may be the opening scene of a dramatic shift to dreams that radically improve your life. Keep your heart hopeful and your dream eyes open.

3

∞

"I'm Not Really Dead" and "Goodbye"

"I'm Not Really Dead"

Dream Message: "I'm Not Really Dead"

Deceased appears; the dreamer is surprised, even shocked, to see him or her alive. The death is often explained away as a mistake. Dreamer may or may not realize that the person is, in fact, dead.

Frequency: Extremely common.

Response after Awake: Dreamer may feel acutely pained on remembering the death is real, yet treasure the moments of dream contact. If person was disliked, dreamer may feel relief.

T he class of dream motif I call "I'm Not Really Dead" may start
out extremely pleasant, but finish in acute pain for the dreamer.
If you are mourning the loss of a loved person, you are likely to
experience this dream message as bittersweet. If your feelings toward the dead person are ambivalent, angry, or hateful, you may
feel a guilty relief that he or she is dead after awakening.

The dream message "I'm Not Really Dead" is extremely common, especially in the early stages of grief. You may have it only
once, not at all, or several times.

Polly's Father Is Home Again

The most common reaction to the dream message "I'm Not Really
Dead" is surprise, as in the following dream.

Soon after Polly's father died, she dreamed (emphasis mine):

*I am with my current family in my father's house. Someone comes
out of the shower—it's my father! I say to him, "You're not supposed to be there! You're dead!"*

If you have this type of dream message, you may feel delight,
dismay, or confusion, in addition to surprise or shock.

Joanne's Father Is Alive Again

Approximately two weeks after Joanne's father died, she dreamed
(emphasis mine):

*I am with my family, including my father. He is still very ill. It is as
if he were dead and came back to life. I remember looking at his
face and thinking about when I saw it in the casket. It seemed then
that I would never see him again and now here he is.*

*The house we are in is not my mother's house in waking life, but
we call it her house in the dream. Dad is on the couch and we are all
gathered around. We talk about how he is alive again and how mi-
raculous it is. Then my brother and I start asking, "Who were those*

ashes we buried?" *We go to see the cemetery director and get upset with him. We don't trust him.*

Here we see confusion and suspicion expressed. Joanne's dream continued with a scene in which she was asked to stay with the body of the woman who had lived next door to her father. Joanne looked at the corpse in the casket and saw the woman's face and shoulders move. *"I knew she wasn't dead either,"* Joanne said.

This kind of repetition of motif in several scenes of a single dream, in several different dreams of the same night, or in dreams over several nights is typical. It is as though the dreaming mind wants to underscore a point—in this case that someone is not really dead—so it is presented in a variety of images. Watch for such repetitions in your own dreams.

The third scene of Joanne's dream contained yet another variation of the dream message "I'm Not Really Dead" (emphasis mine):

I am back with my family again. I think about a dream I have had about a bear that I think is alive when everyone else thinks it is dead. I can see its paw moving and stretching. The eyes look blank as though it is stuffed, but I see it move. I tell my family about this dream and say that I knew the bear was my father.

Joanne explained that although her father was still dying in the first scene of this dream, his face looked fuller and healthier than it had when he died, but she felt the energy flow out of him.

As I mentioned, Joanne's dream with three scenes occurred two weeks after her father died. Three months after his death, another set of images with a similar—yet changed—message emerged in a dream (emphasis mine):

I see my dad at this event. He looks good and wears a yellow sweater. I go into my purse to get the deer skull from Cumberland Island to show him. There is also an old Indian pipe nearby that I want to show him (he used to smoke a pipe before he got sick). It has tobacco in it, and I knock it out, but only part comes out. I think about my dad being dead and wonder if I should say anything, but don't bring it up.

Notice how the appearance of Joanne's father has improved in her dreams in this short time. Also see how the activities of the dream have shifted from focus on the father's being alive or dead to focus on mutual interests, and more of an acceptance of his state.

Like many people who have lost loved ones, Joanne wished it were not true that her father was dead. By repeating the theme "I'm Not Really Dead" and leading to the realization that her father was indeed really gone, she was helped by her dreams to accept this sad fact. As his appearance improved from dream to dream, she was beginning to rebound from her loss. Our nightly dreams are part of a built-in healing process.

My Father Comes Back—Time and Again

When my own father died, my initial dreams about him were symbolic (see Chapter 12, "Nine Major Symbols in Dreams About the Dead"). Perhaps I was not yet able to sustain seeing him without overwhelming sorrow.

Then I dreamed about my father indirectly, about five months following his death, when I encountered a man from a historic battle whom I had thought dead, as he did me; it was years later and he was now an artist (as my father was), who bore a battle wound that I treated.

It took me six months after my father's death before I pictured him directly—in a dream of kissing him goodbye (described in the "Goodbye" section). Nine months after his death, I dreamed of talking with him at a party, making arrangements to visit a friend. As I left him to climb upstairs, I thought to myself that although he's dead I needn't miss him because he's always there.

About a year after my father died, I had a kind of "death anniversary" dream about him in which he visited me and we hugged happily. Dreamers often mark birthdays, anniversaries, and holidays—even when not consciously aware of the special date—with extraordinary dreams about the people they love who have died. You will want to watch for such dreams at these significant times.

You will also want to be aware that dreams about the dead often occur when people are under stress and wish for the support of the absent person, as happened for me fifteen months after my father's death. My husband and I had just moved from Philadelphia to London a few weeks prior to the dream. I was afraid we had made a ghastly mistake. I felt enormously frustrated with the difficulties of setting up a household there, waiting in government offices for papers, and with living conditions in general, when I had this lucid dream:

> My father is helping me to take care of a neglected house. Animals are hurt, dying. A rabbit is limping. One animal must be discarded, another set loose, giving it a chance to live. Some birds need care; they must be given water and have their cages cleaned. Several of them fly over to settle on my arms. There is moldy food. My mother arrives looking young and pretty, but doesn't help. I'm fully aware that I'm dreaming and my father is actually dead, not really there helping me, and I feel filled with weeping because I want him present so much.

I woke up deeply sad from this dream. I had not fully recovered from my father's death. But also, I clearly longed for his practical ability to help me in the current difficult situation.

When nearly two years had passed since my father's death—twenty-one months—my dreams continued to exhibit the same struggle to cope and fear that I could not:

> The screen door bangs again and I look up and see my father. He looks young, but still tired around the eyes. He's wearing a rust-colored cable-knit sweater. "Daddy?" I ask. I wonder whether he is a dream or has come back and is real. He takes me in his arms and holds me very tenderly. "You're going to be free again," he says, "in three days." "Who, me?" I am surprised. He holds me so. He feels thin, like the last time that I saw him alive. I think he is saying that I will die. I wonder if I'm sad. I hug him back and say, "Oh, Daddy, I love you so!" I have a glad, or at least accepting, response. It is so real!

I awoke from this dream very sad about losing my father, and concerned about myself. Was I, too, going to die? People who have had someone close to them die feel more vulnerable themselves. Did I feel like dying? I remained depressed all day.

Although this dream dealt with the continuing grief over my father's death, it was also related to the present difficulty of living in London. I found it hard to accept the aggravations of living abroad—the cold, the griminess, the complications—and this caused some stress with my husband. Don't be surprised if your current troubles reevoke past ones.

This dream contained elements of the dream message "I'm Suffering," in my father's thin body and his tired eyes. Yet he looked young and whole, unlike the battle-wounded veteran and the old, distorted man from my earlier dreams about him. Three days later, my husband and I were on a trip to Paris, and the domestic pressures were reduced—a much pleasanter "freedom" than the one I had feared.

Eventually, in later dreams, I saw my father in good health, doing well, swimming in one dream, driving a car in another. In yet another dream, I received an inheritance from him, and in still another embraced him at a Valentine's Day celebration, which is my husband's birthday. Here, I was probably saying I'm being protected and cared for, as my father protected and cared for me in his lifetime. Thereafter, from about two years following his death, my dreams about my father began to lessen and to take on the more normal quality of his being a positive, helpful presence who makes an occasional appearance in ongoing dreams.

Melanie's Friend Reappears

Melanie, like so many people in today's world, lost a gay friend to AIDS. Sometime after his death, she dreamed (emphasis mine):

I'm at a place where gay men dressed as women are dancing in a show. Money is collected as a way for this collective to pay their rent. I am with some straight friends, just sort of passing through this event. All of a sudden I see my gay friend. We are so glad to see each other, and embrace. I think I cry out of happiness. My straight friends don't realize we know each other and wonder why I'm embracing a gay man.

Later I ask my gay friend, "You're dead, aren't you?" He says yes. Then I wonder if the other men in his household are also dead, and if other people know. I think he says they are dead, but most people don't realize that.

We hang out for days, doing things together. The dream ends as I am talking with my friend, touching his arm, and I can feel him fading—and then he sort of disappears, going back to "the other side."

This dream left Melanie with a "strange spiritual flavor." She wasn't surprised when her friend left in the dream; she knew he wouldn't stay for long. In this case, the dreamer simply accepts the fact that the deceased is, in fact, dead, but she is able to enjoy the pleasure of being together again in the dream.

Celeste's Daughter Dances Again

Celeste's daughter had epilepsy. Tragically, the young woman died when she suffocated during a seizure, alone in her apartment. When we spoke, Celeste had only had vague dreams of talking with her daughter about being dead, and of seeing her dancing. In a dream that Celeste found amusing, her daughter popped out "like Vanna White," wearing her usual outfit of a white turtleneck T-shirt and blue jeans. There were two rows of messages on white cards, but Celeste awoke before she was able to read them. She found these dreams unsatisfying.

Celeste felt jealous of friends and family who were having vivid dreams about her daughter. One of her women friends, who was in charge of cleaning out the daughter's apartment after her death, dreamed:

You daughter's skin is hanging in the closet. She jumps into the skin and starts dancing around, saying, "It's good to be alive!"

As you saw, it often takes time to dream about a person you love when he or she has died suddenly or traumatically. Be assured that such dreams do come in time, often bringing needed consolation with them.

Donna's Husband Is Brought Back

Donna lost her husband when he died from leukemia, following a complex and painful bone marrow transplant. This procedure involves a preparatory step in which the patient is placed in a body mold that inhibits movement for several hours while the bone marrow is destroyed by radiation. After her husband's death, Donna's dreams about him included this process (emphasis mine):

> I see my husband being put into a compartment, probably dead. When he comes out, he is only sick. I am surprised. I thought he was gone [dead], but he isn't. It's confusing. We debate about whether we can talk to one another or not.

Here the major reactions expressed are surprise and confusion. Another feeling that can be evoked by the dream message "I'm Not Really Dead" is that of anger.

Dick's Wife Goes to a Meeting

Dick had lost his wife about a year before, when he dreamed:

> I walk into a place where there are a bunch of people around a conference table. I see my wife seated at the table, busy talking with others. I feel angry and frustrated. How could she be doing this when all the time I'd been missing her! Finally she gets up and comes around to me. She explains it was something she had to do without me hanging on.

People who have lost a loved person are often startled by their feelings of anger toward the deceased. There may be an unexpected resentment at being "deserted," or at being left to deal with difficult problems alone. These emotions are usually characteristic of later stages of bereavement, when the survivor is struggling to adjust to life without the person who died. Don't be startled if they surface in a dream.

Kay's Husband Is Deformed

When Kay's husband died in an industrial accident in which his chest was crushed, her initial dreams about him were terrifying to her. In one, she saw him very far off, thin, "like a soda cracker." She said, "A couple of these dreams scared me to death." In one of them:

> I look into a mirror and see not my face but his, as though it has been scribbled on and erased.

In another of these distressing dreams, Kay's husband wore a navy coat as he moved stiffly toward her, "almost not alive."

Such dreams reflect the sense of distortion and unreality that follow traumatic deaths. They also echo the fear of ghosts common in past times. Kay ceased dreaming about her husband directly and began to substitute the image of a fish caught on a hook, and other negative scenarios that were more bearable to her at the time.

Understanding the "I'm Not Really Dead" Dream Message

Why do we dream that the dead are not really dead? We wish it were so. We hope it is so. We're accustomed to their presence and can't quite believe they are gone. Dream messages that convey "I'm Not Really Dead" force us to give up our denial and face the fact that the death is real, over and over again.

We have seen how dreams of "I'm Not Really Dead" can evoke a wide variety of emotions—surprise, sorrow, confusion, joy, anger, terror. Expressing these feelings in dreams and struggling to deal with them help us to work through the emotional anguish of our grief.

On another level, if there is an afterlife, "I'm Not Really Dead" dreams may portray the continuance of the spirit of the dead, with the gradual improvement in the appearance of the dead being related to some sort of afterlife development. Many people think so.

If you receive a dream message of the type that follows, "Goodbye," you are quite likely to awaken deeply contented.

"Goodbye"

Dream Message: "Goodbye"

Deceased takes leave of the dreamer, saying, "Goodbye," "Farewell," or "I have to leave now," in words, by gesture, or by mental communication.

If the goodbye is not literal during the dream, the dreamer afterward comments something to the effect that "I knew he/she came to say goodbye to me." Often includes physical contact and verbal expressions of love, as well as an affectionate goodbye.

Frequency: Common.

Response after Awake: Wide variation, usually including joy. Dreamer may be persuaded there is an afterlife.

Death as a Journey to the West

In the mythology of most cultures—ancient and modern—death is depicted as a journey to an unknown land, usually located in the west. Native Americans, for instance, use the term "to go west," meaning to die. The west presumably emerges as a symbol for death because it is the place of the setting, the "dying," sun. The ancient Egyptians said that the souls of the blessed complete their journey with the sun god in his bark (a small boat). The journey follows the path of the sun after it disappears, through the underworld, eventually reaching the east, where, like the rising sun, the soul is resurrected. Some groups, such as Tibetan Buddhists, provide a "map" for the dying person, to be memorized prior to death, and then to be read to the corpse (with the assumption that its listening spirit is lingering nearby) to guide the deceased through the space between death and the next rebirth.

Because of these cultural ideas about death as a journey to an unknown land, the comments of people who are dying, the dreams of the dying, and the dreams of people who are mourning the dead are filled with images of travel, preparations to leave, modes of transport, border crossings, obstacles, and ultimate destinations.

Journeys in Comments of the Dying

Dying people frequently speak of the need to get ready for a trip or make a change in their last few days of life. A pair of nurses who care for terminally ill patients for Hospice, Maggie Callanan and Patricia Kelley, document this fact in their book *Final Gifts*.[1] Callanan and Kelley believe that what most witnesses take for confusion in dying people is actually an attempt to communicate their experience of approaching death. They tell of one woman saying, "It's time to get in line," a few days before her death; she and her husband had traveled extensively, backpacking or in tourist groups, often spending much time waiting in lines. One agitated dying woman demanded to know, "Where's the map? I'm lost! If I could find the map, I could go home!" She died the next day. A seriously ill man, who had spent much of his retirement time sailing, asked the nurse, "Well, how's the tide tonight?" He, too, died the next day. Another dying man anxiously said, "I can't find my passport. Do you know where my ticket is?" He died ten days later. A dying man who was an engineer stated, "I'm trying to figure out how I can take the house and everything in it!" His death occurred the next week. A friend of mine who was caring for her mother as she died told me that the dying woman began to talk about "catching the bus," and expressed concern it would depart without her.

Such comments are a kind of announcement that "I'm getting ready to leave." Callanan and Kelley urge caretakers of the dying to be alert for statements of this sort, saying they are metaphors for the dying person's awareness of the nearness of death. They suggest the caretaker "carry the metaphor forward." For example, if a dying former pilot speaks of getting ready to take a flight, ask, "When does it take off?"

Caretakers can help by not challenging the dying person; instead, accept and validate what the person says. Rather than respond with something like, "Don't be ridiculous. You're in no condition to need a passport," say something like, "Sounds as if you feel a change is coming. Is there anything I can do to help you get ready?" Caretakers should provide information about the dying process, reassure the person that he or she is understood, and give whatever comfort is needed to die peacefully.

Journeys in Dreams of the Dying

Dying people not only talk about journeys, they dream about them, as well. Marie-Louise von Franz, the Jungian scholar who wrote *On Dreams and Death,* said, "In my experience the image of the journey in dreams is also the most frequently occurring symbol of impending death."[2] I concur. However, keep in mind that people often dream about taking a journey at several life junctures, not only prior to death—such as starting a new project, going off to college, moving to a new home, at graduations, marriages, and births. The old life is over; the new begins.

Journeys in Dreams of the Bereaved

Those of us who are mourning the loss of a loved one also dream about travel. Dreams about journeys, even if the deceased is not directly depicted, seem to symbolically represent our separation from them. Often we dream of seeing our person getting on an airplane, leaving in a spaceship, setting sail on a boat, catching a train, or boarding a bus. Airports, train stations, bus stations, and docks are common settings for "Goodbye" dream messages. So is traveling down a river or crossing it. Usually, the mode of travel that appears in dreams about the deceased is one that they typically used during their lifetime. Look over this sampling of journey dreams about the dead with the dream message "Goodbye," and you'll probably recognize some of your own.

Ben's Wife Gets On the Plane

Ben's wife, Flo, was in her seventies when she died. Although they had been about the same age, Flo had been the dominant partner. Now Ben felt lost. Two months after his wife's death, Ben dreamed:

> *My wife and I are going to the airport. She looks younger, well, and happy. We reach a gate through which I am not allowed, but she is. She goes onward and when she has almost reached the airplane, just before she enters it, she turns and waves goodbye to me.*

Ben felt relieved when he awoke from this dream. He said that it made him realize Flo had just "gone on ahead" and he would join her later. Ben became actively engaged in life once more, even to the point of remarrying. Notice the barrier that appears between the living and the dead—a frequent symbol in "Goodbye" dream messages. Watch for it in your dreams about the dead.

My Father Stays On the Train

During the first year after his death, I dreamed of my father as being "present" only twice; in other dreams, he was mentioned or was represented symbolically. During the second year of mourning, however, he appeared in twenty-four dreams. Certainly it was less painful to dream of him directly by then. Of the dreams in which my deceased father was present, fifteen percent involved trains or railroad stations—his typical mode of travel when not using a car. For instance, six months after my father died from his second heart attack, I dreamed:

> *I am on a train, sitting to the right-hand side of the car, near the aisle. My mother comes and squeezes between me and the seat back in front of me to get to the vacant seat near the window. I feel almost*

squashed. Later she is showing me something about injections in the sole of her foot that will make her two legs equal in height (her legs are equal in reality). I think this foolish but don't say so.

I get up to leave the train and go to the door. Near it, on a sideways seat, is an old man. I "know" it is my father, even though it doesn't resemble him in the slightest. He stands up, wobbly and bent over, supporting himself with a cane. His shoulder is bumpy and distorted (like my husband's collarbone is from a horseback-riding accident). I kiss the old man goodbye tenderly, feeling a wave of deep sadness. I must get off the train. I wake up weepy.

Among the numerous emotions depicted in this dream is the sense of "pressure" I was feeling at the time from my widowed mother (symbolized by her almost squashing me); my sense that she was acting unbalanced (represented by the unequal legs); the association of fatherlike feelings with my husband (depicted by his broken collarbone on the old man); and the nostalgia I felt over having been deprived of my father's older years (the aged man) by his early death at age sixty-two. Dreams are a pictorial record of complex feelings. Here, I must leave my father to continue his journey alone.

Marilyn's Mother on a Passing Train

Three days after her mother died, Marilyn had a vivid dream about her:

I am on a train going one way. I see my mother on another train going in the opposite direction. It was O.K.

Marilyn had to travel her own way, away from the land of the dead.

In a variation of this motif, one woman dreamed of passing her dead father, who was going up on an escalator as she was going down on a different escalator; later the same night, she dreamed of being on an airplane with him and of being told she had to get off at the next stop while he went on alone. Notice how, in each case, the dreamer has to physically separate from the person who has died. Some dreamers find it very difficult to accept this separation from the loved person and yearn to join them, as Elena did.

Elena's Boyfriend Travels On Alone[3]

In Switzerland, Jungian therapist Verena Kast has collected dreams of mourners and studied how their dreams guide the bereavement process, eventually constructing a new identity for the mourner. In her book *A Time to Mourn: Growing Through the Grief Process,* she gives a poignant dream series collected from a young woman she calls Elena.

Elena was twenty-three when her boyfriend, George, unexpectedly had a heart attack. The night before his heart attack, George dreamed:

> *The Swiss Army. I am supposed to turn in all my equipment because I am about to undertake a long journey abroad. But I must also hand over my cigarettes, a lighter and a manuscript which I have just begun. I argue that these are my personal property. The officer to whom I must give these things shrugs his shoulders and says, "That's the way it is here: orders are orders." I am looking forward to the journey. At last something unpredictable is happening again.*
>
> *Horses are pulling a heavily laden wagon. Suddenly—I have no idea how—the horses have broken free; the wagon remains standing, then rolls backwards into a tree while the horses gallop away. I am happy that the horses have broken free. They continue to gallop across the country but cannot harm anyone.*

Here we see both the imagery of preparation for a journey and that of the "animal soul" separating from its burden (as the body is thought to separate from the soul at death). The significance of animal imagery in dreams about the dead is discussed in Chapter 12. Notice, however, the strain that the dream animals are undergoing before they break free. Imagery of laboring strenuously has been associated with dreams preceding ill health.

Having to turn in all his personal equipment is also an ominous sign in George's dream. Was the "manuscript which I have just begun" George's life story? His life's work? At the time, he saw the dream as a message to make a fundamental change in his life situation, perhaps taking a journey alone, to find something new in himself. He did, however, feel peculiar the morning after this dream. Later the same day, he suffered his first heart attack.

George died suddenly three weeks later, after a second attack. Elena dreamed of him almost every night following his death; these encounters felt like actual visitations from her love, deeply consoling her, but she was always plunged back into mourning when she awoke. Three weeks after his funeral, Elena dreamed (emphasis mine):

> *George writes me a letter. He asks me to visit him and names a train station on the border as the meeting place. I meet him. We are in a train together with others. At a certain place we must all climb out, only George may and must travel on. I attempt by means of the highest authority to arrange that I might also go on, that I might travel with George—but to no avail: the authority wants nothing to do with me.*
>
> *Tenderly we say good-bye—I feel numb.*
>
> *Now I have to find a train to travel back. I search endlessly, running from station to station. All night long I feel like I have been searching for the right train. Then at some point, I find myself in a train that is going back. There are a lot of people in this train: I am afraid of these people—also there is no room for me. I end up between two train carriages and wake up completely exhausted.*

The border in Elena's dream was, of course, the boundary that separates the living from the dead. Only the deceased may travel onward. She could not join him, no matter how she wished for it at the time. The dreamer's tender goodbye to her boyfriend was followed by a difficult return to her life alone. This dream was forcing upon Elena the impassable distance from her beloved that she must accept in order to live. The dream reunion and tender farewell depicted both the bond that still existed between the mourner and her lover and the urgent need to separate from him.

A year later, Elena said that this dream saved her life. It was of decisive importance in turning her back to face her own world.

Eventually, Elena was able to retain a connection with the deceased George as a once-loved figure within her, and simultaneously reinvest her energy in her current life. Her dream was a decision for life we must all make when our world has been shattered by loss.

Lois's Husband Gets Off the Train

Dreams involving trains and the deceased do not always convey the message "Goodbye." Lois's husband, John, had worked for the railroad before he died, and often traveled by train, making the station a normal place to see or meet him. It was very close to the anniversary of his death when Lois dreamed:

> I'm waiting for the train, feeling very nervous, pacing. I see my parents [deceased] sitting on the railroad track. I feel concerned they won't get off the track before the train comes. They need assistance. I'm nervous and pacing because the train is late. It pulls in and my husband gets off. He still looks very thin. His pants are too big. He gives me a really big smile.

Although she was pleased to see the image of her husband, Lois woke from this dream feeling depressed. She yearned for a hug. The sense of loss is often especially strong at the time of the first anniversary of a death. In this case, the dream message was not "Goodbye," but more a "Hi! How Are You?"

Colleen's Father Leaves on a Spaceship

Colleen was away from home, sleeping soundly, when she was awakened at 2:00 A.M. by an astonishing dream:

> I meet my father on a spaceship somewhere way out in space. He is dressed like Captain Kirk and the setting is very similar to the Star Trek Enterprise. Dad comes to me and his exact words are, "I have to leave you now." I am extremely upset and start begging him not to leave. He then tells me, "I have to go and I'm going to marry a

woman named Grace." I am hysterical and he finally takes me in his arms and says, "Now I'm going—I have to, but you have to remember, I won't ever really leave you. I'll always be with you." With that he hugs me, and honest to God, I felt a soul union like nothing I've ever felt on this earth. I am overcome and overwhelmed by love and the merging of our spirits. In the dream I am so overtaken by this love that I pass out. When I "wake up" [a false awakening, as Colleen was still in the dream], I see the spaceship flying off deeper into space.

Then Colleen actually woke up. Her dream seemed so real, and she was so upset about it, that she went and woke up her roommate to tell her about the dream.

Colleen continued, "Four hours later, my aunt telephoned to tell me that my fifty-seven-year-old father had a massive heart attack in the middle of the night and died almost instantly." This kind of dream report seems inexplicable except by some extra-sensory communication, or spiritual contact, between the dying or dead person and the dreamer. There were no indications that her father's health was in danger, nor was she around him to notice if there had been, and he was too young to be expected to die.

Colleen had no doubt that "my dad came to say goodbye to me." Her dream, in addition to the message of "Goodbye," has elements of "I'll Always Love You" in her father's loving attitude, assurance of his enduring presence, and affectionate embrace.

You may be puzzled by the motif that the dying man said he had to go marry a woman named Grace. Colleen explained that in her religion, the Virgin Mary was often referred to as "Grace," and that her father had a special devotion to her.

Colleen was very close to her father and found this dream extremely comforting. Her dead father was traveling to another world to be with the Blessed Mother, and yet his spirit would always remain with his daughter. "I don't think I would have ever accepted his death had this [dream] not occurred . . . it confirmed my belief that there is no such thing as death . . . it changed my life." Colleen felt she had experienced divine love.

Death as a Celestial Marriage

Strange as it may seem, dreamers sometimes portray a death as a wedding as Colleen did. This imagery appeared in the popular film *All That Jazz,* a biographical account of choreographer Bob Fosse's dances, dreams, visions, and hallucinations about his approaching death. In the motion picture, Jessica Lange appeared as an angel in white beckoning the dancer to join her. A prestigious Japanese film producer-director also linked the imagery of a beautiful woman and death in his *Akira Kurosawa's Dreams.* In his portrayal, death was personified as a goddess trying to cover a freezing, dying mountain climber with her veil. In fact, he was being smothered by the snow. Only at the last moment did her exquisite face turn ugly, as she succeeded in covering him with her whiteness.

Socrates' Dream of the Woman in White[4]

These images of death as a meeting with a beautiful woman are not simply the imaginative products of film producers. Two nights before the Greek philosopher Socrates drank his cup of poison hemlock, asleep in a prison in Athens, he had such a dream. His friend Crito awakened him just before dawn. The city was awaiting the return of a boat that would signal the time for his trial and execution. Socrates said he did not think the boat would arrive that day:

> . . . *I do not think it will come today, but tomorrow. I am counting on a dream I had a little while ago in the night, so it seems to be fortunate that you did not wake me. Crito: And what was the dream? Socrates: A fair and beautiful woman, clad in white, seemed to come to me, and call me and say, "O Socrates—On the third day shall you fertile Phthia reach." [a quote from Homer's* Iliad*] Crito: What a strange dream, Socrates! Socrates: But its meaning is clear, at least to me, Crito.*

Socrates was sure that the woman in white in his dream knew the precise day of his death.

Weddings in dreams, or unions with partners in white, may symbolize death. Indeed, a new life begins with each death.

Marie-Louise's Father Stops By[5]

Jungian analyst Marie-Louise von Franz's father died suddenly when she was absent from home. She was "preoccupied with the problem of his departure" when she had this dream three weeks after his death:

> *It was about ten o'clock in the evening, dark outside. I heard the doorbell ring and "knew" at once somehow that this was my father coming. I opened the door and there he stood with a suitcase. I remembered from the Tibetan Book of the Dead that people who died suddenly should be told that they are dead, but before I could say so he smiled at me and said: "Of course I know that I am dead, but may I not visit you?" I said: "Of course, come in," and then asked, "How are you now? What are you doing? Are you happy?" He answered: "Let me remember what you, the living, call happy. Yes, in your language, I am happy. I am in Vienna (his hometown which he loved and longed for all his life) and I am studying at the music academy." Then he went into the house, we climbed the stairs and I wanted to lead him to his former bedroom. But he said: "Oh, no, now I am only a guest," and went up to the guestroom. There he put his suitcase down and said: "It is not good for either the dead or the living to be together too long. Leave me now. Good night." And with a gesture he signalled me not to embrace him, but to go. I went into my room, thinking that I had forgotten to put out the electric stove and that there was a danger of fire. At that moment I woke up, feeling terribly hot and sweating.*

Von Franz told this dream to Jung, who believed it to be about her real father, not her father as a symbol. He pointed out that by being in Vienna, the father's loved hometown, he had "gone home." Von Franz's father had been musical but had not developed this gift to his satisfaction, so he was fulfilling another deep desire. Jung thought that encounters with the world of ghosts gave a sensation of coldness, and that von Franz's sensation of heat in the dream was a defense against the chill of death.

From our point of view, we note the announcement made with the doorbell, the dreamer's presentiment of the father's arrival, the open door, and the suitcase which represents his journey and his brief stopover to visit and say goodnight to his daughter.

Although both Jung and von Franz seemed to feel it risky to embrace the image of the dead person in a dream, many dreamers claim this is the most important moment of all—when they can actually feel, touch, smell, and sometimes hug and kiss the missing loved person. When the dreamer is willing to accept the reality of the death, I believe it can be healing to hold and express love to the dead person in a dream. Perhaps the belief that it is dangerous to touch the deceased makes it appear so to the dreamer, because when one believes it is safe to do so, there seem to be only positive aftereffects, as in the case of the woman who dreamed of embracing her father when he came to say goodbye before taking off in a space-ship.

Jung commented, in a letter to a friend whose brother had died in an accident and who had dreamed afterward of speaking with his ghost, that the continual presence of the dead in our dreams is "only relative, since after a few weeks or months the connection becomes indirect or breaks off altogether, although spontaneous re-encounters also appear to be possible later." Jung felt it was unwise to try to provoke contact with the dead in dreams. "To be on the safe side, one must be content with spontaneous experiences."

This statement may be true, but I think it is important not only to accept encounters with the dead that arise naturally, but also to engage in structured remembrances of the dead, to honor them, and to bless them. In this way, one avoids overobsession with the lost loved person while still providing reliable points of contact.

Understanding the Meaning of "Goodbye" Dream Messages

The participants in my study dreamed of "Goodbye" messages throughout the grieving process, from the exact moment of death until weeks, months, or even years later. You can anticipate a "Goodbye" dream message at any time.

In general, you will find that "Goodbye" dreams are positive and often help you to start resolving your grief. Such messages seem to assist us in accepting the reality of a death, in expressing some of our emotions about it, and by providing a sense of completion. They may leave you feeling that your person who died is well in spirit, even evolving in another realm, thus allowing you to go on with your life.

When bereaved people are able to feel, "Yes, so-and-so is really dead, but his/her spirit truly does live on," the dream messages "I'm Not Really Dead" and "Goodbye" have fulfilled their purpose.

4

"You Fool!" and "Congratulations!"

"You Fool!"

Dream Message: "You Fool!"
Deceased indicates strong disapproval of the dreamer.

Frequency: Rare but important.
Response after Awake: Dreamer often suffers a mood of discouragement throughout the following day.

F ew people find it tolerable to be told, "You Fool!" whether the person uttering it is alive or dead. We want our behavior to be acceptable to people significant in our lives. Although this dream message is fairly uncommon, it still arises too often for comfort. If you experience it, you may find it unpleasant and perhaps alarming. It occurs most often when the relationship between the dreamer and the deceased is strongly ambivalent. Of course, all close relationships have some degree of mixed feelings, but when anger or guilt between the living and the dead remains unresolved, the dream messenger is most likely to shriek, "You Fool!"

In olden times, people who had such dreams felt they had been assaulted by an "angry ghost," and hastened to settle its spirit by special prayers and offerings. Some members of primitive tribes who were troubled by dreams of an angry dead mother or father, followed by misfortune in the waking state, said they had been "bitten" by the angry ghost of the parent. One tribesman from South Africa told of dreaming he was "praying and singing when I saw my [dead] father coming from the wall to me, wearing dark clothes and being angry, wanting to kick me." [1] After he returned to church regularly in waking life, these dreams with the message "You Fool! stopped; then when he had trouble, his father came in dreams to talk to him, without being angry. Other tribal members made sacrifices to angry ghosts, as well as altering their behavior to appease them.

You may feel "bitten" yourself if confronted with such a dream. These dreams, as with some other negative messages we've considered, usually improve over time. Here's how.

Carla's Dead Mother Scolds Her

Carla's mother was dying from complications of breast cancer when, contrary to her express wishes, her grown children decided she would be better off in the hospital. Until the day she was hospitalized, no one in the family had acknowledged how seriously ill their mother was. She died, unexpectedly, alone in the hospital later that same afternoon.

The very evening their mother died, Carla and her brothers and sisters gathered in her room. Burdened with grief and guilt over her premature and lonely death, they shared memories as they went through her closet and sorted her clothing.

That night, Carla and her husband slept in sleeping bags on the living room floor in the mother's house. It was hard for Carla to fall asleep, but eventually she was overcome by exhaustion. A startlingly vivid dream came to her:

I am lying in my sleeping bag on the floor. It is as if I awaken from sleep, but the scene retains its dreamlike quality. I turn toward a noise at the front door. There in the hallway stands my mother. I am aware in the dream that she has died; I am astounded and glad to see her. Her exact words have faded from memory but the tone is clearly one of anger. "How could you have gone through my things?" *She is livid that we "let go" so quickly. I feel very distraught. This feels like our last "earthly" interaction. I don't want the relationship to end on a note of conflict. I awake without responding.*

Carla felt she had been truly visited in this dream by her mother's spirit before it was released. She thought that her mother left this world as an unsettled spirit, in relation to her family, and that a great deal of anger and hurt had been left unspoken. In addition, Carla felt guilty for having gone through her dead mother's clothing so soon; she felt even more so for having taken her mother to the hospital, where she died alone.

Carla dreamed of her mother over the next several months, but without the vividness of the dream the night of her mother's death. Finally Carla had a dramatic dream that helped resolve her mixed and difficult feelings about her mother (The complete dream text appears in Chapter 8):

I hold [my mother] in my arms. We talk of unresolved anger, incidents of conflict from past years. There is a pervasive mutual sense of forgiveness and unconditional love. As I hold her, her body undergoes several magical dreamlike metamorphoses. She becomes a tiny, vibrant pink-skinned infant, an unrecognizable animal form, a grotesquely disfigured elderly woman, then back to herself. I am not alarmed or repulsed by these changes; my posture is one of nonjudgmental acceptance and love.

I am crying in the dream as this transformation unfolds, as I know it is a prelude to her final departure. The tears are not of anguish, but of release for both of us.

Peacefully, and with an exceptional aura of surrender in each of our hearts, she dies in my arms.

This dream fits the format of the messages "I Forgive You" and "Please Forgive Me." From this time on, Carla's dreams about her mother decreased markedly. Later, at a couple of key points in her life, Carla again dreamed about her mother, and her image continues to recur in times of struggle and of joy.

This "dream death" experience of Carla's could, of course, be seen as a simple wish fulfillment—she would have liked to be present at her mother's death and comfort her without reserve. Yet the effect of such dreams is not simple; it is profoundly positive.

Carla believes that her mutual-forgiveness dream has been "a remarkable and effective tool in coming to terms with my mother's death" and in generating a resolution in the relationship that was incomplete when her mother died.

Those of you who may have endured an alarming dream in which you were subjected to the wrath of a deceased person can find encouragement in Carla's experience. Resolutions in dreams can be as satisfying and life-supporting as if they had happened prior to the person's death. Dreams that carry the message "You Fool!" can point the way. They may be followed by dreams of resolution, as they were for Carla.

Joyce Brothers's Dead Husband Vents Anger[2]

Psychologist Joyce Brothers has given a touching account, in her book *Widowed,* of the "angry ghost" in her early dreams about her deceased husband, Milt. Before his death, Milt had been ravaged with complications from bladder cancer. Understandably, he resented the deterioration of his body and his impending death. In the last few months of his life, Brothers writes, Milt directed his anger toward her. In so many relationships, when we know the other person will continue to love us no matter how we behave, we sometimes vent our frustrations onto them. Milt had no one else to express his anger to, and knew that his wife would stand by him. Brothers had resolved not to let it show that her dying husband's anger bothered her, but understandably it did. Mates of dying men and women often feel forced to absorb unkind behavior, which leaves them depressed and anxious.

For a long time after her husband's death at age sixty-two, in a bleak January, Brothers had unpleasant dreams in which Milt was always angry with her. He still looked bone-thin and ravaged. Even so, she felt glad to sense his presence again in these dreams. Awake, she grieved anew. Dreams of her angry husband recurred for months.

Then, the autumn after he died, Milt appeared in one of Brothers's dreams looking and acting more like his old self before the illness. The second spring after his death, Brothers had what she described as "a miracle dream":

We were at the farm, just the two of us. It was snowing hard. The house was toasty warm, a fire blazing on the hearth. There was the spicy fragrance of the fresh-baked gingerbread that I had just taken out of the oven.

Suddenly Milt and I were outdoors. The snow had stopped. The sun was bright. We were slipping and sliding on the snow as we made our way down the hill toward the brook. We were holding hands and laughing. And everywhere there were flowers. Daffodils were blooming on low woody bushes. The trees were in bloom with roses and daisies. It was a fantasy land. We picked some of the flowers to put on the dinner table that night.

As we went back to the house, our arms full of flowers, I told Milt, "How lovely it is to have a second chance to be with you." I totally appreciated what it meant to be with him. It was a wonderful feeling. I knew it was a dream, but even when I woke up, the feeling of pleasure and closeness persisted.

This dream and other pleasant ones that followed, about their times together, gave Brothers much satisfaction. She said that each one of them was "like a gift, a rerun of the happy days I miss so much." She felt that her husband was only "lent" to her in these dreams and that they would lessen, in the usual pattern. This comforting dream message is a variation of the form I call "I'll Always Love You." Notice that the snow is followed by sunlight and flowers, warmth and physical contact—these are often images that arise in pleasurable dreams about love.

Such vivid dreams of delight are turning points as the bereaved person begins to resolve grief. Although sorrow may still linger, the feeling becomes less one of heavy anguish and suffering, and more one of nostalgia and gratitude for having had good times together. Be patient if you receive a "You Fool!" dream message; you may—by time and inner work—bring forth a transformation.

Another effect of "You Fool!" dream messages may be to prompt you to take action to relieve feelings of guilt before another death takes place, as happened with Tom.

Bob's Dead Grandmother Accuses Him

Bob's grandmother had been dead for some twenty-five years when he had an extraordinarily intense dream about her that transformed his behavior.

Bob had become almost completely alienated from his father. He accepted his mother's and sisters' negative comments about the man without question, feeling that his father deserved his hate and resentment.

Imagine Bob's surprise when he dreamed one night:

A face suddenly zooms toward me, leaving a silver thread behind it, as a jet does when it is flying very high. It is the face of my grandmother, lit by a very bright white light. She looks very stern as she says, "Why are you crucifying my son?" She repeats this twice. I am in wonderment. She zooms back as quickly as she came and I wake up, knowing this is more than a dream.

Bob said his dead grandmother looked the same as when he had known her years ago. Her "stern fearsomeness" and the "shocking realism" of this dream made Bob rethink his behavior toward his father. The brightness of the white light suggested to Bob that what his grandmother said must be the truth.

Although it was hard for Bob to believe that his ideas and feelings about his father were mistaken, the dream forced him to question his beliefs for the first time. He reviewed his life and his relationship with his father. He began to understand the man's frustrations, and how his mother had played a role in them. Gradually, over several months of introspection, Bob felt his hatred toward his father melt into compassion.

When Bob returned to his hometown not long after this dream, having been away for several years, he heard that his father had been hospitalized after a heart attack. He went to see his father and told him that he had no further ill feelings toward him or how he lived his life. He was able to thank his father for giving him life; they talked about the good times, rather than arguing about the bad ones.

Bob felt grateful he was able to change his relationship directly with his father while he was still alive. He no longer felt consumed with bitterness toward him, or burdened by the heavy weight that imposed. The father and son were able to respect one another; Bob gained a sense of peace as a result of his shocking dream. In a very real way, his dream that his grandmother accused him of crucifying his father woke Bob up to the truth.

If, in a dream, you find yourself being berated by someone who has died, you need to consider whether there is any truth to their complaints and whether alteration of your behavior is desirable. The accusations may or may not be true. You need not accept the blame if it is not deserved. Remember that dreams exaggerate and dramatize, as if to make us pay attention. In the case described below, we see how Paul Tholey, too, decided there was some—but not total—validity to the dream accusations.

Our dreams about the dead not only may affect our emotions toward the deceased and other people, but also may have a profound impact upon our work life.

Virginia Woolf's Dead Father Snorts at Her Work

British writer Virginia Woolf recorded a classic example of the dream message "You Fool!" in a letter to a friend in 1908, about four years after her father's arduous death. Virginia was only twenty-two and her sister Vanessa twenty-five when their father died; their mother had died nine years earlier. Woolf's relationship with her father, Leslie Stephen, had always been conflictual. On the one hand she admired him as a scholar, literary critic, and historian—he was the editor of the respected *Dictionary of National Bi-*

ography—but on the other hand she resented his harsh treatment of Vanessa over her poor housekeeping skills.

After Leslie Stephen's death, although Vanessa appeared to be relieved, both daughters suffered from guilt. Vanessa undoubtedly felt ambivalent toward her dead father, perhaps regretful he had been so displeased with her in his last years, and at the same time, angry over his hardness toward her. Years later, Vanessa's son wrote that after her father died, his mother dreamed that she had committed a murder. She recognized the connection between it and her guilty feelings over being relieved at her father's death, and, he said, promptly stopped such dreaming.

Woolf first began to try writing fiction in 1908, at age twenty-six; she was preparing the manuscript for a novel when she wrote in a letter to her sister's husband, who was advising her:

> *I dreamt last night that I was showing father the manuscript of my novel; and he snorted, and dropped it on to a table, and I was very melancholy, and read it this morning, and thought it bad. You dont realise the depth of modesty in to which I fall.*[3]

Woolf awoke from her dream feeling profoundly discouraged. She had never written a novel before, or showed an attempt to do so to her father, so the dream situation was imaginary.

On one level, of course, the dream expressed Woolf's own self-criticism as well as the criticism she imagined her father would have about her work. She probably also wanted her sister's husband to reassure her regarding the quality of her manuscript.

Despite this dream disapproval, Woolf went on to become an outstanding novelist. However, she remained supersensitive to any criticism of her work and agonized over reviews of it for the remainder of her life.

When a relationship with the deceased was especially ambivalent, it continues to be so after death. You may find yourself yearning in dreams for approval, which the deceased withheld in waking life. Perhaps you are one of the many people who dream of arguing with or being scolded by dead parents decades beyond their deaths. It is important for dreamers to find resolution. Paul Tholey's case provides an inspiring model.

Paul Tholey's Dead Father Insults Him

Psychologist Paul Tholey, at the Psychology Institute of Wolfgang Goethe University in Frankfurt, has studied lucid dreams (dreams in which we know we are dreaming) since 1959, and uses them as a therapeutic tool for self-healing. Tholey refers to a lucid dream as a *Klartraum* (clear dream). His findings, previously unavailable in English, are helpful. If you receive the dream message "You Fool!" you may find Tholey's suggestions useful, too.

Tholey believes that the most effective technique a dreamer can use to deprive a threatening figure of its dangerous characteristics is "conciliation." He came to this conclusion after a series of dreams about his deceased father:

> After my father's death in 1968, he often appeared to me in my dreams as a dangerous figure, who insulted and threatened me. When I became lucid, I would beat him in anger. He was then sometimes transformed into a more primitive creature, like a dwarf, an animal, or a mummy. Whenever I won, I was overcome by a feeling of triumph. Nevertheless, my father continued to appear as a threatening figure in subsequent dreams.[4]

Until this point in Tholey's experience, the dream messenger was yelling the equivalent of "You Fool!" and Tholey's response was the equivalent of "I Hate You." Happily, a change took place:

> Then I had the following decisive dream. I became lucid, while being chased by a tiger, and wanted to flee. I then pulled myself together, stood my ground, and asked, "Who are you?" The tiger was taken aback but was transformed into my father and answered, "I am your father and will now tell you what you are to do!" In contrast to my earlier dreams, I did not attempt to beat him but tried to get involved in a dialogue with him. I told him that he could not order me around. I rejected his threats and insults. On the other hand, I had to admit that some of my father's criticism was justified, and I decided to change my behavior accordingly. At that moment, my father became friendly, and we shook hands. I asked him if he could help me, and he

*encouraged me to go my own way alone. My father then seemed to
slip into my own body, and I remained alone in the dream.*[5]

Tholey found this dream had a "liberating and encouraging effect on my future dreaming and waking life." He said his father
never again appeared as a threatening dream figure, and in the
waking state, Tholey's fear and inhibitions in dealing with figures of
authority vanished. Would this beneficial result have occurred had
Tholey not first experienced being able to physically overcome his
father in earlier dreams?

I find that confronting hostile dream figures—whether "angry
ghosts" or other types—is remarkably successful in stripping threatening dream figures of their power. Turning to face the tiger, the angry witch, and other such figures has transformed them into a kitten,
a mother, and similar less frightening images. Our fear provides
threatening dream figures the power to grow in size and harmful-
ness; our courage causes them to shrink and become less hostile. It
may be that what is essential is the courage to face the danger, alone
or with help, not to crush it.

Tholey concluded that aggressive behavior by the dreamer in
a dream can have a cathartic effect in a short period of time without being therapeutic in the long run. He says that the good feelings resulting from destroying a hostile figure by killing it were
sometimes mixed with fear and guilt that might continue while
awake. However, submitting to a dream enemy's aggression by allowing oneself to be killed almost always led to fear and discouragement.

For me, as for Tholey, the middle road of confronting the
threatening figure with confidence, and challenging it, proved most
effective. Moreover, in the waking state, many people who had
these confrontation dreams gained in self-reliance.

How to Cope with "Angry Ghost" Dreams

Here are some suggestions for dealing with threatening dream
figures, whether they are deceased parents or other dead persons
(based in part on Tholey's model and in part on my own):[6]

1. *Confront and conquer by force.* When faced with a menacing dream figure, confront it. If it continues to threaten you, or physically attacks, counterattack it, fighting by yourself or getting help. In apparent life-or-death situations, kill the dream figure. If destruction proves necessary, allow the spirit of the conquered figure to continue to exist in a helpful form. When you have successfully proved to yourself that it is possible to triumph over dream enemies, move on to the next step.

2. *Confront with confidence.* Turn around, face the menacing dream figure, gaze directly into its eyes, and challenge it. Ask it "Who are you?" "What do you want?" "Why are you doing this?" Be willing to listen to reasonable answers and discuss them.

3. *Confront with friendliness.* Question the hostile dream figure in a friendly manner, while continuing to maintain eye contact.

4. *Offer reconciliation.* Make a bargain with the threatening figure. Befriend it. Offer to change behaviors if appropriate.

5. *Request help.* Ask the dream figure to give you a gift, solve a problem, guide your future, or grant any other request you wish to make.

6. *Enter the dream figure's body.* Can you understand it better from this perspective?

7. *Enjoy the dream figure.* Interact with it in positive, pleasurable ways—swim with it, fly with it; be happy with it. If reconciliation and dialogue have been fruitless, separate yourself from this dream figure, at least for the time being.

8. *Bless the dream figure.* Surround it with golden light. Open your heart to it. Let it merge with you. Love it despite all.

9. *Seek out any hostile dream figures or situations.* When you feel confident of your ability to cope with dream dangers, then deliberately seek out and find them. Take this step only after considerable success in dealing with the hostile figures that spontaneously arise in dreams. Move from the safe, protected spaces of your dream to the dangerous ones; go from the light into the dark, from high places to low places, from the present into the past. Enter the eye of the storm, go into the tidal wave, face the worst. You may want to carry with you special protective devices and be accompanied by a helper.

*   *   *

Because this is your dream, you may choose to use any or all of these steps for interacting with hostile dream figures. It's up to you. There are opposite actions you may want to take when the dead appear in your dreams bringing good wishes.

"Congratulations!"

....

Dream Message: "Congratulations!"
Deceased indicates strong approval of the dreamer.

Frequency: Rare but important.
Response after Awake: Dreamer usually feels delight, even exaltation. Uplifted mood may last a long time.

If messages of "You Fool!" emerge when dreamers feel self-critical or sense how disapproving a deceased person would be about some action or omission, messages of "Congratulations!" arise when the dreamers feel they have accomplished something that they themselves are proud of, or that would give great pleasure to the dead person.

In times past, dreams of "Congratulations!" would have been welcomed as blessings flowing from the spiritual world: The ancestors are pleased. Today, such dreams evoke strong personal gratification.

Paul Tholey and His Dead Father Merge

We saw, in the last section, how Paul Tholey's dreams of his angry father transformed over time. Here, by repetition, I want to call your attention to the final aspect of that transformation:

. . . I told him that he could not order me around. I rejected his threats and insults. On the other hand, I had to admit that some of my father's criticism was justified. . . . At that moment, my father became friendly, and we shook hands. I asked him if he could help me, and he encouraged me to go my own way alone. My father then seemed to slip into my own body, and I remained alone in the dream.[7]

By shaking his son's hand in the dream, Tholey's deceased father was indicating—at long last—his approval of his son. In a real sense, Tholey had become his own man, having firmly rejected some of his father's criticism of him, having accepted other aspects of it, and having become willing to change certain behaviors. The "liberating effect" of this dream freed him from his fears and inhibitions in dealing with figures of authority, demonstrating the importance of this step in the dreamer's self-development. "You Fool!" had transformed into "Congratulations!"

What are we to make of Tholey's merging with the figure of his father? It seems to me that this element of the dream shows us how the angry-ghost figures of our dreams are—at least in part—our own self-criticisms. We sometimes project onto the deceased's image in a dream our own words and thoughts that we are not yet able to accept. By dreaming that his reconciled father "seemed to slip into my own body," Tholey finally integrated the father part of himself that he had formerly rejected. By incorporating this modified father part, he became whole. Freud might call this a "positive introjection."

If you should have a dream in which the deceased cries out, "You Fool!" you will want to consider, as Bob did and Paul Tholey did, whether there is any aspect of what was said in the dream that is true. If so, alter your behavior accordingly. You may find it frees you for a fuller life.

Sometimes we have to change our lives before dreams of "Congratulations!" arise, as Emanuel Swedenborg did.

Emanuel Swedenborg's Dead Father Approves of His Work

The Swedish philosopher-scientist-mystic Emanuel Swedenborg lived in the eighteenth century, but his relationship with his father was a conflictual one many modern people share. A businessman wants his son to take over the business; instead, the son goes into the arts. A physician wants his son to join him in practice; instead, the son dedicates himself to a life in computer research. Swedenborg's father was a minister and bishop who had always wanted his son to follow his own religious career; instead, the son chose science. His father was irate. They remained distant for the rest of the father's life.

Some nine years after his father's death, Swedenborg recorded in his *Journal of Dreams* an entry that gave him great satisfaction. In his dream:

Father is tying the lace cuffs that I wear.[8]

At that time, lace cuffs were worn only by laypeople, while the clergy wore plain cuffs. To dream of his father assisting him in this manner suggested to Swedenborg that his dead father had finally accepted his son's chosen role as scientist.

However, it is important to know that despite having rejected a career as a minister, shortly before his dream Swedenborg had undergone several powerful spiritual experiences. These prompted him to use his scientific skills to probe the spiritual world. It was probably this integration of an element of the spiritual into his work that stimulated Swedenborg's dream of his father's approval.

When we dream of a dead relative accepting and praising our work, we are likely to feel that what we are currently doing would please the person if he or she were still living. People who hear the dream messenger say "Congratulations!" often feel, as Swedenborg did, that the spirit of the deceased is truly present and made happy by them.

Another area of the dreamer's life that evokes "Congratulations!" dreams, in addition to changes in attitude and work style, is the birth of children, grandchildren, and other descendants that the deceased never had a chance to see. Remember this approval need not be in specific words. A gesture, as was the case for Swedenborg, or a look of pride may convey the message.

Tagore's Dead Mother Praises His Work

A revered Indian philosopher of the nineteenth century named De-
bendranath Tagore was the head of a movement that sought to
modernize Hinduism. He struggled to find a balance between modern beliefs and traditional, sometimes superstitious practices. He
found some of that balance in a dream that followed a sleepless
night of anxiety and trouble in which "my head felt dazed on the
pillow." Finally, Tagore fell into a "borderland between waking and
sleeping" when:

> One came to me in the dark and said "Get up," and I at once sat up.
> He said "Get out of bed," and I got up; he said "Follow me" and I
> followed. He went down the steps leading out of the inner apart-
> ments, I did the same and came out into the courtyard with him. . . .
> From thence he mounted upwards to the sky, I also followed him.
> Clusters of stars and planets were shedding a bright lustre, right and
> left and in front of me, and I was passing through them . . .

The mysterious guide next took Tagore "through a spectral city,
to a quiet, spacious room of white marble":

> I sat silent in that silent room; shortly afterwards the curtain of one
> of the doors in front of the room was drawn aside and my mother
> appeared. Her hair was down, just as I had seen it on the day of her
> death. . . . She said "I wanted to see thee, so I sent for thee. Hast thou
> really become one who has known Brahma? Sanctified is the family,
> fulfilled is the mother's desire." On seeing her, and hearing these
> sweet words of hers my slumber gave way before a flood of joy. I
> found myself still tossing on my bed.[9]

This classic version of "Congratulations!" parallels the modern
dreamer's one of feeling fulfilled by the praise of a dead parent.
Tagore, like Swedenborg, was greatly encouraged in his actions by
this potent dream of his mother's approval.

Ancient or contemporary, primitive tribal member or industri-
alized urban dweller, we are connected to the ancestral stream by

our dreams. Psychologist Kelly Bulkeley, author of *Spiritual Dreaming,* points out that "many of the world's spiritual traditions consider dreams of the dead to be the single most direct means of relating to sacred powers and realities."[10]

Here's how your dreams about ancestors may connect to the next generation.

Jorge's Dead Father Meets His Grandson

Jorge was very close to his elderly father despite the physical distance between them; he lived with his wife in the United States while his father and mother continued to live in Mexico. When his father died in his eighties after a second heart attack, Jorge traveled home for the funeral. The first thing he saw when he arrived at the family house was his father in his casket. "The image stuck," he told me.

For some two and a half years after his father died, Jorge did not dream about him at all. Like so many people, he found it too painful to reexperience the loss even in a dream. Jorge thinks it was because whenever he thought about his father, he saw him dead in the casket. Meanwhile, Jorge's wife, who became pregnant a few months after the father died, gave birth to a healthy son. Finally, Jorge dreamed of his father:

> We are in a garden. I am standing so close to my father I can smell his aftershave lotion. My son (then about one year old) is playing around in the flowers and grass. I introduce my father to my son. He is so pleased. "See? I told you! It's great to have a child!" he says. My father is so real. I feel his presence. We smile and talk. I tell him that we're planning another baby. He is really happy. It's wonderful to be with him.

Gardens were a special place to Jorge's father, who taught his son much about the care of plants. Observe the sensation of smelling the father's aftershave lotion. Fragrances are often associated in dreams with powerful emotions; they evoke the feel of reality.

Jorge's father had lived to see his son marry, after a wild youth, and was very fond of his son's wife. The last time Jorge and his father were together before his death, the father asked when he and his wife were going to have a baby. "We're thinking about it," replied Jorge. "Don't think too hard" was the father's response. Jorge's dream brought a fulfillment to himself and, he feels, to his father's spirit. Such dreams leave the dreamer feeling blessed.

Joanne's Dead Grandfather Meets Her Nephews

Joanne, who had had several dreams about her deceased father bringing the message "I'm Not Really Dead" (described in Chapter 3), eventually had a dream in which he symbolically said "Congratulations!" Three and a half years after her father's death, Joanne dreamed:

> I am with my nephews, holding the younger one. He tells me a lot of nice things, including that he loves me. My brother has brought them to me to take to see my father. Then I am holding my older nephew, and my father is there. I give my nephew to my father and say, "This is your grandpa." As they are together, I tell my younger nephew about my grandfather. As I do, he steps out from behind my father. Surprised, I say, "This is my grandpa!" They spend some time together.
>
> When we get back, my brother is waiting there and my younger nephew runs to him, saying, "I met your grandpa!"

This dream is a favorite of Joanne's. We can understand the pleasure of being able to introduce children from the new generation—in Jorge's case, his son to his father, who had never seen his grandson, and in Joanne's case, her nephews to her grandfather, who had never met them.

Numerous other dreamers have told me dreams of introducing dead relatives, such as a grandmother, to their newborn infants. Some dreamers describe being visited by a deceased favorite aunt, or some other dead relative who shows up to report approval of a new mate or a new home, and convey love.

Accepting the Blessings of the Dead

You have seen how many types of dream messages can complete the unfinished aspects of your relationships with the dead. Dreams of "Congratulations!" provide an opportunity that was denied us in waking life—by the death of the older person—to introduce our significant people to one another. These dreams impart a feeling of completeness, of joining the circle of the future to the past.

Whether we dream of the dead coming to approve of—or at least accept—our behavior, our work, or the new life that has come forth since their deaths, we rejoice. These dreams of "Congratulations!" feel real because they *are* real experiences. Perhaps it is the actual spirit of the lost person touching ours again for a moment. Perhaps it is our conception of him or her. Whichever it is, the results are life-affirming.

If "You Fool!" carries the condemnation of the dead to the dreamer, "Congratulations!" dream messages bring their blessing. Like a loving godparent at a graduation, a marriage, a baptism, or a birthday celebration, dream messengers who say "Congratulations!" are most welcome guests in our dreams. Their benedictions bestow a sense of special favor; their praise uplifts us.

When you dream about an ancestor commending your work, you may be applauding your own search for higher moral or spiritual values. Or you may be directly contacting some higher power. No matter.

In a real sense, by accepting the blessings of the dead in dreams, we release our innermost energies for outer life. We feel encouraged, even inspired, to fulfill our lives in the time we are given.

5

∞

"You'll Be Sorry!" and "Here's a Gift"

"You'll Be Sorry!"

Dream Message: "You'll Be Sorry!"
Deceased curses the dreamer.

Frequency: Extremely rare but important.

Response after Awake:
Dreamer most often feels excessive remorse or fear that
may linger or escalate thereafter.

If the dream message "You Fool!" brings the dreamer the condemnation of the dead person, "You'll Be Sorry!" brings his or her curses. The difference between the messages is one of severity. In the case of "You Fool!" the dreamer usually feels guilty, as with the woman who sorted through her dead mother's belongings the evening of the day her mother died. In the case of "You'll Be Sorry!" the dreamer is tormented by excessive guilt—with or without justification. These are the dreams of the survivors of horrific accidents, the sufferers of post-traumatic stress syndrome, especially when the dreamer somehow feels responsible for the tragic death of another. These are also the dreams of the repentant murderer.

The Furies and Nemesis

Such dreams of torment are like the modern version of the Furies of ancient Greece. In the classic Greek tragedy of Aeschylus' *Oresteia*, Orestes, the son of Agamemnon and Clytemnestra, slew his mother. His guilt was somewhat alleviated by the fact that his mother and her lover had killed his father; also, Orestes was ordered by the gods speaking through the oracle at Delphi to avenge the death of his father.

Nonetheless, the sin of matricide, or the murder of any blood relative, was considered so heinous as to deserve severe punishment. Thus the Furies—the three avenging deities of retribution— were called from the abyss to pursue and torment Orestes. The task of these children of the goddess Night was to punish crimes beyond the reach of human justice. Their duty was accomplished by dogging the footsteps of murderers until they were driven mad. Howling and hissing, these female spirits pursued Orestes from land to land, never letting him rest. At long last, after many adventures and much suffering, Orestes took refuge in the temple of Athena (the goddess of wisdom, called Minerva by the Romans) at Athens. There a trial was held. When the judges of the court were equally divided over Orestes' guilt or innocence, Athena herself commanded that he be set free.

Another figure of punishment in ancient Greek tradition was Nemesis, the goddess of vengeance. She was depicted with wings, holding the wheel of fortune, and riding in a chariot drawn by mythological creatures called griffins. Nemesis had the power to invoke the Furies and set them upon a wrongdoer. When we refer to some threatening person as "our nemesis," we are using the name of this ancient goddess.

Today, we are less likely to think of the Furies or of Nemesis, and more likely to speak of our own internal sense of wrongdoing. No wonder people who have committed crimes beyond the toleration of society—and eventually themselves—sometimes turn to religion, with the hope that repentance will bring forgiveness for their sins.

Expiation for a great wrong is sometimes found by other means than a religious conversion, as we can see in the case of the contemporary American author William Vollman.

William Vollman Is Pursued by His Drowned Sister

William Vollman, who wrote *The Rainbow Stories* and other books based on his personal experiences in the underworld of prostitutes, winos, and skinheads, suffered for years from a nightmare of the "You'll Be Sorry!" form.

Vollman is the oldest of four siblings. When he was only nine years old, he was left in charge of his six-year-old sister on the edge of a pond in New Hampshire. He knew that the shallow bottom of the pond dropped off abruptly; and he knew that his sister could not swim. At one point, the boy stopped paying attention. "I was lost in some kind of daydream," he said in a 1994 interview with a *New York Times* reporter.[1] Sadly, this moment of carelessness resulted in the drowning death of Vollman's sister.

The feelings of profound guilt that followed his sister's death invaded Vollman's sleep:

> I had nightmares practically every night of her skeleton chasing me and punishing me, pretty much through high school.[2]

After this tragedy, Vollman felt unwanted at home, and was too miserable to talk to his parents about this and other feelings. He left as soon as possible, choosing a tough working ranch/college that would take him away from his hometown area.

Eventually, Vollman became a writer who lives out a special kind of expiation. He focuses on experiencing bizarre, even dangerous styles of living; then he describes them vividly in his novels, stories, and poems. He mingles his life with his work, using his body and personality as an experimental field. For instance, in an abandoned weather station at the magnetic North Pole, alone in the middle of winter for two weeks, he nearly died before a rescue plane arrived, but he got the understanding of loneliness and fear he wanted for a book describing how the explorer Sir John Franklin and his party starved to death in the Arctic in a doomed attempt to find the Northwest Passage.

In the Tenderloin district of San Francisco, Vollman paid prostitutes to tell him their stories. Finding they would not trust him unless he shared their drugs, he smoked crack and drank wine with them, seemingly without addicting himself. He has wandered the brothels of Thailand and Cambodia without proper protection; it seems that many prostitutes there object to condoms. He has taken similar risks in researching stories on transvestism and attempted suicide.

Vollman appears to be on a mission to help people, to save them, as he was unable to save his sister. In one instance, he kidnapped a sex slave—a child prostitute from a brothel in the south of Thailand—and took her to Bangkok, where he enrolled her in a vocational school. He extracted a receipt from her father, stating that technically she belonged to him. Acts such as this involve serious hazard because it is said that local pimps usually murder their child whores once they are worn out—certainly they would not appreciate having their product abducted before extracting all possible income from her. Vollman said to an interviewer, "I'm a real sucker for that stuff, you know, because of my sister, if she's a girl and she's in trouble, then anything I can do . . ."[3]

Vollman's writing has a large cult following. He is producing a seven-volume book called *Seven Dreams,* re-creating the history of the North American continent, three volumes of which have been published. He has been described by the *Washington Post* as "the most prodigiously talented and historically important American novelist under 35."[4]

Yet whether or not Vollman will survive his chosen lifestyle remains to be seen. Certainly his drowned sister's dream "curse" has haunted his life. We can hope that the skeleton of his sister no longer chases him in his nightmares as he acts out his efforts to save others who appear to be lost—perhaps himself among them—and to drag them out of the deep pond to the safe edge of shore.

The Ghosts of Nero's Mother and His Wife Haunt Him

The Roman emperor Nero, who was born in A.D. 37 and died at the age of only thirty-one, was considered one of the most debauched and cruel of the twelve caesars. He was notorious for the lecherous passion he held for his mother, Agrippina, which he partly satisfied by selecting a mistress who was his mother's "spitting image." It is unclear whether he committed incest with his mother—some historians believe he did—but he certainly seduced freeborn boys and married women, raped the vestal virgin, had a slave boy castrated to make him more like a woman, and "married" him in a mock wedding ceremony, in addition to acquiring three wives.

Agrippina retained great power over her son. Eventually, Nero came to resent her ever-watchful eye. He deprived her of honor, expelled her from the palace, and forced her to retire to the island of Rhodes. Later he tried three times to poison her, but she had always taken the precaution of swallowing an antidote in advance. He then tried to have his mother drowned by arranging for a boat in which she was traveling to sink, but she swam to safety. Finally, he had her assassinated. He then carefully examined her corpse, commenting on her good and bad points.

Nero's cruelty toward his family members and friends would make him seem invulnerable to guilt. He poisoned various other relatives, and had one of his wives, Octavia, executed; he kicked another, Poppaea, to death while she was pregnant, and had her child by a former marriage drowned.

Yet Nero's murder of his mother haunted him. He often admitted that he was hounded by his mother's ghost and that the Furies were pursuing him with whips and burning torches. He arranged for Persian magicians to try to conjure up his mother's ghost and entreat its forgiveness.

I have mentioned that the crime of matricide was especially abhorred in olden times. In ancient Rome, the punishment for the murder of either parent was to be sewn up in a sack with a dog, a cock, a snake, and a monkey, and then cast into the river Tiber or the sea to drown. As Nero came to be universally loathed, someone draped a sack around the neck of a statue of him, with a note saying that such drowning was what he deserved.

Before having his mother killed, Nero was said not to remember his dreams. Afterward, his dreams terrified him. It is recorded that Nero dreamed:[5]

- that someone tore the tiller of a ship from his hands, preventing him from steering

- that the statues of the nations in the Theater of Pompey surrounded him and he was unable to escape

- that his favorite horse was transformed into an ape that whinnied a tune

- that the doors of the Mausoleum opened and a voice called: "Enter, Nero!"

Clearly, Nero was fearing retribution for his crimes. His dreams, which were viewed as omens of evil for the dreamer, suggest that he felt he had lost control of his life (in losing the tiller of the ship); that he feared being trapped by his people (the female statues, personifications of the provinces of Rome, that moved in to surround him); that his instinctual life (his favorite horse) had become base (an ape) and foolish (whinnying a tune); and that death was calling out to him (the open Mausoleum, with a voice entreating him to enter—Romans believed that tombs were the dwelling places of the dead). These were inauspicious dreams indeed.

From the point of view of "You'll Be Sorry!" dream messages from the dead, the following dream of Nero's is most telling:

His [deceased] wife Octavia dragged him down into darkness, where he was covered by swarming winged ants.[6]

This dream of Nero's seems to be another version of the Furies hounding him. In this case, it is his wronged wife—whom he tried to strangle on several occasions before he had her falsely accused of adultery and executed—who drew him into the abyss where he was tortured by swarming ants. Octavia had good cause to threaten the dreamer that he would be sorry for what he did to her. Nero had good reason to fear he would somehow be punished for his behavior.

Nero is most remembered for having had Rome set on fire, while he played his lyre—he fancied himself a great musical artist—and watched the city's destruction with pleasure.

Understandably, various provinces began to revolt against Nero, sending armies to conquer him. Nero awoke in the palace one night at midnight to find that his bodyguard had deserted him. Even his friends kept their doors closed and would not answer his summons. With a few of his staff, Nero attempted to escape in disguise to a friend's suburban villa. Crossing a briar patch and crawling through a tunnel, he finally reached the villa, with cavalry in close pursuit. Realizing that he would be captured momentarily, Nero, to avoid inevitable public execution by being flogged to death, stabbed himself in the throat with the help of his secretary. He died, "eyes glazed and bulging from their sockets, a sight which horrified everybody present."[7] Thus Nero himself carried out the curse of his dream messenger, "You'll Be Sorry!"

When word of Nero's death reached the people, citizens ran through the streets in celebration.

Did Nero's dreams predict his future? Were the angry ghosts of his murdered victims haunting him? Or were his agonized dreams reflections of his own guilty conscience? No matter. Nero paid the price of his misdeeds, asleep and awake.

Macbeth Sees the Ghost of a Man Whose Murder He Arranged

In William Shakespeare's tragedy *Macbeth,* the murderer Macbeth is confronted at a banquet by the ghost of a friend he has had killed. Macbeth says: "Thou canst not say I did it: Never shake/Thy gory locks at me." Lady Macbeth tells her husband, "This is the very painting of your fear . . ." and hurriedly breaks up the banquet.

Later Macbeth learns that although his friend, Banquo, has indeed been killed as planned, the lord's young son has escaped the murder plot. Macbeth feels as imperiled as before. He sleeps little thereafter.

Lady Macbeth's sleep, too, becomes disturbed, her mind unhinged by her crimes. She sleepwalks, and talks piteously as she performs a ritual washing of her hands, trying to rid herself of the blood of her husband's victims—for it was she who urged him into the initial act of violence. Her eyes are open, "but their sense is shut." As she pantomimes washing her hands, Lady Macbeth pleads, in the famous line, "Out, damned spot! out, I say!"

Those who are familiar with the play know that eventually Lady Macbeth commits suicide to escape her guilt, and Macbeth, who has become a complete tyrant, is vanquished in single combat with Macduff, his head cut off to stick upon a pole.

Although Shakespeare's tragedy is fiction, the elements of guilt, vision, and acted-out nightmare are based on reality. Shakespeare's genius may have been in part his ability to render real human responses to emotions, in this instance guilt and remorse.

Coping with the Curses of the Dead

If we have survived a harrowing situation in which other people have died or been badly injured, we may find ourselves anguished by feelings of guilt and/or nightmares in which the dead seem to berate or curse us for our behavior.

You saw how William Vollman suffered nightmares about his sister's skeleton chasing him after her accidental drowning. War veterans may be tormented for years by horrendous dreams of dying comrades they were unable to save.

In contrast, if we have deliberately caused another person's death, nightmares involving his or her curses are more justified. Nero knew he was committing crimes that deserved retribution. His nightmares proved this, and eventually he paid with his own life. Whether modern murderers dream about their victims demanding retribution is unknown.

In the folklore of most cultures, the most devastating curses possible are those of a father and those of a dying person—a dying father's curse being the worst of all. This evil-saying—a malediction, in contrast to a benediction, a good saying—is a key feature of Italian operas.

The power a curse invokes is felt even by those contemporary people who deny divinity, the devil, and magic. The accursed will see any future illness, destruction of belongings, or physical danger to self and family as the result of the fulfilled curse. People who have been cursed may fear loss of their immortal souls. The wishing of evil upon another person stirs age-old fears: the belief in an evil spell still lingers beneath civilized surfaces.

One would think that if the curse is unjustified—if something bad happened to another through no intention of one's own—the person who was cursed could dismiss it. Yet the curse, once uttered, seems to have a life of its own. Brought into existence, it remains a threat to the accursed, any relatives, and sometimes the curser as well.

There is said to be little defense against a curse unless the accursed person either propitiates the power invoked or brings a stronger power to bear against it.

Religious persons have various options. Making a confession, being truly repentant, seeking absolution, and making atonement for one's wrongdoings may relieve feelings of guilt. This is probably why people in jail, or running to escape, sometimes experience religious conversions, hoping to find emotional relief.

All people may reduce remorse by asking for forgiveness from the person or the spirit of the wronged person. Making retribution to the extent possible also may help. If the wronged person is no longer alive, making restorative efforts to his or her living relatives can bring relief. Those involved in twelve-step programs will recognize this important step.[8]

In addition, it is vital for us to forgive those who have mistakenly cursed us. (See the last chapter for suggestions.) The case described below is a good example of how this can take place in dreams. The spoken magic of a curse is paralleled by the spoken magic of a blessing.

"Here's a Gift"

Sandra Is Gifted with Floral Corsage from Her Murdered Friend

Sandra had a remarkable experience with a dream gift. She had had a friend from first grade through high school who was also named Sandra, nicknamed Sandee (not her real name). This loving and outgoing young woman had been murdered at the age of twenty-four by serial killer Ted Bundy. While living in Hawaii, where her husband was stationed in the navy, Sandra learned of the death of her friend from a relative who sent her a clipping describing the discovery of Sandee's remains in some woods near Seattle.

Sandra was so shaken by her friend's death that she was unable to even think about it or express her profound grief and fears. It was years later, when she began to record her dreams in journals, that she began to dream about Sandee. These dreams led Sandra to her minister's office, sobbing, and her process of delayed mourning began. Sandra wanted to believe that her murdered friend was at peace, but she could hardly accept that, when Sandee had had such a violent death. She felt great anger toward Ted Bundy, who was then on death row in Florida, having been convicted of murders there, too.

For the first time, Sandra was able to talk about her feelings with her minister, and shortly afterward had a dream that helped her heal:

I'm at a Christian women's retreat for the weekend. We haven't been allowed to wear our watches so that we can experience freedom away from the constraints of time. One of the ladies can't stand not knowing what time it is, and dials the telephone number to find out, but another woman disconnects her before she can discover the time.

Everyone here has been given flowers and greens, and I see that some of the women have woven them into wreaths around their heads. They look so beautiful!

Now I see my old friend Sandee, wearing the most beautiful wreath of flowers in her hair. She looks so radiant. I go over to get my flowers to try and do the same thing, noticing that I have mostly the greenery and a few delicate purple flowers. I try weaving mine together and ask Sandee to help me. She makes it into a corsage for me instead of a wreath so that I can wear it over my heart.

Sandra awoke from this dream with a profound sense of peace. Because the women in her dream were forbidden to wear watches, and the one woman who tried to find out the time was disconnected, Sandra realized that she had to accept not knowing when she will die. She felt the dream taught her that "we are all mortal, we all will die nonetheless. The timing is not for us to know either."

Although Sandra does not discuss the impact made by the fact that she and her murdered friend bear the same name, such a parallel is always important in understanding dreams. If you dream of something happening to someone with your name, you can be sure there is a powerful identification with that person. The brutal death of Sandee provoked feelings of vulnerability in Sandra. This dream gift helped her accept the uncertainty of life.

Another aspect of the dream that comforted Sandra was that her friend looked radiant. Now she really felt sure that Sandee was all right, as in the more frequent dream message "I'm O.K." But this dream went further. Wreathed in flowers, almost like angels with halos, the dream women looked beautiful. Yet it was not for Sandra to wear the wreath. Her gift, from the hands of her murdered friend

Sandee, was a corsage made of the same materials to wear over her heart.

Greenery often symbolizes healthy new growth in dreams. Sandra commented that the color purple represents spirituality for her. Thus the dream corsage, combining greenery and delicate purple flowers, is a composite signifying new spiritual growth. By wearing it over her heart in her dream, Sandra indicated emerging new heartfelt emotions.

Eventually, Sandra worked through her anger toward Ted Bundy. For a paper in a theology class, she researched the pros and cons of capital punishment. She finally read a book about Bundy and his victims written by someone who knew him as a friend; it left Sandra with more sadness than anger. She then had a dream about Bundy that made a strong impact:

I am standing next to Ted Bundy thinking maybe he can change. All of a sudden, his eyes fill with incredible hatred and evil and he is going to bite me. Instead of running in fear, I stand my ground and yell at him, "No, no, no!"

Sandra sensed that the hatred and anger she felt for Bundy was threatening to overshadow her own life, and that it was time to stand up and say no. As hard as it was for her to do, Sandra began to pray for Bundy in all his sickness and distortion. She hoped he might confess the murders for which he was convicted. Hours before he was executed, Bundy did indeed confess to several murders, including that of Sandee.

The morning Bundy was executed, Sandra had a kind of vision in which she saw her murdered friend walk in the light with a wreath in her hands and give it to Ted Bundy.

In contemplating this vision, Sandra felt that her friend Sandee was showing unconditional love and forgiveness to her murderer. Sandee's dream gift to Sandra was, of course, more than a corsage symbolic of new spiritual growth; it was also the gift of the ability to forgive and to love.

No matter what our religious persuasions, or absence of them, we need the capacity to let go of hatred, anger, and resentments, and to give love.

We also need to learn to accomplish our life's special work. For several people, this knowledge emerged through dreams.

Alice Evans Sees Her Dead Grandfather's Well-Crafted Objects

Poet Alice Evans's dream gift came from her deceased grandfather. He was a serious, quiet, kindhearted person with a wry sense of humor, who had high standards and good taste. As a highway engineer, he oversaw the construction of new, good roads: roads over wagon tracks, Indian paths, and game trails, as well as highways that removed dangerous curves and made safe passages from country to city.

Alice was only twenty-six years old when her grandfather died at age seventy-six. She never felt much of a connection with him during his lifetime, yet she began to have significant dreams about him some ten years after his death. His presence in these dreams "showed me how to accomplish my work, how to build my own road."

As we discussed her grandfather, Alice's identification with him began to emerge. She saw herself as being perfectionistic, as he was, and as sharing his sense of responsibility. "If I'd been a man, I might have been like him." In a Jungian sense, her grandfather probably represented her inner male energy. Through her dreams about him, and through imaginary dialogue with the images that arose in these dreams, Alice came to view her grandfather as her personal "wise old man" figure.

Alice has written a series of sensitive and touching poems based on her dreams. It's not possible to quote them in their entirety, but I excerpt here a few stanzas, to give you the flavor of what was involved in transferring dream images into literature. One of Alice's poems began:

Grandfather
what's this you're trying to tell me
now that you are ten years dead
and this unbridgeable distance between?

In memory, I drive the old highway
which you built in Roosevelt days

into the mountains of Kentucky
where kudzu grows
and trees meet above blacktop in green tunnels
but no road I take now will bring me any closer
to where you never were
you who were ghost in the flesh
when I knew you
one of God's frozen people
have come into my dreams seven times
in recent months
to look at me in silence
and show me polished figurines, bookcases,
a Grandfather's clock . . .[9]

In a later section, the poet made clear the connection between her dead grandfather and herself, and the gift he brought her, as your dreams can bring gifts for you:

Grandfather
I am a woman with ideas.
They fairly fly from my mind
at times they are so fast
I barely get a glimpse of them
leaving me and sailing off into space.
But where is the ground I stand on
how do I capture these ideas and put them to use?

You were a man with blueprints.
You brought forth ideas by bulldozer,
carried them scoop by scoop
out into the light and held them down
with gravel and oil,
not to be borne away by wind . . .[10]

After giving highlights from her grandfather's life, Alice described more from a dream about him and showed what its images meant to her:

Forgotten, Grandfather,
so much forgotten already.
In my dream you stand silently beside bookcases.
I examine their emptiness.
I notice the fine craftsmanship
with which they were made.
I admire the figured grain of the red cherry
polished to a high shine.
I listen to the clock echo the knowledge
that I, who was reading books at four,
newspapers at five, who knew at seven
that I was born to be a writer
am now middle-aged, and I have written no books
my words instead are scattered
from bedroom to kitchen to study
stored in file drawers
on microfilm and computer discs
awaiting my devotion for completion.[11]

In the fourth section of her grandfather poem, Alice remarked on the anger held within this quiet man. She described a dream of herself struggling to pull a great fish from a dark pond and asking her grandfather for help. In the final section, she likened him to an eagle:

Grandfather Eagle,
I see you circling a ring of purple rocks
careful always to stay clear of
the fire in the center.
You raise your eagle wings
You lower them, and together we dance
while fire light throws shadows
on the red rocks.

Step by step we measure out the distance
on my path, the road I am building
around this circle of rainbow rocks.
You show me how to
raise and lower

raise and lower
wings
teaching me to keep my feet on earth
until muscles are strong
and can bring me back down.

Grandfather, I teach you to breathe,
to trust the strength found in darkness.

You, my companion now,
on this bridge we build together
between darkness and light.[12]

By using her dreams about her grandfather as the structure of a long poem, Alice came to an understanding of their meanings for her. The key images from her dreams about her grandfather were:

- the beautiful wood of her grandparents' furniture
- some polished, carved figurines
- a beautiful grandfather clock made of medium-light wood with a figured grain pattern
- asking her frail granddad to help her move a tall bookcase

In the first of these dreams, Alice felt her grandfather was trying to show her something, to tell her something, to give her something. She came to believe that in the image of the grandfather clock, her grandfather "showed me I'm running out of time. I need to do it now." The wonderful grains and patterns of the wood in her dreams probably represented the patterning in Alice's poems. She saw that her grandfather could teach her to build well-crafted things too; that she could "fly" and still be "grounded." Through her dream images, her deceased grandfather became an advisory figure, a teacher about life. Alice imaginatively integrated these dream images with their deeper meanings and crystallized her understandings into a poem that guides her future work.

Li-Young Lee Is Given Seeds by His Father

Poet Li-Young Lee, like Alice Evans, received an important dream gift from the dead. In his book *The Winged Seed*, Lee described waking one night to recall:

In my dream my father came back, dressed in the clothes we'd buried him in, carrying a jar of blood in one hand, his suit pocket lined with black seeds. "The seeds are for remembrance," he said to me.[13]

Lee marveled about the image of the seeds for years after the dream. He is, of course, his father's "seed," and as such, he realized he must make sense out of his and his father's memories.

Lee's family had escaped from Indonesia after severe difficulties—his father was accused of being a spy, was imprisoned by Sukarno and later confined to a mental ward in a hospital. Eventually, the Lee family reached America, where his father became a minister to a rural congregation in Pennsylvania; there Lee cared for his father during his last weeks of life.

In his poetic language, Lee struggles with his legacy of remembrance contained in the black dream seeds his father brought to him. The lifeblood in the dream jar is of value only if the remembrance is fulfilled.

Every one of us receives an important emotional legacy/gift from our ancestors. You may wish to try synthesizing your dreams about deceased loved ones into poetic form as these poets have. Even if your efforts may not have the same evocative power for the public, they almost always do for the dreamer.

Many writers have discovered their muses through the tutelage of dream figures.

The Muse in Your Dreams

The ancient Greeks explained inspiration to write poetry, compose music, and express arts as the result of contact with one of the Muses. These nine mountain goddesses, the daughters of Zeus and Memory (Mnemosyne), presided over song and the different styles of poetry, the arts, and science. When we are inspired to create, the Greeks thought, we are responding to the whispered teachings of the Muses; we are "breathing in"—the literal meaning of the word "inspiration"—their rhythms and harmonies. When we visit a museum, we are entering a temple of the Muses, their sacred space. When we make music, we are giving them voices. Even today, poets may speak of searching for their personal muse, as Milton did when he wrote, "My wandering Muse, how thou dost stray!" Poets, writers, musicians, and artists need look no further for their muse than their nightly dreams. You may find yours there as well.

In our dreams, the Muse often takes the form of an ancestral voice. Sometimes these voices allow us to forge our future lives.

Isabel Allende Learns from Her Grandparents

Writer Isabel Allende, who achieved worldwide acclaim for her first novel, the international best-seller *The House of Spirits,* says she has been guided in her work by her ancestors. In one account, she told of the struggle to complete her first manuscript. She was forty, living in self-imposed exile in Venezuela after the assassination of her uncle Salvador Allende in her native Chile. She was dissatisfied with her marriage, had been disillusioned in a love affair, and felt she had not yet done anything significant with her life aside from birthing two children. She was bored with her work at a school. She summarized her life with one word: mediocrity.

When Allende received a call from Santiago saying that her admired grandfather, her Tata, who was now nearly one hundred years old, was dying, she began to write him a lengthy letter. In exile, she could not return in person. That letter metamorphosed into her first novel, telling the story—partly fictionalized—of her family. She became obsessed with the project, going around in a trance during days full of obligations, and writing much of the evenings and nights.

Word of her grandfather's death arrived when her novel-letter was almost complete, but Allende was having trouble with the epilogue. She says she wrote it many times without finding the tone she wanted. "It seemed sentimental, or sounded like a sermon or a political tract. I knew what I wanted to tell but didn't know how to express it, until once again ghosts came to my aid." One night Allende dreamed:

> *My grandfather was lying in his bed with his eyes closed, just as he was that early morning in my childhood when I crept into his room*

to steal the silver mirror . . . I lifted the sheet and saw he was dressed in mourning, complete with necktie and shoes, and realized he was dead. I sat down by his side, there amidst the black furniture [which he in fact had had painted black after the death of his wife], to read him the book I had just written, and as my voice narrated the story the furniture turned blond again, blue veils fluttered over the bed, and the sun came in through the window.[14]

Allende says she awoke from her dream, startled, at three o'clock in the morning, with the solution to her difficulties with the epilogue. She would describe Alba, the granddaughter who was her alter ego, writing the story of her family beside the body of her grandfather, who was to be buried the next morning. Allende went directly to her typewriter and in less than two hours wrote the complete ten pages of the epilogue. She felt that her long period of paralysis and muteness had ended.

Allende showed her finished manuscript to her mother, made some changes suggested by her, and began the search to find a publisher. Eventually, she reached a literary agent in Spain who placed the work in a couple of days; Allende's career was launched. The most prestigious publishing houses in Europe, from Finland to Greece, bought translation rights; in the United States, a film of the book was later produced, starring Meryl Streep and Jeremy Irons. It was an almost unheard-of reception for a first novel.

To this day, Allende—who has since written five more books—begins each new work with a tradition of invoking her ancestors' help. She always starts a new book on the same day, January 8, that she began her first one. She tries to arrange to be alone and silent for several hours on that day to rid her mind of noise and confusion. "I light candles to summon the muses and guardian spirits, I place flowers on my desk to intimidate tedium and the complete works of Pablo Neruda [a beloved Chilean poet] beneath the computer . . . In a secret ceremony, I prepare my mind and soul to receive the first sentence in a trance, so the door may open slightly and allow me to peer through and perceive the hazy outlines of the story waiting for me."[15]

Allende reported, in an interview for the Discovery Channel program *The Secret World of Dreams*, that she often dreams her clairvoyant grandmother, her Memé, is watching over her shoulder as she writes. Or that she is looking over the shoulder of her grandmother, who is writing a story. Clearly, Allende feels in contact with her ancestral spirits in her dreams. She is not alone.

Carol Edgarian Hears an Ancient Voice

When novelist Carol Edgarian was a student at Stanford University, she spent her junior year at the college's campus in Tours, France. There she lived in an "unheated gray cell of a dormitory room." One night in that cold room, she dreamed about an old woman with a haunting voice, one that she felt sure she had never heard before. Edgarian told an interviewer, "There was something about this old woman. I had to find out about her."[16]

For an honors thesis, Edgarian combined the voice of the old woman she had heard in her dream with some research she had done in high school on the history of her Armenian ancestors. Years later, this thesis became the early chapters of Edgarian's first novel, *Rise the Euphrates*. The voice of the old woman became the voice of Casard, the grandmother who, as a child, survived the Armenian massacre by the Turks. The four-generational family epic Edgarian wrote received rave reviews and launched a new career for its thirty-one-year-old author.

As a bonus, Edgarian met and eventually married the New York editor who published her novel. Edgarian says that her novel is not autobiographical, but there are many parallels between her and the narrator of the tale, Seta Loon, the granddaughter of the old woman. Was Edgarian hearing the voice of an ancestor in her dream? Was she being touched by the whispered words of her muse? Was the dream simply the stirring of her own creative depths? Whatever the answer, Edgarian listened. Her life reaped the benefits. So can yours.

Ancestral Voices in Your Dreams

In the experiences of novelists Isabel Allende and Carol Edgarian, you can see how the images of their ancestors still live in their dreams. Sometimes it's more difficult to recognize their presence in our own. Yet you, too, have grandmothers and grandfathers, great-grandparents, and other relatives from the past—known and un-known—whose voices sometimes filter through your dreams.

Elsewhere in this book, I mention various gifts from deceased loved ones that appeared in dreams. One woman, after being offered jewelry by her deceased father, chose a kiss instead; a man was given a Mexican bowl by his dead lover; another woman was presented with an exquisite Buddha brooch by her deceased father; a widow was gifted with pink roses from her dead husband. Yet another woman dreamed of receiving a silver necklace from a dead male friend. In one of my dreams about my father, I was shown a handsome Chinese urn and other objects of art that I knew represented my father's artistic talents being gifted to me.

There are many striking accounts in literature of gifts received from deceased relatives and friends. Here's a sampling:

- The English poet-artist William Blake said he was taught in a dream an inexpensive method of engraving by his dead younger brother Robert.

- An Irish actress who had been given a picture of a heron by the English actress Mrs. Patrick Campbell dreamed Mrs. Campbell stepped from a train to ask her, "Have you found my gift from the grave yet?" Awake, she removed the backboard of the painting and found a valuable signed Max Beerbohm caricature of Mrs. Campbell, the news of whose death arrived a few days later.

- One woman, after dreaming that her still-living sister's walnut cabinet had secret drawers containing valuables, searched it a year later, after her sister had died, and found a cache of diamonds.

- Another woman's deceased father appeared in a dream, telling her to look in an old gray shirt of his that had been discarded; later her brother, to whom she had told the dream, retrieved the shirt and found that a roll of bills had been sewn inside it.

Some of these dream reports border on the supernatural.

Dante's Son Finds the Missing Cantos after a Dream

One of the most startling historical accounts of finding a missing item by means of a dream about the dead concerns the dream of one of Dante's sons, Jacopo. No one could locate the final thirteen cantos of the one hundred known to be in Dante's great work, *The Divine Comedy*. His survivors were sure they had been written, but where were they? The fourteenth-century poet and scholar Boccaccio recorded how Jacopo found the answer. Near the hour of matins (the period between midnight and dawn), Jacopo had in his sleep:

> seen his father Dante come to him, dressed in shining white garments and his face resplendent with unwonted light. And it seemed to him that he asked him whether he was alive, and heard him answer: "Yes, but with the true life and not this of ours." Wherefore he dreamed that he went on to ask whether he had finished his work before passing into the true life, and if he had, where was the missing portion which they had never been able to find. . . . "Yes, I finished it." And then it seemed to him that he took him by the hand and led him into the room where he used to sleep when he lived in this life, and, touching one of the walls with his hand, said, "Here is what you have been searching for so long." And as soon as those words were spoken, it seemed to him that his sleep and Dante departed from him together.[17]

Jacopo dressed and went at once to the home of a pupil of his late father's. After he related his dream, they went together to the place where Dante had lived before his death, roused the current occupant, and found a cubbyhole in the wall behind a mat in the place Dante had indicated in the dream. Inside were papers so moldy from dampness they would have rotted away if they had been left longer. The men cleaned off the mold, found the pages were numbered, rearranged them, and ascertained that they were indeed the thirteen missing cantos. The masterwork of decades was complete. It was a dream gift for the centuries.

Welcoming the Blessings of the Dead

Dreamers need to hear the voices of the dead in dreams, to listen to their messages, supernatural or not, and to act upon them when appropriate. In a very real sense, ancestors in our dreams are our "elders," our inner sages.

When their messages are not literal directives of where to find something, we need to strive to understand the symbolism of their dream gifts. What do they represent? Do these gifts come from spirits of our ancestors? Are they from personal muses or angelic beings? Are they from higher parts of ourselves? We know with certainty only that their gifts are special blessings.

We need to acknowledge and honor these ancestral voices with understanding. If we do not write poetry or books based upon their teachings, we may, in our own way, enrich our lives with these dream blessings.

To be given a blessing once meant to be marked by the sign of the cross—originally with blood—and thereby to be made holy. Today, we are more apt to think of receiving a blessing as the bestowal of a special favor, a gift, or some other good thing. As mentioned earlier, a blessing is a benediction (a good saying) in contrast to a malediction (an evil saying) or curse. We ourselves may offer blessings as an act of devotion or worship, awake or asleep. Blessings, in dreams or waking, may confer bliss, a taste of heavenly joy.

Symbolically, by receiving a gift from the dream messenger, we are being encouraged, or being given approval, to proceed with some action. By accepting these blessings of the dead we are freeing powerful inner energies for our later lives.

Sometimes the blessings from the dead take the shape of concrete gifts in a dream, as we have seen. Pink roses, shapely urns, beautiful brooches—such gifts may represent talents, or skills, or be signs of acceptance from the deceased. Often these presents received in dreams symbolize love. Dream gifts involve the transfer of emotional energy from the deceased to the dreamer.

Recognize the dream blessing. Then accept it with gratitude. Welcome it. Use it while awake to benefit yourself and others.

6

⚮

"Stop!" and "Go Ahead!"

"Stop!"

Dream Message: "Stop!"

Deceased warns the dreamer to cease some behavior.

Frequency: Relatively rare.

Response after Awake:
Dreamer usually feels surprised or frightened.
May change plans that were under way, and
years later, appreciate the warning.

People who receive the dream message "Stop!" from the dead are getting a warning to watch out for danger. Such a message may take a comparatively mild form, as it did for a woman whose dream messenger said, "Tell your mother to get the cobwebs out of her hat," presumably urging her to cease her old-fashioned ways of thinking. At the other extreme, these dream messages may range to absolutely forbidding the dreamer to perform a certain behavior.

It is these stern commandments to cease an action that cause dreamers the most trouble. They impose a kind of taboo.

The Taboos in Your Dreams

Since the "Stop!" type of dream message from the dead is fairly rare, you may not ever experience it. However, it is good to know about, in case you should become exposed to it.

In primitive groups, taboos (also spelled "tabus") were—and sometimes still are—imposed by the king, the chief, or by a priest. A taboo sets apart some person, thing, place, name, or action as unmentionable, untouchable, unsayable, or not to be done. There are various reasons for imposing a taboo: because something is sacred, or it possesses a mysterious power, or it is unclean; or to ensure protection of it; or to prevent interference with certain institutions of society, such as marriage.

Tabooed locations are still sometimes indicated by a symbolic mark or sign, usually consisting of a branch of a certain tree placed across a door or hung in the prohibited place, or bunches of certain leaves or wands set there, or the presence of crossbones. Lest you think taboos are a long-forgotten practice, consider how today's scientists puzzle over how to mark atomic-waste burial sites to warn away from poisonous areas future generations who may not speak our languages; various international warning signs are being considered.

The word "taboo" is Polynesian; the same religious or social prohibition goes by other names in different societies. The Irish of olden times called them a *geis* or *gessa* (plural). The so-called curse of the Egyptian mummies against those who violate their tombs is a variation of the taboo. The evil eyes drawn on Middle Eastern sacred places, to prevent desecration, serve a similar purpose.

In any culture, to break a taboo is to be overtaken by misfortune, disease, and death. The taboo does not need to be punished by man; taboos avenge themselves. Sometimes a taboo may be removed by the authority who imposed it. Even today's dreamers are loath to go against a strongly voiced message to cease and desist, as can be seen in Kitty's case.

Kitty Receives an Order from Her Dead Father-in-Law

Kitty was born in China, where ancestors have long been revered. She probably would have remained in her country and married there, had the Communist revolution not occurred soon after she graduated from college.

Kitty's parents, fearing for her safety, urged her to leave the country. Her older sisters had already gone to study in the United States. Kitty hoped she would be able to return to her parents soon, so she went to work in neighboring Hong Kong. There she was pursued by a man whose father was a Chinese from Taiwan, and whose mother was Japanese. She had met him earlier when he visited her parents' home on business. She did not want to marry this man, but after a few years, it seemed the best thing to do.

Kitty's parents continued to tell her to stay away from her homeland. There was no way they could help her at this point; they had lost everything to the revolution. In her loneliness and confusion, Kitty agreed to visit her suitor's family in Taiwan, and liking them, finally agreed to marry. She felt it was the best decision she could make. Things might have been all right had the couple continued to live within reach of her new relatives. However, Kitty's husband soon demanded that they move to Japan. As a proper wife, she could hardly object to his wishes.

The newly married couple settled down to live in Japan, where her deceased father-in-law had been a prominent businessman with widespread holdings. His distinguished face gazed out at her from family portraits and images in public places.

Once in Japan, she was completely isolated, in a strange country with strange customs, unable to speak the language, and pregnant with the first of her two sons.

"In Japan, the man is king," Kitty told me sadly. She soon discovered, along with many a Japanese wife, that her husband had far more interesting things to do than spend his evenings at home. He gradually became immersed in innumerable affairs, kept and traded favorite mistresses, and left Kitty in splendid isolation. The women in her husband's life, sensing her weak position, tormented her with telephone calls and letters trying to drive her away. Yet Kitty considered it shameful to divorce.

Although she had ample money for a comfortable life on a material level, Kitty was miserable. In Japan, any children belong to the father. She could make no attempt to leave without losing her boys. "I felt like a dog with a collar," she said. With no resources, and a cultural acceptance of such behavior in men, Kitty grew desperate. "I would have killed myself, but I didn't even feel like a human being."

Finally, late one night when she had been sitting up waiting for her husband's return, Kitty made a decision: she would leave everything, including her two sons, and join her sisters in America. She staggered to sleep in exhaustion, and had a dream that changed her life:

I am at my father-in-law's house, very large, very dark, facing a river. I walk outside to the veranda that surrounds the house. From there I look down to the grass between the house and river, where I see two men fighting.

My father-in-law is very tall and distinguished-looking, with a stern expression. He seems all white, with his white hair, and wearing a white judo costume. In his hands he holds a leafy branch with which he fights the other man, who holds something sharp, perhaps a sword.

Suddenly the opponent cuts through the branch in my father-in-law's hand. I am amazed. "Why is the branch not falling?" I wonder. I look clearly and see my father-in-law holds the base of it. The cut part hangs suspended in the air. Even though it's cut, with him holding the base, it will not fall.

Kitty awoke with a start. Then she saw a vision of her father-in-law directly before her in her bedroom. "He was sitting in meditation, his face very sharp, looking straight into my eyes. I knew I did something wrong. I told him, 'I know! I know! I will not betray you!' I knew why he came. I knew what he wanted me to promise."

Kitty explained that the dream made her realize she could not leave the family. She was like the branch of the tree in her dream. Even if she was separated from the base, the spirit of her deceased father-in-law would support her. As long as she stayed, he would care for her and the boys. She promised her father-in-law that night she would never leave his grandsons.

Many times through the next years, Kitty railed at her deceased father-in-law for forcing her to stay. "Now the dog collar had a leash tying me to the house." Yet she felt his protection. "He became like a god to me." She carried his photograph with her. She prayed to him, asking, "Why did you tie me to this family?"

From then on her behavior was different. Instead of fighting so strongly against her husband, she became more humble. She focused on the welfare of her boys, their schooling, their advancement. She studied the Japanese language, she made friends among Japanese women. She learned to survive.

Despite the fact that Kitty's husband's behavior grew worse, she refused to be driven away. As she saw it, her duty now was to shield her children. She felt that she had been ordered to do so; she had been forbidden to leave by her father-in-law. Her loyalty and devotion evoked sympathy from her Japanese friends.

Once, she traveled on a four-month trip to see her sister in the States, leaving her sons in the charge of their trusted governess. When she returned, she found that her husband had moved his current mistress into the house the day after she departed. On her return, the mistress moved out and Kitty's husband soon followed. Nonetheless, Kitty stayed in the house and took care of her sons. She worked many extra jobs to ensure that she would have enough money in case her husband withdrew his support. Finally, her husband recognized that she would not desert the boys to divorce him, and so he gave her permission to leave with the children and promised his support.

Kitty and her sons lived in the States for several years before she could bring herself to ask for a divorce from her philandering husband. Eventually, she visited her in-laws in Taiwan, asking permission of her husband's brother to divorce. Kitty also visited the grave of her father-in-law, where she prayed fervently, "Can I be free?"

Kitty felt she received an affirmative answer from her dead father-in-law when she opened her makeup case during the journey and found that the mirror had shattered. In Chinese tradition, a broken mirror signifies the finish of a marriage. Kitty went ahead with a divorce. "It was just like getting out of prison," she told me.

Kitty continued to care for her sons, and had the satisfaction of seeing them graduate from college and launch professional careers. Then she had a chance to marry again, a kind and gentle man she had known from her childhood in China. With her sons' blessings, Kitty began a belated happy life. After more than two decades, Kitty believes that her deceased father-in-law finally carried out his part of the bargain. She still treasures his guidance.

Woman's Dead Son Tells Her She's Destined to Live

A woman whose sixteen-year-old son was killed instantly in an automobile wreck received a "Stop!" dream message one week later. In her dream:

> I am in someone's living room. When I look up, my son is standing across the room. I know that it is his spirit and say to him, "I wondered when you were going to show up." He comes to me and takes both of my hands in his. We both fly upward into a star-filled night sky. We then fly through something that feels like a force field. I feel a kind of suction as we pass through. I remember thinking that we are on "the other side." We fly around this open sky for a time and then come back, passing through the suction of the force field again.
>
> My son says to me, "You know, Mom, I can't keep doing this." I know that he must go to do his soul's work. He tells me that there are three little girls whose mother doesn't watch them carefully. His job is to watch over them. I know that it is time for him to go. I tell him to take me along, that I don't want to complete this lifetime without him. He tells me, "Mom, you're here till you're seventy-one."

The bereaved mother awoke from this dream with a complete feeling of peace. Clearly, she had been anticipating a dream visit from her son's spirit and accepted it with ease.

Yet the woman's wish to die to join her dead son is a feeling many survivors experience, especially with the loss of a child or a lover. Kitty had the same wish to die to escape a dreadful situation. It is then that the deceased loved one may appear directly in a dream, or some other image such as an angel—the word means "messenger of God"—to urge the dreamer to return to life. For Kitty, it was a greatly respected figure that forbade her to escape or abandon her sons. In responding to such dream messages, the dreamer begins the process of getting on with life.

Return to the Living

At times the order "Stop!" arises when the dreamer attempts to follow the image of the person who has died. One woman was following a dream path her dead mother had indicated when she found herself confronted by a bright angel who blocked her way, saying, "Don't come now—turn back and continue walking." Another dreamed of sitting peacefully beside her dead father in an airplane that was taking off. After a bit he said to her, "I'm sorry, but you'll have to get off now, as you cannot go where I am going." The plane landed in a wheat field, where she and her husband disembarked; the plane then continued its route with her dead father.

Remember the dream of Elena, described earlier, in which the young woman dreamed of getting on a train at the border with her deceased fiancé, George? At a certain place all the passengers were required to disembark, with only George permitted to travel farther. Elena tried to persuade the highest authority to let her go with George, but was unsuccessful; she must return.[1] She said goodbye to George and found a train back.

It is as if the land of the dead is taboo to the living. If you dream of the dead advising you to "Stop!" it's a good idea to comply. Dream reunions bring comfort, but eventually we must separate from the dead. The physical bond is broken. We need to accept their departure. The deceased then become part of a guiding force within us.

"Go Ahead!"

Dream Message: "Go Ahead!"

Deceased urges the dreamer to proceed
with some behavior.

Frequency: Relatively rare but important.

Response after Awake:
Dreamer usually feels comforted and encouraged.
May make or proceed with plans suggested by
the dream encounter.

Mary's Dead Son Helps Her Proceed with Her Life

Mary's beloved son Greg died from melanoma when he was only
forty-two. Losing a child is probably one of the most difficult deaths
to endure. Shortly before Greg fell ill, Mary's husband suffered a
stroke and became incapacitated. During the same period of time,
Mary was having her own health problems, as a result of a deteri-
orating hip joint. Her troubles seemed to be overwhelming. Greg's
death was almost too much to bear and Mary felt his loss keenly.
Her grief was agonizing. A bright, active woman in her early sixties,
she felt her life grind to a standstill.

It was almost a year after Greg's death that Mary had a dream
about him that helped her to heal:

> I am standing outside a house which is built high above a chasm. The
> house is California style, of dark wood with large windows sur-
> rounded by a wide deck which, in front of the main entrance, extends
> out beyond the rim of the river making a kind of crow's nest. The sun
> and air are warm, but the river is frozen. Slabs of ice overlap the
> noisy but invisible water.

I am watching the sky, rocks, and blocks of ice below when Greg comes up behind me. "Hi, Mom," he says, and I turn to hug him. As always, I think how tall he is and how good it feels to be hugged by a tall man. "Help me, Mom," he says. "We've got some work to do."

We walk out to the end of the deck and I see some piles of fairly large rocks, big irregular hunks. Greg picks one up and heaves it out and down into the river. It hits, breaks through the ice, and disappears into a fountain of water spewing up through the hole. "Come on, Mom, help me," he says.

I pick up a medium-sized rock and heave it out into the air. It hits a different spot and again the ice breaks and water sprays out. We take turns tossing rocks and smiling at our results. It feels wonderful to work alongside Greg in the easy rhythm of pick up, throw, and watch. We laugh when our rocks make simultaneous splashes.

Slowly the piles of rocks grow smaller until there are only two stones left. Greg smiles and says, "Together, eh?" and over they go. We stand, side by side, watching the river now running freely through the canyon.

I ask, "Why did you come back, Greg?" and he answers, "Oh, Mom, I thought you needed some help to break up the ice in your heart."

Mary awoke from this dream thunderstruck. It was a turning point in her recovery.

As we discussed her dream, Mary explained that water has been significant in her life. In her middle years she was active in canoeing and sailing; she still swims three times a week. In addition, Mary's astrological sign is Pisces, the fish that needs flowing water to live. Obviously, then, frozen water would not be good in her dream.

Mary also told me that she was rather uncomfortable with heights, that her son used to tease her about it. However, she likes tall people, being herself a tall woman. Being hugged by a man taller than she is feels especially good.

Mary mentioned that the dream took place when she was visiting friends in Popham Beach, Maine, a place she described as "heaven on earth"—an appropriate spot to meet the dead. The dream house was a western style that is her favorite type of housing.

Therefore, in Mary's dream language, she was in a very special place (the house), facing something uncomfortable for her (the height above the frozen depths below), when the spirit of her son asked her to help him work. Their tools were rocks, hard enough to break through the slabs of ice. Mary commented, "If the river had been blocked with stones, it couldn't flow again, but ice can melt." By their mutual effort, Mary and her son were able to make the river run free again. She felt blessed to have help "to break up the ice in her heart." Mary's life river began to flow in the waking world as well.

By sharing her dream with her grief support group, and with her many friends through her annual holiday letter, Mary touched hundreds of people who found themselves moved by the dream's imagery. Later, in television talk shows we appeared on together, Mary's dream reached thousands of people. The imagery of the heart always speaks to other hearts.

Mary became active again, doing volunteer work, joining a writing class, and using her multitude of talents. Her dead son's message to "Go Ahead!" with her life made all the difference. You, too, may be given such a signal.

Woman Sees Her Dead Father in Glorified Form

One woman described an unusual version of the "Go Ahead!" dream message. About twelve years after her father's death, at a critical juncture in her life, she dreamed:

> I see my Father standing before me. He is my biological father, but he appears like, and radiates the energy of, God. He is bathing me with compassion, and speaking words of comfort that I find overwhelming. I cry, and am deeply moved that my Father sees into my situation so clearly, and is able to offer me such deep love and encouragement. He says to me, "I know what you're going through is difficult, but you are learning. Continue with your work . . ." or words to that effect.

The woman said that when she awoke from this dream, her first impulse was to discount the visitation. In fact, she felt somewhat resentful, in that her father had had difficulty being compassionate during his lifetime. "You imposter! How dare you come in and impersonate God," she thought. However, as she began to consider the message more carefully, she opened her heart to her father, and "received him, tearfully, painfully, joyfully." She was able to accept the dream message, enriching her life.

Woman Meets Her Dead Idol in Heaven

Another woman, when she was contemplating the possibility of moving her business and was anxious about the change this might bring, dreamed of waiting in a huge house. To her right was a beautiful white and golden staircase that curved upward. Above her hung a grand chandelier. Suddenly a man began to walk down the staircase to meet her. She felt a strong spiritual attraction to him. When he got closer, she recognized one of her television idols, who had recently died. He grinned and put his arms around her, as if to say, "You are my sister, and I'm proud of you. Don't be afraid to move on." The woman awoke slightly frightened, but quite convinced she'd visited heaven.

Most of the time, the dead wear their own garments, or only slightly more luminous ones, to dispense their guidance. And they are most likely to meet us in beautiful earthly settings rather than celestial ones. But considering that in Christian prayers the words "God the Father" frequently appear and in Chinese tradition deceased ancestors are said to be "with the gods," perhaps we should not be surprised if our dead loved ones sometimes robe themselves in glory to speak to us in dreams. If you receive such a message of comfort, or encouragement to go on with your work, welcome it.

Alan Siegel's Dead Grandfather in the Orange Grove

Dreamworker and colleague Alan Siegel described in his book *Dreams That Can Change Your Life* how he struggled with his grief over the loss of his grandfather. At first, his deceased grandfather appeared in dreams as he looked before his death from stomach cancer—gaunt and ravaged with illness. Siegel felt worried about his grandfather and tried to start a conversation, but the dreams usually ended before he could talk with him. These dreams made Siegel realize that his feelings of loss over his grandfather were still unresolved; reflecting on the dreams helped him clarify important parts of their relationship.

Approximately a year after his grandfather died, Siegel dreamed:

> *I am walking in an orange grove and talking to my grandfather. There are many ripe oranges on the trees, and the grass and trees seem very green. My grandfather is talking with me and giving me some advice about my career, encouraging me to finish school or to pursue something. He seems rotund and healthy, and I am surprised that he is alive, but somehow it makes sense.*[2]

In this dream, Siegel felt his grandfather was acting like a mentor, giving him advice and encouragement, just as he had done in life. He was still advising him, urging him to go ahead with his life.

Observe the symbols of fertility and new growth in Siegel's dream: the many ripe oranges, the extraordinarily green grass and the trees. Such images are often present when the dreamer is experiencing new growth within himself or herself. Not only is the deceased grandfather restored to health in the dream, but also the plant life is flourishing. There are no distressing feelings plaguing the dreamer here; he has recovered from the most disturbing part of mourning. Now Siegel was able to focus on relating to the positive qualities his grandfather embodied while he was in good health. These qualities could continue to guide Siegel, as they had prior to his grandfather's death. Each one of us can find nurturing and supportive principles in our dreams about our ancestors.

Jeffrey Mishlove's Dead Uncle Brings a Song

Colleague Jeff Mishlove, author of *The Mind's Eye* and host of a popular television series, *Thinking Allowed*, experienced a profoundly moving dream about his favorite uncle the same night that his uncle died:

Uncle Harry comes to me. He talks to me about my life, about my girlfriend, and other significant life events. I have the impression he is communicating to me with a yinyang symbol (the Chinese symbol for change), which is strange because he is Jewish. I am touched by the exchange with him and begin singing an old Jewish melody. As I wake up, I find I am crying and still singing the words, "Our father, our king, have mercy on us . . ."

Mishlove was so impressed by this dream that he wrote to his uncle's family to inquire about Harry's health, and received the news that his uncle had died three days earlier, the night of his dream.

This kind of experience—a dream about a specific loved person which is simultaneous with that person's death—is called a "crisis apparition" in nineteenth-century parapsychology literature. We have encountered it a few times before in this book. It always makes an indelible impression upon the dreamer, sometimes convincing him or her of the verity of an afterlife and the reality of a spiritual world.

In Mishlove's case, the image of his deceased uncle seemed to be saying goodbye by using the yin/yang symbol that indicates change. He offered advice, as he did during his lifetime, suggesting Mishlove should "Go Ahead!" with his life. The ancient melody and words of prayer emerged from a deep emotional level, perhaps stirred by the passing of a soul. It was this dream, in part, that inspired Mishlove to make his life's work in parapsychology.

Listening to the Voices of the Dead

Mary found the strength to go on, after dreaming that her dead son helped her melt the ice in her heart. Another woman was encouraged to continue her work, after dreaming that her dead father, as God, urged her to do so. Yet another felt able to move her business, after dreaming that her dead television idol told her not to be afraid to move on. Alan Siegel was heartened to pursue his career, after dreaming that his dead grandfather supported it. Jeffrey Mishlove went into a new career, after dreaming that his dead uncle advised him about his life.

Still another woman dreamed her dead sister appeared in the form of a bright light shining through trees, assuring her that it was all right for her former husband to remarry; and another woman dreamed her dead husband gave her permission to marry again.[3] Yet another found a dream note with her dead father's name on it pinned to a bulletin board; she felt he was encouraging her to devote her life to the study of dreams as a spiritual path.

Whatever your lost loved ones have to say in such dream encounters, you should listen, ponder, and cherish. Their words may transform your life.

7

"Join Me!" and "Your Turn Is Coming"

"Join Me!"

> ### Dream Message: "Join Me!"
> Deceased entices the dreamer to join him or her in death.
>
> ### Frequency: Extremely rare, but important.
>
> Response after Awake:
> Dreamer is either terrified or deeply depressed.
> There may be a risk of suicide.

Why should survivors be tormented by dreams of a dead person entreating them to die? When a survivor receives this rare type of dream message, it is usually because the dreamer:

· identifies strongly with the deceased

· is profoundly depressed over the loss of the deceased

· or, feels extreme guilt about the deceased

People who dream that the dead person entreats them, "Join me!" may temporarily feel that life has lost all meaning. The dead person seems irreplaceable.

Someone who has been severed by death from a lover, a long-time beloved mate, or a cherished child, usually feels despair and may have fleeting thoughts of suicide. These disturbing thoughts typically diminish over time. The griever's life force strengthens as renewed meaning to life is found.

Man Is Split Apart from His Dead Mother

A psychiatrist friend who was emotionally close to his mother was out of the country when she died. The evening he received word of her death, he was able to sleep for only a couple of hours. When finally he did fall asleep, he had a disturbing dream:

> Dealt with an Arab country. . . . There was a big event—a mountain had split. A large, round hill or mountain had split into two pieces, and there were some arrangements to be made. Maybe a funeral—anyway [I had to] come to terms with it. The breaking, the change.

Many of us who are close to a loved one who dies experience his or her death as a wrenching apart, a breaking of a unity, as this dreamer did with the mountain that split into two pieces. All of us must learn to come to terms with the change that results. It can be a painful procedure.

Mother's Nightmares About Dead Son

Parents who have lost an adored child may be plagued by nightmares with the message "Join Me!" These distressing dreams are particularly poignant because parents may feel that the deceased child "needs them on the other side."

Marlo Thomas played the role of a bereaved mother in the CBS television movie *Reunion*, based on a novel, *Points of Light,* by Linda Gray Sexton about a mother who lost her son to a bizarre accident.

The boy had awakened in the night and she had comforted him, allowing him to sleep with his favorite toy, a horse that had a rope attached in order to pull it. Although the horse was meant to be a "day" toy only, the mother relented and let the boy keep it in bed for once.[1]

To the mother's horror, when she went to check on her son in the morning, she found him dead, with the rope still attached to the toy horse but twisted tightly around his neck. The combination of grief and guilt nearly undid this mother.

Despite her two healthy children, she became obsessed by her dead son. She began having hallucinations as well as nightmares about his calling to her, "Mommy! Come here! I need you!" Months of torment followed. Again and again the boy appeared, begging his mother to follow him. Not only was the mother's life at risk, but also her two other children's. She wanted desperately to go to her son. Eventually, however, she was able to pull back from the brink, recognize her instability, and get the help she needed.

Thomas identified with the bereaved mother because she was still reeling from the sudden death of her father, comedian Danny Thomas, at the age of seventy-nine. "A death—especially the sudden death of a loved one—is a violent act on your body. I felt very much as if I'd been hit by a plank around the shoulders and chest. My head felt heavy. It was a stunning experience," she told an interviewer.[2]

Thomas felt that playing the role in *Reunion* verified what she had learned as she coped with her father's death. "The real reunion is to reunite with the rest of your family, to take your loss and fold it into your life and make it part of who you are," she said, adding, "It's just not enough to be a survivor—you have to thrive."[3]

This conclusion of Thomas's is true, and, although Sexton's book is a novel, the description of the struggle of a grieving parent to bear the unbearable also is true. In whatever form it appears, "Join Me!" is a dangerous dream message that must be understood in order for its message to be denied.

Twin Is Tortured by Hanged Brother

When a twin dies, the surviving twin has a particularly difficult bereavement. Identical twins, especially, have an intertwined connection. When death has been violent or unexpected, "survivor's guilt" may plague the remaining twin. Death of one twin by suicide can leave the other twin at serious risk.

In Chapter 2, I described the wedding eve nightmare experienced by Robert Samuel, whose identical twin, Richard Daniel, committed suicide at age eighteen. You may recall the barbed wire decapitation and the talking head, saying, "*Now* are you sorry?"

Richard Daniel had been the dominant twin, a sports hero and extremely popular. Following a car accident that injured him and prevented his participation in sports, and shortly after being disappointed in a youthful love affair, he hanged himself in a place only his twin would know where to find him—as happened. This tragic event shadowed Robert Samuel's life into his middle years. Even when he is happiest, there may arise a nightmare in which his twin's image seems to mock him for daring to be happy. Like other people who have lost someone especially intimate, Robert Samuel suffered from the fearful thought of joining his dead "other self." He has survived, however, and prospered, into his forties.

When mourning is this complex, professional therapeutic help is required.

Confused Identities with Twins

Psychiatrist George Engel wrote a fascinating article describing his reactions to the death of his identical twin, Frank Engel, at the age of forty-nine. The article, written ten years after his twin's death, tells how he felt that "to be separate was to live, to be joined was to die."[4] He developed the idea that he could not possibly live more than a year after his twin died from a heart attack. Engel's first symptoms of heart trouble appeared on the plane flight to his brother's funeral. Indeed, he did suffer a heart attack about eleven months after his twin died.

When he survived the heart attack, and surpassed the self-imposed life span of one more year, Engel then began to fear that he would die at the same age as his father had, at fifty-eight. As he approached this age, Engel realized he now was feeling as if he were "becoming a twin" to his father. Happily, he survived beyond the age of his father's death—it was a year later that he wrote the article.

To Engel, "death meant reunion." He explained how during the first days of grief over his twin's death, and periodically thereafter, his own "ego boundaries" were vague. He noted this in dreams which were "characterized by an extraordinary sense of confusion as to who was who and which had died." In these dreams, Engel says, he had to struggle to separate himself from his dead twin. He would awaken with a feeling of surprise and relief.

Twins grow up being a single unit, first being "the twins" in contrast to first being individuals, especially when the twins are virtually indistinguishable. There is a long period of conflict for twins between being a unit and becoming separate persons. Many twins develop a private language and use their power to confuse other people about their identities in order to influence others' behavior. Small wonder that dreams after the death of one twin are marked by profound confusion between the self and the other twin. Again, ability to separate may mean survival.

William's Dream Saves His Twin

On the other hand, this same identification between twins sometimes saves lives. William and Lawrence were identical twins who had always been together in school and, later, in work. When they retired, they built mirror-image houses. After Lawrence's wife died, he lived on alone in their house for seven years. One night, William dreamed that his twin was in danger and calling him.

William startled awake, dressed, and rushed next door, where he found Lawrence had taken his deceased wife's leftover sleeping medication. William called an ambulance. Lawrence was rushed to a nearby hospital, had his stomach pumped, and survived. His physician refused to dismiss Lawrence until the hospital psychologist approved and he agreed to continue psychotherapy.

As a result of William's dream, not only did Lawrence physically survive, but the therapy he received changed him from a silent, repressed man into a loving, open-hearted one. His grown children and the rest of the family welcomed this transformation, and Lawrence's remaining years were much happier. Identification can rescue life as well as put it in jeopardy.

Lost Lovers

The bond between sweethearts can be almost as intense as that between parents and children, or between identical twins. The death of a lover can put the survivor at high risk.

Remember the Swiss woman, Elena, whose fiancé had suddenly died of undiagnosed heart disease? She credited her dream of having to get off a train at the border while her boyfriend, George, was permitted to travel onward, with saving her life. It helped her recognize that she must "turn back" and attend to living. Doing so is very difficult when the dead lover seems to be calling to the dreamer.

Dream messages of "Join Me!" by a deceased lover have the flavor of the mythological evil spirit called "the demon lover."

The Demon Lover

In medieval times in Europe, people believed in a devilish spirit referred to as the demon lover. This malevolent spirit was said to come to women in the night in the shape of a handsome, virile man—sometimes with a flaw such as cloven hooves. The demon's purpose, supposedly, was to seduce the sleeping woman into making love. The demon lover often was thought to sire a child by means of his seduction. Offspring born of such unions were said to be deformed, to be twins, to be evil spirits such as witches or other demons, or, at the very least, to be exceedingly cunning. The wizard Merlin was said to be the son of such a demon.

The hapless woman who became a victim of a demon might die of exhaustion as a result of her lover's nightly attentions. Witches were thought to desire, even evoke, such a lover, but the innocent maiden was advised to avoid his advances by protecting herself with herbs such as Saint-John's-wort, vervain, and dill.

In Christian times, the demon lover was thought to seek sexual intercourse as an emissary of the devil, or even to be Satan himself. Many pre-Christian cultures had parallel figures, such as the satyr in ancient Greece, a mythological creature said to love wine, women, and nymphs. Many cultures believe that the ghosts of the dead form a class of demons, especially if the deceased has died by violence.

In ancient times, these malicious spirits were called incubi (singular, incubus), from the Latin word meaning "to lie upon." The corresponding female spirits were called succubi (singular, succubus), from the Latin for "to lie under."

The term "incubus" was equivalent to the word "nightmare." The incubus was said to "ride" his female victims in the dark, pressing them under his body, weighting them down. The succubus lay under her male victims, provoking them with lascivious movements into nocturnal emissions (wet dreams). In modern psychology, the term "incubus" may be applied to the type of nightmare that produces a feeling of heavy weight or oppression on the chest or stomach. This sensation is an actual physiological response to some bad dreams; in the past, the explanation was that the weight of the demon lover caused the pressure.

The idea of incubi and succubi also may have evolved in part from the pagan notion that the gods sometimes have sexual intercourse with human beings. In those cases, however, the resulting offspring were considered half divine rather than demonic. Evil offspring, like that depicted in the novel *Rosemary's Baby,* which was later made into a film starring Mia Farrow, are more typically portrayed than divine ones.

Richard Wagner's opera *Der Fliegende Holländer* (*The Flying Dutchman*) was his version of the medieval legend of a dead captain forced to sail a phantom ship, luring other vessels to their doom, until redeemed by the love of a woman who would be faithful unto death.

Some contemporary dreamers are tormented by the same impulse as Wagner's heroine, to join the dead when deprived of a loved one.

Young Woman's Dead Fiancé Beckons

After her fiancé died, Stella began having disturbing dreams:

I see him beckoning to me, asking me to join him.

Stella's distress was intensified by these nightmares, and she wisely sought psychological help. As long as a year after her lover's death, this young woman was still anguished by an occasional dream of him wanting her to join him in death. This romantic image can be very seductive. Fortunately, Stella's therapist was providing support that assisted her in dealing with these dreams and guiding her toward other values in her life.

Somehow, some way, we must find life worthwhile after the death of a beloved. The lost loved one needs to become part of us, a treasured part, but no longer essential.

If you or someone you love is troubled by dreams about the dead in which the message "Join Me!" appears, obtaining psychological help is important.

Older Man's Dead Wife Urges Death

Of course, it is not only the young person setting out on a married relationship who may mourn the loss of a mate. A gentleman in his seventies confided to me a nightmare he had a day or two after his wife died:

> My wife is urging me to kill myself.

The elderly dreamer awoke, terrified. As he thought about this alarming dream, he realized the imagery was an expression of his own wish. Losing his loved spouse of many decades left him feeling bereft. His despondency continued for several months, he told me, until he had an experience in a church. While he was praying, he sensed his wife's spirit nearby, not her form but a golden light. He felt certain for the first time that she was well. This "encounter" and the resulting belief in her well-being released him from his fears.

Widow's Dead Husband Comes to Fetch Her

A seventy-year-old widow named Matilde, a member of the Mapuche Indians of Chile, told this dream to an anthropologist:

My dead husband came to take me away. He came to the creek nearby our hut. He told me he had everything ready and I should rush because we couldn't waste any time. He told me to dress properly, to wear all my jewelry and my best dress. He would wait for me at the creek. I went to the house and I got ready. When I went to the creek, he was already waiting for me in his carriage. When he saw me, he gave me his hand so I could get hold of him to jump into the carriage. But I lost my balance and I couldn't grab his hand. He told me he was afraid that the carriage wasn't working and he would have to leave the carriage there and take only the horse. He was going to help me to get on the horse, but I woke up.[5]

In terms of Matilde's healthy survival, she was probably lucky not to have joined her dead husband on the dream horse. The woman in the following story was not so fortunate.

Widow Is Clutched by Husband's Hand from the Grave

A fifty-one-year-old woman, in a case described by Russian psychiatrist Vasilii Kasatkin, had lost her husband three months earlier. She developed heart trouble and was recuperating from a heart attack she had suffered two months after his death. During the day preceding the nightmare, she had experienced a slight pain in the region of her heart:

I am in the cemetery where my husband is buried. I sit down on his gravestone. Two bony hands reach up out of the grave. One hand grasps my throat. The other puts its bony fingers around my heart. It's hard to breathe. I try to scream but can't for a long time. Finally I manage to scream.[6]

The dreamer awoke in fear, with a fast heartbeat, a pain in her heart, and a spasm in her throat. Clearly, her physical condition had worsened during the night. The imagery of her morbid dream depicted the typical suffocating sensations and squeezing pain of some heart attacks.

Yet this nightmare did more than put the widow's physical sensations into vivid images. Her dream seemed to be saying that her husband's spirit was reaching out of the grave to clutch her life away and drag it to him. It reminds us of the myths of malevolent ghosts. Her husband's dream image was not coaxing her to join him; it was attempting to force her to do so. Surely it felt that way to the bereaved woman.

Freud's "Work of Mourning"

Sigmund Freud introduced the term "work of mourning" in his classic 1917 paper *Mourning and Melancholia*.[7] In it, he drew a distinction between normal grief and melancholic depression. Although both conditions may begin with the loss of a loved object and share several characteristics (painful dejection, loss of interest in the outside world, loss of the capacity to love, inactivity), melancholia has the additional element of greatly lowered self-esteem.

In the normal work of mourning, according to Freud, a person is forced by reality to recognize that the loved object no longer exists. Yet the wish to cling to it is strong. A struggle ensues. Eventually reality wins, and the mourner gradually withdraws the attachment to the loved person. But this task is carried out slowly, bit by bit. Each one of the memories and hopes which were bound to the loved person is brought up, lamented, and detached. It is an excruciating process. When the work is complete, often sometime between one and two years later, the survivor is free to invest emotions elsewhere. While mourning lasts, the process absorbs all one's energy. But one must sever one's attachment to the lost person in order to live fully again.

Resisting the Call to Join the Dead

Several classics tell the story of a brokenhearted lover trying to follow the dead beloved into the Land of the Dead in order to retrieve his or her spirit, as did the mythological Greek musician Orpheus, who sought his dead wife, Eurydice. Many folktales contain the motif of a dead lover returning, taking his sweetheart behind him on horseback, and attempting to carry her with him into the grave,[8] just as Matilde dreamed her dead husband was trying to do. The theme of such tales and legends is similar to our modern dreams: We may reunite momentarily with dead lost lovers, but we cannot bring them back to life. Nor should they take us with them.

If you find yourself tormented by dreams of a dead person coaxing you to join them, you need to resist. Techniques for confronting threatening dream figures may be useful, as described in Chapter 4, in the section "You Fool!" If such dreams persist, seek out professional guidance.

Contrast to "I'm Waiting for You"

You are not likely to confuse the seductive or destructive images of the dead urging you to "Join Me!" with the beneficent images of the deceased giving reassurance of continued caring presence, and of patiently waiting for you.

Many dreamers report soothing dreams of the dead in which the deceased says something to the effect of "I'm watching over you," "I'm waiting for you," "I'll be here when it's your turn."

In time, the lost person becomes a cherished part of the past. Survivors may gradually come to feel that the lost loved one is waiting patiently and lovingly—not urging an early departure—on the other side. This feeling can be a comfort toward the closure of one's own life.

"Your Turn Is Coming"

Dream Message: "Your Turn Is Coming"
Deceased informs the dreamer when he or she will die.

Frequency: Relatively rare.

Response after Awake:
Dreamer may feel some concern, but more often
feels peaceful acceptance.

The Fixed Life Span

The hourglass of Father Time has been a long-established symbol of the fixed measure of time available to each of us. Is there a predetermined limit to our lives? Does destiny fix our fate? If so, can we extend it under certain circumstances? Can we add a few grains of sand?

Life spans seem to vary from country to country, and within a country, vary in different social and cultural groups. In the United States, the average life expectancy for a white woman born in 1994 is 79.6 years; for a white man it is 73.2 years; for black males it is 67.7; for black females it is 75.7.[9] Of course, individual life spans vary too, depending upon one's health and one's genes.

The biblical standard seems to be "three score and ten," that is, seventy years—a marked deterioration in length from the patriarchs, who were reported to live to the century mark and beyond.

According to scientific standards, barring accidental death, our lives will last a certain, predetermined number of heartbeats, or a certain predetermined number of cell divisions.

I found it strangely unsettling, when I was working on a genealogy program on my computer, to click on the life expectancy button. My age appeared, calculated to the day, with the comment that I would live another twenty-six years, provided I was not a smoker. Certainly I know that the figures in the program must be based upon actuarial tables used by insurance companies, but there is something very odd about being told one has a precise time limit. It may be even odder to gain this information in a dream.

The Welcoming Spirits

One of the most consistent characteristics of dreams and visions of people who are dying, and of people who have had near-death experiences, is that of being welcomed to the afterlife by the spirits of dead loved ones. We have all heard stories of a dying person seeing apparitions of a long-dead father, a cherished deceased sister or brother or mother, a child who died in infancy, a dearly loved friend, or a beloved dead mate.

In a study of deathbed visions done in 1977 (by Karlis Osis and

Erlendur Haraldsson and described in their book *At the Hour of Death*), it was found that in the overwhelming majority of cases, the visions reported were perceived by the dying patient as being the presence of some sort of escort to "the other side."[10] These escorts were sometimes God or an angel, but more often they were deceased relatives. The apparitions seemed to the dying persons to be present in the room, to talk with them, and comfort them. The authors had deliberately excluded cases in which the dying were heavily sedated and appeared to be confused or disoriented. Death usually followed fairly soon after the appearance of the "escorts."

When the person who was expected to die momentarily, or had appeared to die but was resuscitated, and recovered, the escorts seemed to vanish.

Hospice nurses Maggie Callanan and Patricia Kelley say, in their book *Final Gifts,* that the most prevalent theme as dying people become aware that death is near is the presence of someone not alive.[11] Sometimes this happens weeks prior to death, but more often it is days or hours before dying.

The dying person seems to see and hear and talk with someone who is not visible to others in the room. Usually it is some significant figure from the person's life, but it may be a religious figure. There may be several figures clear only to the vision of the dying person.

Dying people often describe what they see and hear to the living people in the room. Here are a few samples:[12]

· Oh, look! Here comes Steve. He's come to take me swimming.

· Would you wait, I'm not ready yet!

· Do you know who the little girl is? The one who comes to see me.

· There was an angel by my bed.

· When I woke up there was an angel sitting in the light from the window.

· My sister and my husband are calling me to come.

· I woke up with a start when I felt a warm, caring hand on my shoulder. I looked around behind me and there was my aunt smiling at me as she touched me. It made me feel so good and safe.

In all these cases, the dying person was speaking of people who were dead, sometimes even without knowing they had died. Callanan and Kelley recommend expecting dying people to experience the presence of someone not alive. They urge helping dying persons by not arguing with them, but by speaking the truth. Paraphrasing Callanan and Kelley, and saying simply, "Remember, he [or she] died a few years ago?" can be helpful, but trying to convince the dying they could not possibly have seen someone who is dead can only be disturbing or productive of anger.

Two months before my friend Laura's mother died, in her late eighties, she began having visions of a large black man. First, he was in the far corner of the house, then in the kitchen, and later in the door to her bedroom, getting closer each time. The dying mother explained that "the black man is here to take me home to Poppa." For white people, as we will see in the chapter on symbolism, the image of Death often has a black face, representing the unknown.

Whatever may be the source of such visions and the dreams that parallel them, their effect is calming. The dying person feels the presence of a loving guide. Those who have died before, or some good spirit, will be with them on the journey to the other world.

Let's look at how approaching death has been depicted, and what the welcoming spirits might say, in dreams.

"Your Turn" in Literature

Many of the dreams recorded in literature take the form of "Your Turn Is Coming." This is probably because the predictions contained in such dreams make a strong impression upon the dreamer, who writes the dream in a journal or letter, or tells it to friends who write it down. When death follows soon after the dream prediction, people are invariably impressed. Thus, these dreams get recorded in anthologies and other published books and passed on in various ways.

Lady Margaret Harrison Gets Life Extension

Lady Margaret Harrison, for instance, who died in 1640, had seemed certain to die fifteen years earlier. She had been violently ill with a fever three months after her daughter was born. For almost two days she was taken for dead, but was actually in a coma. When Lady Margaret emerged from her deathlike trance, she confided to her husband and her minister that she had been in a place where she felt troubled by the "sense of leaving her girl." Suddenly two women clothed in long white garments had appeared. She thought she fell down with her face in the dust before these welcoming spirits. They asked her why she was troubled in such great happiness. She replied, "Oh, let me have the same grant given to Hezekiah, that I may live fifteen years, to see my daughter a woman." The two women in white answered, "It is done." In that instant, Lady Margaret awoke. Her minister, who preached her funeral sermon, confirmed that Lady Harrison's death took place exactly fifteen years after that dream.[13]

Lady Margaret had been referring to the account in the Bible of a king of Judah named Hezekiah who, as he lay dying, was granted a life extension of fifteen years by God, who heard his prayer. This ancient account had so impressed Lady Margaret that many centuries later, when she was almost dead, she was able to recall it and ask for the same favor.

Are such notions answers to prayers? Is the belief that one has been given a life extension enough to activate healing powers? Is the belief that one will die at a given time sufficient to guarantee it? Many times the answers seem to be yes. Perhaps there is a part of us that senses what is happening to our life forces.

Minister Is Touched by Death's Dart

An English minister in the eighteenth century described a dramatic dream of his father's with the message "Your Turn Is Coming." (Some accounts attribute the description to Reverend John Coleridge, others to S. T. Coleridge in a letter to Thomas Poole in 1797.)[14] The father had traveled to Plymouth, with another son, to get him settled as a midshipman. Then the father returned home directly, explaining to friends when they urged him to stay overnight that he was eager to get home because of an impressive dream:

> Death had appeared to him as usually painted and had touched him with his dart.[15]

When the father reached home, he repeated this dream to his wife, had some punch, gave an account of his travel, and went to bed in high spirits. However, he soon complained of a "pain in his bowels" and drank some peppermint water his wife brought; then he said he felt better and lay down again. In a moment, his wife heard a noise in his throat and called to her husband in vain. Then she shrieked, awakening her son. When he heard his mother's scream, the boy, who knew his father was expected but not that he had returned, felt "certain that Papa is dead," as he was.

What causes such dreams? Is there a subtle recognition of impending ill health? A precognition? All we know for certain is that they do occur.

Abraham Lincoln Sees Self in State

Perhaps the most famous dream prediction of a time and manner of death is that of President Abraham Lincoln. A few days before his assassination, Lincoln recounted:

> About ten days ago, I retired very late. I had been up waiting for important dispatches from the front. I could not have been long in bed when I fell into a slumber, for I was weary. I soon began to dream. There seemed to be death-like stillness about me. Then I heard subdued sobs, as if a number of people were weeping. I thought I left my bed and wandered downstairs. There the silence was broken by the same pitiful sobbing, but the mourners were invisible. I went from room to room; no living person was in sight, but the same mournful sounds of distress met me as I passed along. It was light in all the rooms; every object was familiar to me; but where were all the people who were grieving as if their hearts would break? I was puz-

zled and alarmed. What could be the meaning of all this? Determined to find the cause of a state of things so mysterious and so shocking, I kept on until I arrived at the East Room, which I entered. There I met with a sickening surprise. Before me was a catafalque, on which rested a corpse wrapped in funeral vestments. Around it were stationed soldiers who were acting as guards; and there was a throng of people, some gazing mournfully upon the corpse, whose face was covered, others weeping pitifully. "Who is dead in the White House?" I demanded of one of the soldiers. "The President," was his answer; "he was killed by an assassin!" Then came a loud burst of grief from the crowd, which awoke me from my dream.[16]

This dream of Lincoln's was recorded by a friend, Ward Hill Lamon, to whom he described it one evening at a small social gathering. In this case, we do not have a deceased figure announcing that "Your Turn Is Coming." Rather, the dreamer seems to be shown the future event with his own corpse.

Surely Lincoln, like other presidents and prominent political figures under great pressures, had received threats of assassination. He knew there were many people unhappy with his policies, as well as those who applauded them. One could not help but anticipate the results of such danger under these circumstances. But that his assassination could follow so soon after his dream that appears to predict it is startling.

We have the record of the dreams of two other leaders whose murders took place even sooner: the next day.

Julius Caesar Shakes Hands with Jupiter

On the night before he was assassinated, the Roman emperor Julius Caesar dreamed he was soaring above the clouds, and then shaking hands with Jupiter.[17] In this dream, Caesar saw himself being welcomed into heaven by the highest-ranking god. Meanwhile, on the same night, Caesar's wife Calpurnia dreamed:

The gable ornament, resembling that of a temple, which had been one of the honours voted him by the Senate, collapsed, and there he lay stabbed in her arms![18]

Calpurnia awoke suddenly from this dream and the bedroom door burst open of its own accord. These dreams and other omens led her to plead with her husband not to attend the Senate that day, and indeed he hesitated, perhaps in part because of his own dream. But eventually, Brutus persuaded Caesar that he should not disappoint the others, and he went to his death.

Caligula Is Kicked Out of Heaven

The Roman emperor Caligula, too, must have sensed the growing antagonism toward him when, the night before he was assassinated, he dreamed:

> *he was standing beside Jupiter's heavenly throne, when the god kicked him with a toe of his right foot and sent him tumbling down to earth.*[19]

Caligula, like Caesar, received his dream message directly from the highest-ranking Roman god. The difference between these dreams—being welcomed in heaven and being kicked out of it—is that Caligula had already declared himself to be a god. He was well aware of his many crimes and, according to his dream, felt he would not be welcomed in heaven after his death. Caesar, in contrast, was a righteous man and had reason to expect that he would be accepted in heaven.

The Roman historian Suetonius recorded these dreams, and others of the twelve Caesars, because it was believed that dreams of prominent heads of state were highly significant. Certainly these emperors must have sensed the imminent risk to their lives.

Henry James's Sister's Dead Friends Beckon

The novelist Henry James, and his brother the psychologist-philosopher William James, had an invalid sister named Alice. She was said to be as talented as her siblings, but her chronic physical and nervous illnesses made it difficult for her to develop her abilities. She kept a diary in which entries were recorded with all the skill of her brothers. Eventually, when she was in London dying of breast cancer at the age of forty-three, Alice dictated her comments to her close friend Katharine up until the last few hours before her death. She asked Henry to cable to their brother William and his family in Cambridge, Massachusetts, saying, "Tenderest love to all. Farewell. Am going soon." Alice also dictated a dream that she had two nights before her death:

> She saw two of her dead women friends standing up in a boat, putting out to sea in a storm. They seemed to pass from under the shadow of a cloud into sunlight. They looked back at Alice on the shore, as if beckoning to her to join them.[20]

When a person is dying, dreams of the dead calling the dreamer to join them are deeply comforting, in contrast to such dreams when the person is in good health but feelings of depression suggest an end to life. Alice surely felt her dead friends, as welcoming spirits, would provide shelter on her journey.

Elizabeth Barrett Browning's Spirit Predicts Her Sister's Time

The poet Robert Browning recorded a dream told to him by Arabella, who was the sister of his dead wife, the poet Elizabeth Barrett Browning. Arabella Barrett dreamed:

> She was walking with her beloved sister, Elizabeth, who had died two years before. As they walked, Arabella turned to her sister, who in the dream was very much alive, and asked, "When shall I be with you?" Her sister replied: "Dearest, in five years."[21]

Robert Browning recorded this dream on July 21, 1863. In June 1868, nearly five years after her dream, Arabella Barrett died.

"Your Turn" in Contemporary Dreamers

Modern dreamers, too, receive dream messages that "Your Turn Is Coming." Sometimes these are specific predictions, as in the dream the woman had about her dead son telling her to go back to life, that she was to live until she was seventy-one. For other dreamers, the message is more general.

Dorothy's Dead Father Beckons

Artist and dreamer Dorothy had a momentous dream at the same time her mother died:

> I am walking on the beach. It is early morning and the air is clear. I am dragging a long stick that I periodically use as a cane to lean on. When I look ahead, I can see that the beach comes to an end, but it also continues. Something tells me that the continuation of the beach is not of the same place or of the same dimension.
>
> As I get closer to the end of the beach, I can see my dead father beckoning to me to cross over to the other side, over to the continuation of the beach. When I do, I find myself at a wonderful fair or carnival. There are tables covered with all kinds of brightly colored wares. My father takes me up to one of the tables. It is covered with jewelry made of jade. He shows me a particular piece of jewelry, a white Buddha brooch.
>
> I pick it up and look at it very closely. It is very beautiful. The jade is quite translucent and a single fine bright green vein runs through the side of it. I hold it in the palm of my hand and it feels cool against my skin. I sigh and express my appreciation for the piece. Then I tell my father it is time for me to go back. He takes my arm and says, "No, not this time."

Dorothy woke up surprised to see the state her bedding was in. The blankets were bunched up and on the floor. It looked as if she had been struggling with something. She had no dream recall until later that morning, when her sister called to inform her that their mother had died in her sleep. Immediately, the memory of her dream flooded back. She recalled how her mother had used a cane the last few years of her life; she knew then that she had played the role of her mother in the dream, as she dragged the stick through the sand. She thought that her dead father's saying she / her mother wasn't going back meant death. Perhaps, she pondered, the state of her bedding was a result of her struggle, her resistance, in letting her mother's spirit go. Clearly, she was strongly identified with her mother.

Dorothy's parents always had been close. Since her father died ten years earlier, her mother had lost all interest in life. The crossing over, from one beach to the beach of a different dimension that continued on the other side, represented her mother joining her father in death. The wonderful, colorful carnival of paradise was there.

Dorothy said, "I was fortunate to have this dream to help me with my grief . . . it assured me that my mother was where she wanted to be, with my father." The dream brought her consolation during her grief.

Dorothy's dream, in addition to being a variation of "Your Turn Is Coming"—more of "Your Mother's Turn Is Now"—also carries the message "Here's a Gift." The exquisite jade Buddha Dorothy was given in the dream was a gift from her dead father that she has not yet fully understood. We may need time to live with such gifts from the dead before their meanings become as translucent as the dream jade was. Surely part of the gift was a spiritual compassion, characteristic of Buddha, bringing solace to the dead parents' daughter.

Man Hears His Dead Friend in the Hall

When Zal, my husband, was in his late sixties, he was saddened by a series of deaths among his family and friends. Such events, in addition to the grief one feels about the lost persons, stir fears about one's own mortality.

This concern was evident in a nightmare he experienced a few months after the death of David, a close friend:

I am in my office in the middle of the night, working. I hear a noise like a person. I look out and see a sort of shadow of a person—it's very dark—going down the hall toward the coffee room.

"Come here! Come here!" I hear myself calling. "Come here, David!" Then I see the white hair of a patient of mine who has serious

health problems; then the profile of a former patient, who has all kinds of health and other problems.

As I call out, I have real trouble getting my voice to articulate. It's thick and grumbly . . . and then you woke me.

Zal rarely has nightmares, or even recalls dreams, so his making harsh sounds while he slept aroused me, and I in turn woke him.

Several elements in the dream are characteristic of dreams about the dead—the darkness, the shadowy figure, the hallway.

It was clear to both of us that this dream was not only a response to his friend David's death, but also expressive of a concern about the future of his own health and life span. Although Zal's genetics suggest longevity of over one hundred years, witnessing physical changes as he ages, along with observing the deaths of good friends and family members, causes concern. Our turn may not be next, but it *will* come. Our dreams help prepare us.

Elderly Woman Visits Her Dead Mother

Older people often get glimpses in their dreams of what lies beyond. Elizabeth, in her early eighties, dreamed about seeing her mother:

I am at a bus station. I can see Mother inside the glass door. She looks out and says to me in surprise, "What in the world are you doing here?"

We have observed earlier how frequently dreams about the dead are set in places of transportation, "terminals." We also noted the recurrence of a barrier, such as the glass door, that stands between the dead and the living in dreams. The unusual aspect of this dream is the surprise expressed by Elizabeth's mother. This element suggests it is not yet time for Elizabeth to make the "trip" that will reunite her with her dead mother.

On another occasion, Elizabeth dreamed:

I am spending seven days with my mother. But I am going to leave tonight. I am not sure of the departure time.

In these dreams, Elizabeth seemed to be preparing herself for her own "departure." The time was not yet, but perhaps soon. Elizabeth is now in her late eighties, past the age at which her mother died. When we reach the age at which one of our parents died, there is an inevitable wondering—awake and in dreams—whether our time, too, has come.

Accepting Our Time Whenever It May Be

The best stance to take is to accept the fact that our lives have a limited span. Rarely will we know the exact time of our deaths. Yet even as we struggle against the limits of our lives—by exercise, healthy eating, and lifestyle—we must acknowledge them. We can choose to live well within these limits whatever they may be. We can seek love and meaning in the face of death. We can find purpose even in our old age; we can manage to contribute something positive, embody our ideals, enrich our realities, admire what is beautiful, and love what is good. We may live long enough to grasp the meaning of our dreams, to understand the content of our lifetimes, and to comprehend the meaning of our own life stories— then share these stories with others.

8

"Please Forgive Me" and "I Forgive You"

"Please Forgive Me"

Dream Message: "Please Forgive Me"
Deceased asks the dreamer for pardon or expresses regret for some action.

Frequency: Relatively rare, but important.
Response after Awake:
Dreamer feels either comforted or elated. May state that an apology was made. A sense of completion or satisfaction lingers a long time.

B ecause so many close relationships are ambivalent, people often die before conflicts are resolved. You may not only be left with feelings of grief for the deceased, but also feel hurt, resentment, or anger that seems impossible to ever express or resolve.

Happily, a resolution sometimes takes place within a dream, as it did for Gloria.

Gloria's Dead Father Settles His Account

Gloria had become alienated from her father, to whom she had been close for most of her life. This happened because during her marriage to her first husband, Gloria reached a point where she felt she must divorce. She dreaded telling her parents. They lived a considerable distance from her and she did not wish to worry them with her marital problems.

Unfortunately, her soon-to-be-ex-husband took it upon himself to write to her parents, and gave them his version of the divorce. Her father then wrote to Gloria, expressing his bitter disappointment in her and her behavior. The letter caused Gloria great distress, but she could never bring herself to discuss it in the times she was together with her father over the next twenty years. Although Gloria sensed that he eventually understood why a divorce was necessary, she still felt wounded over the things her father had said in the letter, and the fact that he never apologized.

Then Gloria's father developed Alzheimer's disease and was unable to recognize his daughter, much less apologize to her for a long-ago letter. After he died, her grief was extreme.

Approximately two years after her father's death, Gloria had an extremely vivid dream about him that brought comfort:

> My father "came" to me as I remember him about thirty years before his death. He was smiling and dressed in khaki work clothes with a hat sitting jauntily on his head. He put his right arm around my shoulders and asked me to walk with him, saying he was going to the bank to settle his account. As we walked along, he drew me closer and said, "Everything is fine," and then he walked away, presumably toward the bank.

Gloria awakened with "the most wonderful feeling of peace." She cried uncontrollably with relief. She said she could still "feel Dad's love surrounding me." Although Gloria continued to miss her father, the dream eased her awful grief. She was convinced that her father "came back to let me know that he apologized" for the things he said in the letter.

In Gloria's dream, the deceased father's wish to "settle his account" at the bank was probably a metaphor for settling his emotional account with his daughter. This dream has many of the elements we recognize as characteristic in dreams about the dead—her father's youthful appearance, his happy, loving manner, and his assurance that everything was fine. That this is more than an "I'm O.K." dream message is seen by the impact it had on the dreamer, especially the belief that the deceased father had returned to apologize. This dream brought the peace the dreamer craved. A similar resolution of resentment may arise in one of your dreams.

Mary Lou's Dead Uncle and Dead Schoolmate Ask Forgiveness

Which of us does not have memories of childhood hurts, snubs, or injuries? The incidents themselves may be small, but the reaction to them large.

Mary Lou carried a lifelong hurt from school days toward an older boy who had physically injured her with a snowball, and then smirked over the pain he had caused. She also had been emotionally wounded by an uncle who paid attention only to his son while ignoring Mary Lou and the other cousins; his behavior made her feel "invisible." This woman was in her late sixties when she had a dream that helped dispel these heartaches:

> The boy from school and my uncle were both in the dream, one after the other, very briefly, but—without words—as if they knew all and asked my forgiveness.

Mary Lou awoke with a vivid sense of having been in the presence of both males, dead many years before. She said, "I felt as if the pain of my childhood had been recognized." Mary Lou knew the hurt she had suffered was healed at last. Such painful memories held through the years can do us harm. In a dream, vanquish any you hold when you have the chance.

Your troublesome feelings may include guilt, as they did for Carla.

Carla Holds Her Dying Mother

Perhaps you remember Carla (described in Chapter 4), who had the upsetting dream of her dead mother screaming at her after she and her siblings had gone through the mother's belongings. That dream had taken place the night of the mother's death.

Carla was burdened with feelings of guilt about having put her mother in the hospital against her will, the fact that her mother died alone, and having sorted through her things so soon after her death. These thoughts might not have been so troublesome had the basic relationship been good. But in addition, Carla felt her mother had left the world with "an unsettled spirit" regarding her family, that there was a great deal of anger and hurt left unexpressed.

Carla said that she dreamed about her mother many times during the months after her death, always with an awareness that she had died and the visit was temporary. These dreams culminated in the dramatic dream several months after the mother's death that I described in Chapter 4. I repeat it here in full to underscore how forgiveness may occur in a dream.

> *I am walking into the dining room of the family house where I grew up. My mother is lying on a bench in the corner of the room. She looks peaceful but very weak. I am aware that she is dead, and that I am to accompany her through a "dream death."*
>
> *I hold her in my arms. We talk of unresolved anger, incidents of conflict from past years. There is a pervasive mutual sense of forgiveness and unconditional love. As I hold her, her body undergoes several magical dreamlike metamorphoses. She becomes a tiny, vibrant pink-skinned infant, an unrecognizable animal form, a grotesquely disfigured elderly woman, then back to herself. I am not alarmed or repulsed by these changes; my posture is one of nonjudgmental acceptance and love.*
>
> *I am crying in the dream as this transformation unfolds, as I know it is a prelude to her final departure. The tears are not of anguish, but of release for both of us.*
>
> *Peacefully, and with an exceptional aura of surrender in each of our hearts, she dies in my arms.*

Carla said she felt that this dream was "a realization of the un-met goals of our relationship at the time of her death." Observe how the image of the mother underwent shape shifting, through forms from different stages of the life cycle, and even an amorphous an-imal figure. These changing images may have been metaphors for the many-sided nature of her mother, characteristic of all people. Through each metamorphosis streamed love. In a way, this peak dream of Carla's contains two messages, "Please Forgive Me," as well as "I Forgive You."

From this time on, Carla's dreams of her dead mother lessened. She reappeared in a dream when Carla graduated from medical school, and years later, in a time of turmoil and major self-exploration, she appeared in a dream bringing words of reassur-ance. Her visits recur in times of struggle and joy. There has truly been an evolution in the relationship between this dreamer and her deceased mother. Fortunately, many of us can share that positive change, although it may take a long time, as it did for Rae.

Rae Looks into Her Dead Father's Blue Eyes

Rae was in her middle seventies before she had a dream that helped her feel better about her father, who had died almost a quarter of a century earlier. Rae and her father "had never had a comfortable life experience with each other." She dreamed:

> I am awakened one night, at two a.m., by hearing my name being called. I jump out of bed and start to walk around the bed when a very bright light appears in the bedroom door—and there stands my father! He is smiling and I am impressed with his big blue eyes.

Although this dream was fleeting, it had a deep impact on Rae. She thought about it for days afterward, and recalled taking part in a workshop years earlier in which the participants were encouraged to sit quietly and await the presence of a deceased person who needed forgiving. In her imagination, Rae had seen her dead father appear; from his big blue eyes a bright light emanated. He smiled and sat down. She went through her forgiveness exercise and he left as quietly as he had come.

Rae felt that her father had come to her again in this dream to assure her that all was well. Although no words were spoken or touches exchanged, the dream has the flavor of a response to forgiveness. Sometimes forgiveness is easier after death, as Susan found it to be.

Sarah's Dead Brother Apologizes

When Sarah's younger brother tried to kill himself on the eve of her wedding, she felt anger as well as sorrow at his distress. He succeeded in committing suicide a few weeks later. Sarah, who was pregnant at the time, miscarried a few days after her brother's funeral.

Sarah was understandably angry at her brother. She railed at him for the loss of her baby, and for the pain and grief he had caused her and the family. She decided to "speak with him" and found, to her surprise, it was easier than when he was alive and tormented by hate. Sarah was reluctant to share his exact words, but explained:

> When he is talking with me, his spirit is above my head to the right facing me. I don't see his "earthly" features but feel him. He has apologized, given information, and told me how he is now. He's at peace and only brings messages that put others to rest. It's so unlike his earthly, angry self, but it is him . . .

These experiences of Sarah are sometimes dreams and sometimes "waking visions of clarity and reality." Whatever they may be, they have brought her ease.

Sarah believes that her brother's spirit is "reconstructing" and will eventually move on. She hopes that someday one of her children may have a son who will be a happier reincarnation of her dead brother. It appears not only that there has been an apology for the misery the dead brother caused, but also that Sarah has forgiven him. Her own anger toward him, as well as her dead brother's lifetime anger, has dissolved. Forgiveness, like love, needs to flow in both directions.

"I Forgive You"

....

Dream Message: "I Forgive You"

Deceased offers pardon to the dreamer, or expresses regret
for some action. Conversely, the deceased may
communicate forgiveness to the dreamer.

Frequency: Relatively rare, but important.

Response after Awake:
Dreamer feels comforted or elated. May state that the
dream has caused feelings about the dead person to
change. A sense of completion or freedom from
guilt may endure.

Geoffrey Forgives His Dead Father

Geoffrey, in his late forties, continued to have negative feelings
about his father long after leaving home at the age of nineteen. He
considered him "supercritical, authoritarian, pushy, bossy, know-
it-all, and disparaging." He said that his father estranged everyone
in the family and that he and his sisters considered their mother a
martyr for staying with him. A dream about ten years after his father's death helped Geoffrey change his mind:

*I am in the house I grew up in, in England. I am upstairs, walking
into my bedroom (where I slept from age fourteen to nineteen). I am
my present age.*

*As I walk into the room, I am surprised to find my father sitting
on the bed in front of me. He looks totally different from the way I
have always seen him. Instead of looking severe and old, he looks
young, friendly, pleasant, and quite calm. He turns to greet me. I am
very surprised but he is not. I am amazed at how different he is from
how he was when alive. He is easy to talk to and we chat pleasantly.*

After a while we say goodbye and I kiss him goodbye, feeling good about him, and leave.

After this dream, Geoffrey's attitude was transformed. "I no longer felt the resentment (which I didn't approve of but undoubtedly still had) towards him. I felt able to see him as a human being rather than a tyrant, and [was] even a *little* bit fond of him, as opposed to antagonistic." Geoffrey also had a sense that his father's spirit was on a more positive spiritual path than before, and that he no longer had to worry about him as a being.

Geoffrey felt certain that this was an actual meeting. He believed he was able to see his father as he really is, and that they were "making friends," which they should have done during his lifetime but never did. He thought the long gap between his father's death and the dream was necessary for his father's spirit to be evolved enough, and friendly enough, to initiate contact.

Geoffrey shared this dream with his mother, hoping it would help her handle any negative feelings that remained. He finds himself still working on eliminating some of the unwelcome characteristics his father used to have, which he occasionally sees in himself.

Being able to forgive a dead person who has mistreated us frees us to recognize the ways in which we might resemble that person, and to be able to dispose of those traits. You remember how Paul Tholey was able to admit the validity of some of his dead father's criticisms after he dreamed of rejecting his threats and insults and declared his father could no longer order him around? Only then was Tholey able to shake hands with his dead father in a dream and become friendly. Freedom from anger and guilt allows us to become more ourselves.

Francine Releases Her Guilt over Her Grandmother's Death

Francine's grandmother was living with her family when the older woman became ill. One night, Francine heard her grandmother begin to moan and call out to her aunt (who also lived with them). Everyone in the house was asleep. It took Francine a minute to realize that the cries she heard were not part of a dream. She got up and went to her grandmother. The grandmother told her to wake the aunt because she thought she was having a stroke. Francine did so, and then ran downstairs to tell her mother, who called an ambulance. A few days later, Francine's grandmother died in the hospital.

Francine felt enormous guilt. Although she never told anyone, she thought that her grandmother had died "because of my laziness in not getting out of bed sooner and waking my aunt when I heard [her] cries." She would berate herself, saying, "If only I had gotten help sooner." In reality, the time lag was short.

Several months after her grandmother's death, Francine was sleeping on the couch in her living room with the telephone on a table beside the couch, just inches from her head. It was early morning on Easter Sunday. She dreamed:

I meet my grandmother in space. Completely black space. She tells me that she is going to call me on the telephone.

At that very moment, Francine woke up and looked directly at the telephone. It rang. She picked up the receiver and said, "Hello." The connection was very bad, as if the call were coming from far away. Over the static Francine could hear the voice of an old woman saying, "Hello," again and again. She asked who it was, but there was no answer. Then the connection went dead.

In the morning, Francine told her mother about her dream. By then, she felt sure the telephone probably had not rung, that it must have been part of her dream. To her great surprise, Francine's mother confirmed the reality of the experience. She, too, had heard the telephone ring, and had picked up the extension and heard, as her daughter had, the voice of an old woman saying, "Hello," repeatedly.

We have seen that many dream messages from the dead are delivered via telephone. So are messages from waking apparitions. This dream and the experience that followed it brought much-needed relief to Francine. She has continued to feel that the dream and the experience afterward were her grandmother's way of "helping me put an end to the guilt I had been carrying around with me for so many months." Easter Sunday, the day of the resurrection of Christ, was a good day for being freed from guilt.

In this case, it was the deceased who seemed to communicate to the dreamer, "I Forgive You," thus making it possible for her to forgive herself.

Gwen Rocks Her Deceased Father

Gwen's relationship with her father had been tenuous. She felt that "he was finished with me at age twelve." She left home when she was quite young. Later, through her husband, Gwen felt she had made some big steps toward resolving issues with her father, yet they were far from close. Then her father died, when he was in his fifties, during a second bypass operation on his heart. Gwen felt unprepared because he had seemed so healthy. She was not present at his death, which took place far from where she lived, because everyone told her not to come until after the surgery. She was glad that at least she had been able to talk with him by telephone.

In the midst of her grief, Gwen was particularly troubled by the fact that her father had been a declared agnostic. She, in contrast, had become dedicated to her religion. It pained her to think that her father—basically a good man—might be deprived of a peaceful afterlife.

About five months after her father's death, during the month of his birthday, Gwen had an intense dream:

> I am struggling in the waters of a very wide river. I can see the rocky shore. Three or four people are in the water—family members, perhaps my daughter. I am fighting the water, pulling on it, trying to stay in one place. My feet are off the bottom. I'm swimming, but out of control. My father is behind me, downstream. The water is lapping against the rock cliffs, big, rugged, broken boulders, and sharp pebbles. Beside the river is a forest. The water is very cold.
>
> I get an overhead view of my father's body lying on a cross. I am pulling some kind of weight. Then I realize it is Dad. After that there is no more struggle. The cross with his body on it is drifting in a circle.

Gwen awoke from this strange dream with a feeling of peace. She associated the river in her dream to crossing the river Jordan. She said she felt that she was "having to drag" her father into heaven. At the end of the dream, she told me, what was happening was what was supposed to happen. If one has faith and lets go of the burden—in the dream, the burden was her father on the cross—the burden will take care of itself. She said she was able to let go of a "cheated" feeling she had about him, and accept that there was no changing it.

In a sense, by relinquishing the burden in this dream, Gwen was also forgiving her father. Notice the sharpness and hardness of the rocks, the coldness of the water—metaphors for her cold, hard feelings—and how her emotional struggle with her father became a literal one in the dream. The imagery of forgiveness was even clearer in a dream she had a little later:

> At the end, I am sitting on the ground with my legs folded. I'm in a blue flowing gown with my hair hanging down. My father is an adult, lying on the ground. I hold his torso and I rock him.

Gwen explained that the vivid blue of the gown in her dream was her favorite color, which was also the color of her father's eyes, soft, and the color of the sky. Having her hair down, straight, unpretentious, rather than done up for the world, was her "mother image." At this stage of her life, Gwen was able to better understand her father, to be caretaking, to offer comfort and forgiveness. Here the "rocks" were no longer sharp and hard, but an entirely different sort of rock, one that was a source of soothing motion.

The Power of Forgiving

For our own sake, if no other, we need to find the way to accept the apology of those dead people who have wronged us in the past, and—even without their apology—offer forgiveness to them.

Most major religions provide rituals for asking for and receiving forgiveness. Catholicism offers confession of sins and absolution. One of the basic tenets of Protestantism is affirming belief in the forgiveness of sins. Special days are set aside for repentance and forgiveness. Ash Wednesday (the first day of Lent) is considered the appropriate time, in the Episcopal orders of service, to express penitence. In Judaism, Yom Kippur (the Day of Atonement) is thought by many to be the most important day of the year, the culmination of a ten-day penitential season; it precedes the start of the Jewish New Year, offering a last chance to ask forgiveness for any hurts or wrongs committed during the year. Buddhists regard the quality of compassion as essential.

Asking for forgiveness and offering it to others is essential psychologically, whether or not one follows a spiritual practice. The grudges and resentments we hold against others—even deservedly—harm ourselves. Our bitterness and anger can poison our bodies and our goodwill toward humanity.

It is possible to forgive persons who wronged us without condoning their behavior. Such forgiveness can dissolve anger and free us to live fully and joyously. To be truly sorry for some wrong of our own is a prerequisite to being forgiven. There probably is someone—dead or alive—you need to forgive or be forgiven by. If so, you may find the nondenominational suggestions in the last chapter helpful.

9

"I'm Evolving" and "I'm Being Reborn"

"I'm Evolving"

> #### Dream Message: "I'm Evolving"
> Deceased informs the dreamer that he or she is progressing on the other side.
>
> #### Frequency: Relatively rare, but important.
>
> #### Response after Awake:
> Dreamer usually feels comforted, even joyous. A belief in the afterlife may result from this dream.

Assuming there is an afterlife, what happens during it? Does the spirit hover in or near the grave containing the bodily remains or the ashes, or near the site of death? Is there a state of confusion in which the spirit is uncertain whether or not the body has died? Does the spirit linger alongside loved ones for a period of time and then depart to some other realm? If so, what happens there? Is there a resting phase? Is there a Last Judgment? Does the spirit have work or study? Are there rebirths that follow an individual death?

All of these questions are unanswerable from a provable, scientific position. But there are beliefs about the afterlife to suit every taste. Each belief finds expression in people's dreams about the dead. One of the most enduring and appealing of these is the idea of reincarnation.

Putting on the Robe of Flesh Again: Reincarnation

The word "reincarnation" derives from Latin words for "flesh" (*carnalis, caro, carnis*). To "incarnate" is to invest with flesh or bodily nature and form. According to many beliefs, when we are born our spirits put on bodies, much as we might put on a coat. When we die, it is said, we simply shed this bodily garment and continue to exist as spirit. Elisabeth Kübler-Ross describes the body as a cocoon, from which the soul is released as a butterfly.

To reincarnate, then, is to participate in the process of putting on a body over and over again. Reincarnation—also called transmigration or metempsychosis—is the belief that the souls of the dead successively return to earth in new forms or bodies.

When I looked up "reincarnation" in the *Encyclopaedia Britannica*, I found the belief attributed mainly to Asian religions (Hinduism, Jainism, Buddhism, Sikhism) and Asian philosophies, to primitive religions, to some ancient Near Eastern and Middle Eastern religions (the Greek Orphic mysteries, Gnosticism, Manichaeanism), and to some modern religious movements, such as theosophy. I had to smile, because in today's United States of America, there are many people who believe in the concept of reincarnation. They may express it reluctantly and privately to trusted friends, but they hold it among their treasured faiths and it takes form in their dreams about the dead. You may at least hope for reincarnation, if not have faith in it.

Most people are unaware that reincarnation was part of the Christian doctrine until the sixth century, when a group of church officials decided to eliminate it from approved recognition.[1] It has not been dropped from the dreams of the living.

Going to School: Evolution in the Afterlife

You have seen how there is an advancement in the appearance of the dead in dreams about them. Soon after the death, you are likely to depict the deceased as still suffering from the cause of death, looking frail or ill. Later on, you will tend to dream of the deceased in vastly improved health. We observed that not only do physical infirmities disappear, but also a new radiance and vitality seem to emanate from the image of the deceased. Old conflicts and unresolved issues with the deceased may be resolved in dreams. Eventually, the deceased may take on the dream role of wise guide or sage teacher.

In addition to these changes in the appearance and behavior of the deceased, the frequency of dreams about them alters. At first, you might have several intense dreams about the dead person. Later, especially after two or three years, your dreams about the deceased will diminish in vividness and frequency.

One way of looking at these patterns of change might be that as the grieving person slowly adapts to the loss of the loved person, this acceptance is depicted in an improved dream image. The fervor of the relationship lessens, and so does the number of dreams. Another possibility is that the spirit of the deceased person is actually evolving—learning, developing, studying, working, moving from one level to an ever-higher level. The spirit is busy elsewhere and thus appears less in earthbound dreams. This is how a great number of dreamers conceive of an evolution taking place for the spirit of the dead.

Dreams About Evolving in the Afterlife

Beverly's Dead Friend Recognizes She Is Dead

Beverly's close friend Denise died when she was only nineteen, following a long coma. In her dreams soon after Denise died, Beverly would see her friend, recall that she was dead, and become so frightened that she awoke. Later, when Beverly had developed the skill of lucid dreaming, she was able to remain in dreams about

Denise to discuss their activities, unresolved issues, and eventually, her death. In one of these:

> *I asked Denise if she knew she had died. Yes, she knew now, she replied, but not at first. She had been confused. The realization that she was dead came on gradually.*[2]

Beverly thought Denise's confusion about whether she was dead or not was due to her being in a coma for a long time prior to death.

However, this state of confusion about whether or not one is dead is often described, regardless of the presence or absence of coma. Accounts from people who have had near-death experiences suggest that when death has been sudden or violent, the separation between soul and body is shocking and sometimes perplexing. The "guides" or "escorts" who are said to appear to the dying person, and in near-death experiences to those who survive, explain what is happening to the person, and why it may not yet be time for them to die.

Various religions have taken into account this possible confusion of the spirit immediately after death. Tibetan Buddhists, for example, state that the spirit lingers near the body for some forty days. An important function of Tibetan Buddhist monks is to read the Tibetan *Book of the Dead* to the dying person, then to the corpse and to the family of the deceased during this forty-day period, so that the spirit can "find its way" in the afterlife. Among Orthodox Jews, the period of intensive mourning and special prayers is set at seven days—the word "shivah" means "seven." The thirty-day period after the funeral, called *sheloshim,* involves continued special mourning, but with other activities like work or school permitted. Other religions posit different lengths of time that the spirit is said to tarry, and set forth various means to help it depart in peace. The funeral pyres, for instance, used in many Eastern funeral ceremonies, are partly intended to force the spirit to flee the body.

If there is an afterlife, perhaps the first characteristic is a period of confusion for the spirit of the person who has died. If so, religious rituals and prayers may indeed give guidance.

In cases of violent death, the survivor may be grateful to see the dead person showing any improvement in a dream.

Mark's Murdered Brother Waits to Move On

Mark's brother Paul was also his friend; Mark was in despair after he was murdered. A dream about Paul made the separation more bearable:

> I am standing on a bluff overlooking a beautiful valley. I turn around and my brother is standing there. I am so overjoyed to see him I cry and hug him. We talk for a while. My brother tells me he is neither happy nor unhappy, that he is waiting with the others to go on. He tells me that it is all right to be there, that he lives with a group of people who work together while they wait. No one is allowed to wear shoes. He knows who killed him. "It's O.K.," he tells me. Then we are in a kitchen with these other people, men and women. They, too, seem neither happy nor sad, just content to be there until it is time for them to go on. A man walks in; he just brushes all the dirt off his feet. We all joke and laugh.

Although the dead person in this dream is far from the luminous images we may encounter, it is nonetheless a vital depiction of someone who has been murdered. The dead brother is not suffering, but waiting and working with kindly people. The soles—souls?—of their bare feet still touch the earth. The brother is able to say goodbye to his brother/friend before going onward. Surely Mark drew comfort from this dream.

Irene's Dead Mother Moves to Another Level

Irene was deeply troubled after her mother's suicide in her forties. About a month after her mother's death, Irene had a series of dreams that helped her cope.

In the first dream:

> I see Mother looking like she did in her thirties, not very happy. She tells me she is O.K., but doesn't like the house they have her staying in.

Again, we see the feelings of negativity in the early dreams. One has the impression of the mother's spirit being confined, perhaps agitated.

Shortly afterward, Irene dreamed:

I see Mother looking better. I ask her what it is like where she is. She explains that it's very much like it is here, except everything is much lighter. Everything is a lighter vibration, a lighter density. She makes it clear she can't stay long.

Irene awoke from this dream feeling soothed, "absolutely as though we'd sat down and talked." The dream felt exceptionally real to her. Here we have the visible improvement in the deceased's appearance and well-being.

In the third dream:

I see Mother on a bus, waving goodbye. She feels much better and is going on to work on another level.

As often happens, there is a departure of the deceased to continue work elsewhere. Irene said she has dreamed of her mother since, but none of the dreams have had the same vividness as these, which were like real visitations to her.

Howard's Dead Brother Improves

Howard's brother committed suicide with a shotgun after a long period of depression. He telephoned Howard minutes before his death. The hapless man rushed to his brother's side to try to prevent the suicide, but it was too late. For several days, Howard awoke at the same early hour as the telephone call from his brother had occurred. Finally Howard had a dream that eased his agonizing over his brother:

At the same hour, my brother appears standing at the head of my bed. He says, "Howard, why are you feeling so sad?" I ask him, "Why didn't you tell us you were that desperate and we could have helped?" He replies, "It's too late to worry about that. I am better off than I ever was in life."

Howard felt able to "release him and get on with my life" after this dream. He asked, "Was this all a dream or did my brother's spirit visit me one last time? It feels like the latter." Whatever this dream/experience was, it brought needed consolation to the survivor.

From showing mere improvement in early dreams about them, the dead may demonstrate dramatic progress.

Matthew's Dead Brother Travels Fast

Matthew was devastated over the sudden death of his older brother, only thirty-something. Two weeks after his brother's death, Matthew dreamed:

I meet my older brother. He has the most healthy, beautiful tan I ever saw. I'm amazed how good he looks. We communicate telepathically. I ask if I can hug him (I'd had an impulse to do so last time I saw him alive, but didn't). We hug. It's startlingly real. I say with excitement, "This is really happening! You're really here! I'm not crazy and this isn't a dream!" He smiles and nods.

Matthew awoke with a start, his heart pounding. As he thought about the dream/experience, he decided perhaps his brother's tan meant that his spirit had gone to Florida, where he'd always wanted to visit.

In a later dream, Matthew's brother seemed to be able to go wherever he wanted:

I'm in my old room when my older brother appears and says that he likes his dimension because he can go anywhere he wants to in eight seconds.

Matthew thought this remark very characteristic of his older brother, to be so exact. Speed of travel seems to mark several of these dreams. Perhaps it displays the newfound freedom of the spirit.

Bea's Dead Father Zips Through the Stars

Shortly after Bea's father died after a long illness, she dreamed:

> I'm talking with my father, although I can't see him. He gives me a visual experience of what's happening to him. I see him traveling through space at a high rate of speed. There's no vehicle, just a sensation of him shooting out through the stars to infinity, saying something like, "See, there's nothing to fear in death or dying. Away I go."

Bea felt that her father's spirit was giving her a message that she needn't worry about him because he was experiencing something wonderful.

Joyce's Dead Grandmother Finds Happiness

Joyce was very close to her grandmother, who died in her late seventies. Seven months after her grandmother's death, Joyce dreamed:

> I'm falling through a long lit tunnel, pulled toward an end I can't see. It feels very pleasant. All at once, I'm standing in a double doorway looking in at my grandmother. She is seated at a table with a famous couple of singers. I'm very drawn to enter the room but know I cannot. A great feeling of joy comes from within the room. My grandmother turns to me and radiates such beauty and contentment from her face. She says, "I have never known such happiness. One day you will be this happy too."

This dream gave much reassurance and pleasure to Joyce. We recognize in it images characteristic of dreams about the dead: the lit tunnel (also often found in near-death experiences); the forbidden area into which the living person cannot enter; the radiance of the transfigured deceased; the joy of contact.

Along with witnessing the happiness of the deceased (or at least improvement), you may dream that the spirit of the dead person has work to do.

Woman's Dead Son Departs to Do His Soul's Work

Perhaps you remember the woman whose sixteen-year-old son was killed in an automobile accident. Elsewhere, we considered her dream about him taking her hands and flying upward into a star-filled sky. You may recall that she desperately wanted to join her beloved son in death, but he informed her, in the same dream, that she had a life span of seventy-one years. Here I want to underscore that her son also said he could not keep visiting her in dreams, that he had to watch over some little girls whose mother didn't take care of them properly. The woman felt certain in this dream that her son must leave her to go on "to do his soul's work." Hard as it was for her to let go, this bereaved mother felt comforted that her child had important work to do and was developing in another realm.

She is not alone in her belief that the spirits of those who died can become guardians and helpers of the living. Spirits of the dead who guide the living were a central belief in ancient religions, but many contemporary religious groups also assert that the spirits of the dead become guardian angels, or have assignments on the other side. Perhaps, after a period of confusion and then recognition of the state of death, the spirits of the dead have to go to work.

Christine's Dead Mother Gets a New Job

Christine's mother died at only sixty-two. The older woman had remarried after a divorce, leaving her only child feeling robbed of her love and attention. The mother had been an attractive, intelligent woman whose health had deteriorated so badly in the time before her death that she looked like "a very old, sick person." It was hard for the mother, and difficult for her daughter to watch. Christine's dream made a difference:

> My mother brings me here to her new apartment. She is very enthu- siastic about her life, decorating the place, getting into painting and sculpture. She is so young—early thirtyish—and vibrant now. She's delighted to be on her own. She has a new job right down the street.

This dream gave Christine a feeling of happiness and closeness to her mother. She said she understood there was "no such thing as time." To see her mother enthusiastic about her new life was par- ticularly impressive to Christine. The dead in dreams seem to find opportunities to do things that may have been denied to them in life, or continue to do the things that they loved to do.

Jerry's Dead Friend Checks Out Math Theories

Jerry's older friend and master's degree adviser specialized in the study of mathematical economic statistics. Jerry learned that his friend had been hospitalized with a heart condition and visited him; he seemed to be getting better. One night Jerry had a sur- prising dream:

> I see a bunch of symbols streaming by either side of my face, coming fast. I know it's a message from my friend, along with some things I don't understand. The message is, "It's great here—I have a chance to learn a lot—I've been able to check out some theories. I'm finding a lot of answers and formulating new theories."

Two days after his dream, Jerry learned that his friend had died. He was devastated. He attended the funeral and was invited to visit his friend's home. There he looked over some of his friend's notebooks and writing. "To my amazement, the mathematical symbols in the notebooks matched the symbols that I'd seen in my dream!" Jerry felt elated and somewhat comforted. He regretted not having real- ized his friend was so near death. This dream gave him the personal message that he desperately needed; it eased his pain over not being near his friend at the end. Surely his friend was busy pursuing one of his great pleasures.

The spirits of the dead not only go back to work in dreams, they may also attend school.

Gerrie's Dead Husband Attends Class

Gerrie lost her husband from a sudden heart attack that followed a predictive dream she had about his dying. After the funeral, she was concerned for the welfare of his spirit (whom she felt had appeared to her, then vanished). She decided to help guide him. At bedtime for several days, Gerrie read aloud from a book she found inspirational. Like the Tibetan monks, she felt that her husband's spirit could hear her voice.

Gerrie had been widowed for a couple of years when she dreamed of meeting her dead husband in a restaurant and greeting him with a hug:

> I ask him how he is and what he's been doing. He says he has been away attending classes and is learning much. I ask if he'd listened to what I'd read to him. He replies that it helped. I'm glad it did. We turn to join others in the restaurant.

A year later, the widow dreamed:

> I am watching people in a park dressed in costumes from all parts of the world, joined in singing, and doing a dance that resembles tai chi and yoga combined. My husband appears dressed in a pure white suit, and around his neck and in his hair are flowers. I greet him and say, "Let's join them. It looks like fun, and good exercise." He agrees and we turn to join the dancers.

Gerrie awoke from this dream with gladness. "He was progressing rapidly," she said, "and someday I'll join him. Then he can show me the way."

It was five years after her husband's death when Gerrie had another significant dream about him:

I'm at an archeological site, on my knees clearing away dirt. I look up and see my husband, in casual western clothes. This time in his hair are eagle feathers. He turns to leave. I say, "Aren't you going to give me a hug?" We exchange a goodbye hug. He turns back and says, "Forget me," and is gone. A friend comforts me, saying, "Cheer up. Life's too short."

This dream left Gerrie feeling lonely, but also with a new sense of freedom.

Whenever we find ourselves in dreams exploring old ruins or participating in archeological digs, we are bound to be looking into our past. In Gerrie's dream language, she was examining her life, recalling her affectionate relationship with her spouse, and letting him go.

Gerrie's behavior and her series of dreams show several of the characteristics of belief in reincarnation: her reading to his spirit to guide it shortly after his death; her dead husband's dream statement that he'd been attending classes and learning; his pure white apparel and flowers around his neck and in his hair; his eagle feathers—said in Native American lore to mark the presence of the spirit; and his admonition to forget him, as if giving her a final goodbye.

Some people would dismiss this series of dreams as wishful thinking. Of course, they might say, it would be nice to believe our dead loved ones are in a better world, learning and developing and becoming able to help us when our time comes.

Yet to dismiss such dreams would be to miss the beneficial consequence they have for the dreamers. They not only bring comfort to the dreamer, but at times pure joy, even rapture, and ultimately a feeling of freedom and release. The recurrence of this type of dreaming among many peoples and cultures makes it necessary to consider the possibility that they describe real experiences in the afterlife. In any case, they surely make this life better for the survivor, as you may have already discovered.

Joanne's Friend Teaches Her to Help the Dead

Joanne, a devoted dreamer and a skilled artist, recorded the series of dreams she had after her father's death. A few years prior to his death, she had a dream that seemed to help her prepare for the loss:

> I am walking into a town with my friend Ellen. There has been some sort of terrible tragedy in this town and many people have died. Ellen and I come to a dark room with four people who are already dead, but they don't realize it because so many people have died.
>
> Ellen is teaching me how to help them die. First there is an old lady sewing. Ellen rips the sewing from her hands and she disintegrates into thin air. The next man keeps fussing with large burgundy velvet drapes. He is closing them so that no light can come in. Ellen pulls them open and he vanishes too. The other man is arranging cups and saucers on a table. She pushes the cups to the floor and he disappears. I forget what the last one is doing, but whatever it is, Ellen disrupts it and he dies too. I remember feeling like we are really helping these people.

Again we see the inability of the dead to recognize they have died. By disrupting whatever activity they were engaging in Joanne's friend showed how she released the spirits of the dead. Notice the draperies in particular. The image of fabric separating the dying person from the other side is a symbol that recurs often in dreams about death, as we will explore later. Like the ancient Greek Fates, who were said to spin and snip the threads of destiny for each life, Joanne and her friend seemed to impart to the deceased the ability to let go of the present life and pass over.

Bikou's Dead Father Teaches Her

Vivid dreams about the deceased can occur anytime. Bikou had an intense lucid dream about her dead father some twenty years after his death. Her dream was about being on a high plateau on a hot, sunny day, with the sea below, meeting her father, and slyly suggesting they swim, knowing that it was impossible, because the cliff was so high and that this was not his favorite sport. To her surprise, he took her hand, and the two of them ran to the edge and jumped off, unafraid:

> *As we descend slowly, he says, a little annoyed, "Hey, aren't you aware of anything?" I'm jolted to appreciate the slow descent and tell him. Deep down in the water we hug. It's joyful and perfect. I have the feeling everything is all right.*

In this dream of Bikou's we see the deceased moving into the role of teacher or sage. Her dead father pointed out the beauty of the slow fall. Their underwater embrace filled her with joy. She was finding a reunion with the father part of herself.

Each one of us has the opportunity to learn from the spirit of a lost loved one throughout our lives.

The Pattern of Dreams About Evolving in the Afterlife

You can see there is a pattern to these dreams about evolution in the afterlife. The elements often—but not always—included are:

- Confusion about whether or not one is dead

- Gradual realization that one is dead

- Visible improvement in appearance and behavior

- Development of skills in the afterlife (such as ability to travel at great speed, or ability in art)

- Departure for further work, performance of duties, or advanced study

- Occasional appearances as wise guide

In the series of dreams we just examined, we saw most of these elements. Do these things actually happen to the spirit of the person who has died? Or are they projections of our wishes for them and, hence, for ourselves? All we know for sure is that they appear in the dreams of survivors and that these dreams bring solace, even intense pleasure, and may change the dreamer's views about life after death.

Perhaps the culmination of dreams about evolving in the after-life occurs in dreams about rebirth.

"I'm Being Reborn"

Dream Message: "I'm Being Reborn"

Deceased informs the dreamer that he or she is about to be reborn. Circumstances such as sex and place may be given.

Frequency: Extremely rare, but important.

Response after Awake:
Dreamer usually feels comforted. May be inspired to believe in an afterlife.

Melinda's Dead Brother Is Reborn in Mexico

Approximately two years after her younger brother Jeff died from an illness, Melinda had a stunning dream:

I'm walking on my front porch on a bright, sunny day, and as I go down the steps to the mailbox, I become lucid [aware of dreaming]. I'm in a playful, excited mood, and I say to myself, "Well, I wonder what's in my lucid mailbox!"

At first I see ads with perfume samples, and I think, "Oh well, just junk mail." Then I see an oddly folded card, folded in three sections. Slowly I open this up, and read, "Dear Jep (an endearment name for my brother), Make real, native Mexico a real joy." There's a signature which I can't make out, yet I know it to be a guide or counselor for my brother in his after-death state.

I read this in shock. I immediately understand the implications. This is a copy of a communication to my brother, sent to me to let me know what is going on. He's ready to reincarnate into Mexico. I'm filled with great concern for his well-being in a land of poverty, begin to cry, and awaken.

Melinda's startling dream was followed by an equally unusual experience. She said, "Once awake, I bring his spirit forward and argue with him. 'What do you think you're doing!' I say. 'I mean you just got over a terrible death and illness and now you're going to an undeveloped country, God knows if you'll even survive your childhood!' I tell him, 'I'm going back to sleep. I want to hear from you!' I calm down and somehow manage to get back to sleep."

Melinda returned to the dream state:

I immediately see an image of an adult Mexican man in the fullness of his prime adulthood of thirty to forty. He looks sturdy and solid, with a rounded face and broad chest. It's clear to me it's Jeff. He's well dressed in a clean white native shirt and looks very well cared for. He says two words, yet with them comes a flood of understanding: "To recover."

I suddenly realize this is a life which will bring him healing and recovery—he knows what he's doing—and as I feel this, all my fears for him dissipate. I sense this is also Mexico of the past; in fact, the land he lives in is California in our future. It is a simple, happy, healthy existence of close family ties in a beautiful environment.

Melinda awakened feeling not only reconciled to this new life for her beloved brother, but also trusting his spirit's decision. She had no more concern. She said, "The dream has a lasting effect on my sense of peace for him."

Some people might have difficulty accepting Melinda's marvelous dream and experience as a true account. Yet there is no question that dreamers who are able to become lucid (aware, during the dream, of the fact that they are dreaming) are able to call up people and things of interest to them. Lucid dreamers are also sometimes able to return to sleep and continue dreams on the same topic.

Melinda wanted to have a communication from her dead brother; the mailbox was already part of her dream scene, and so provided the means. By descending her front porch steps, Melinda was symbolically going deeper.

What is one to make of the card with three folds? I suggest, in view of Melinda's later impression that the dream referred to Mexico of the past, and California in the future, that the card's three folds represented past, present, and future.

Once again, such astounding dreams do more than reassure dreamers that their dead loved one is well, and bring solace for their grief. This dream was not simply the fulfillment of Melinda's wish that her brother could have had a healthier life, and a fantasy that he will have one now. The encounter with the dead loved one *feels* real. It is a real experience—one with as much validity as a forceful waking encounter.

Is it a true contact with the dead? That is impossible to prove. But the meeting brings peace, and changes lives, with as much impact as if it were. It may be. Transcendental experiences have ever been difficult to describe and impossible to convey. Perhaps only you, the dreamer, can say for yourself. If you have such a dream, it will not matter to you what others believe.

"Avenge My Murder" and "I Give You Life"

"Avenge My Murder"

Dream Message: "Avenge My Murder"

Deceased informs the dreamer that he or she was murdered. Reenactment of murder or site of murder may be depicted.

Frequency: Rare but important.

Response after Awake:
Dreamer feels impelled to act on victim's behalf.

The First Murder: Cain and Abel

The biblical story of Cain and Abel describes the first murder, according to our Western tradition. A quick reminder: In the account of Genesis, Cain, the elder son of Adam and Eve, was a "tiller of the ground," while Abel, the younger son, was a "keeper of sheep." Each brought offerings to God of their produce, Cain bringing fruit of the earth and Abel firstborn sheep. The Lord respected Abel, who was a righteous man, and accepted his offering, but rejected Cain's, because his heart was not right. Cain was angry; when alone with his brother in the field, he rose up against him and slew him. When the Lord asked Cain where Abel was, he replied, "I know not; Am I my brother's keeper?"

Then the Lord said, "What hast thou done? the voice of thy brother's blood crieth unto me from the ground." He cursed Cain, told him that the ground would no longer yield for him, and that he would be a fugitive and vagabond in the earth. Cain protested that this punishment was greater than he could bear, that everyone would try to kill him. The Lord replied that vengeance would be taken sevenfold on anyone who slew him, and set a mark upon Cain so that those who met him would recognize but not destroy him.

When a murder or accidental homicide took place in ancient times, the nearest—usually male—relative of the victim was expected to avenge the dead person. He was called "the avenger of blood," and had the right to slay the murderer without retribution. In modern countries, where civil life is regulated, the duty of vengeance is taken over by courts of justice.

O.J. Simpson's Dream of Killing Ex-Wife Nicole Brown

Despite trials by jury and judgments in court, there are many instances of someone's "blood crying from the ground." When someone has been murdered and their murderer is not caught or goes free, there is even greater suffering among the family members who have lost a loved one than from the death alone. Witness the agony of the Goldman family after the acquittal of O.J. Simpson at the end of his double-murder trial. In our system of justice, the verdict of "not guilty" proves only that there was not enough evidence to convict; it is not proof of innocence.

We may never know whether O.J. Simpson is the murderer of Nicole Brown and Ron Goldman. If he is not the murderer, time may confirm his claim of innocence. If he is the murderer, tradition holds that he will suffer such guilt that the mark of Cain might as well be on his brow.

During the Simpson trial, the jury was told by one of the witnesses, Ron Shipp, a former Los Angeles policeman who was a personal friend of Simpson's, that O.J. confided to him he had dreamed about killing Nicole.[1] Certainly, this does not necessarily make him guilty of carrying out the action, but it does speak to his anger toward her and is consistent with the domestic violence he was charged with previously.

Surprisingly, some murders are solved on the basis of dreams.

Hamlet's Father's Ghost Requests Revenge

We meet this in fiction in the Shakespearean tragedy *Hamlet*, where the ghost of Hamlet's father urges his son, "If thou didst ever thy dear father love—Revenge his foul and most unnatural murder." Hamlet had been told that his father had died naturally. Later he learned from his father's ghost that the king had been poisoned by his brother, who proceeded to marry Hamlet's mother, becoming the king of Denmark. The whole tragedy revolved around whether or not Hamlet could believe what the ghost of his father told him, and if so, whether he should then take vengeance.

In real life, the dream messenger occasionally delivers the same dismal message, "Avenge My Murder." Sometimes the actual solution to a murder emerges in dreams, as in the case of Mrs. Martin.

Mrs. Martin's Murdered Daughter Reveals Her Secret Grave

Maria Martin left her parents' home, early in 1827, to run off with William Corder, a local farmer and reputed womanizer.[2] The couple, unmarried, fled to Corder's farm, some distance away. Maria's parents were outraged and shamed by the scandal this created in the village. Still, the young woman continued to visit her parents occasionally.

Then in the early fall Maria's visits stopped. She disappeared.

Corder said he had no idea where she was, that she had left no note. Maria's mother suspected trouble, and she visited the farmhouse in secret. There she found withered vegetables on the table and sour milk in the cooler, but no trace of her daughter. She contacted the local sheriff, who dismissed the idea of foul play.

Maria's parents searched the countryside trying to find a clue to their daughter's disappearance, without any results. The following March, Maria's mother had a terrifying, lifelike dream:

> She found herself standing in Maria's kitchen watching her daughter being murdered. Paralyzed, she saw every detail. Then the scene shifted. The murderer, identified as Corder, had constructed a shallow grave beneath the floorboards of a barn. As she watched, he placed Maria's body in the opening. Abruptly the dream ended.[3]

Mrs. Martin awoke with a startle. She recognized the barn she had seen in her dream as a red one belonging to a neighbor, on a knoll near Corder's house.

For three nights in a row, Mrs. Martin had the same dream. She shared it with her husband, begging him to contact the owner of the barn and ask permission to search beneath the floorboards. Her husband finally approached his neighbor, saying he wanted to hunt for some of his daughter's missing clothes.

The red barn had been used for grain storage since the previous fall. By now, enough grain had been removed to make a search possible, and permission was granted on April 19, 1828.

Together Mrs. Martin and her husband went to the barn, and she pointed out the spot in the floorboards she had seen in her dream. Mr. Martin removed the floorboards and dug, soon uncovering a piece of green-and-red fabric that looked like the outfit his daughter had worn the last time they met. At a depth of eighteen inches, he hit a portion of a human body. The horrified couple rushed to the sheriff.

The body found under the floorboards of the red barn was identified as that of Maria Martin. Her murderer had placed it there before the grain was deposited for storage the previous autumn.

William Corder was arrested. He eventually confessed to killing Maria in an argument over another woman, and was executed.

Mrs. Martin's dream revealed the manner of her daughter's death, as well as the hidden grave where she had been buried. Her series of dreams had come at a time when it was possible to gain access to the secret grave.

Although Mrs. Martin's daughter remained just as dead as before her body was found and her killer caught, there is a relief survivors feel from finally knowing exactly what happened to their missing loved ones. People who live with uncertainty about a death—those who have relatives who are "missing in action," or those whose loved people have been kidnapped or have mysteriously disappeared—suffer exquisitely. Being able to know a death is certain, however painful, seems to be preferable to living with the unknown. There is a sense of completion.

Also, in some cases, society is spared the continued risk of a murderer at large who may well act again, as in the next case.

J. W. Green's Murdered Son Reenacts Death

J. W. Green, a rich landowner in Montana, traveled on business to Portland, Oregon, in April 1916.[4] He had to remain almost a month, transacting the trade of a large ranch in Montana for a hotel in Portland. Dallas, Green's nineteen-year-old son, had stayed in Montana to take care of details regarding the sale of the ranch. After several weeks, Green had a ghastly dream about Dallas:

He saw his son killed by a stranger wielding an axe. He watched with deep sadness as the man buried his son's body in the Montana timber.[5]

Green woke with alarm. He had not heard from his son for some time. He made hasty arrangements to return to Montana, and when he arrived, he learned that his son had disappeared nearly a month earlier. Green contacted the police, who accompanied him to the ranch to search for Dallas.

The young man's body was found buried in a shallow grave in a thicket of heavy brush and timber at the edge of a creek that ran through the ranch property. He had been shot in the head with a single bullet, rather than killed with an ax, as in Green's dream. Such slight dream distortions of facts are not uncommon.

The last person seen with Dallas before his disappearance was a man named John Miller. This same man had been observed recently selling some of Green's horses. He was arrested for murdering Dallas. In July 1917, John Miller was convicted by a jury in Libby, Montana, of the murder of Dallas Green.

So far, the dreams and murders we have considered happened a long time ago. But dreams continue to help solve murders today. Not all dreams about a murder provide such complete detail as Mrs. Martin's and J. W. Green's dreams did. Sometimes they serve as an incentive to unveil a known murderer, as exemplified in the contemporary case described next.

Margarita's Murdered Sister Pleads for Justice

Margarita Booth, a thirty-three-year-old homemaker in Indiana, came forward after nearly twenty-five years of silence to accuse her mother of killing her little sister, Anna Marie.[6]

Tortured by recurrent nightmares of the pleading face of her baby sister, Margarita could no longer bear keeping her dark secret. She went to the police in 1992 with the purpose of making her nightmares stop. Also, she said, she had made a promise to her sister when she witnessed her death, that "someday I would go and find her and bring her back to give her a real burial."

At a trial held in 1994, Margarita told the jury that in 1969, when she was eight years old, she saw her mother kill Anna Marie Arguello in their home in Frankfort, Indiana. The two-year-old Anna Marie was being punished for wetting her bed. The mother beat her and forced her to remain in a cold bath all day long.

After Anna Marie died during this abuse, Margarita saw her now-dead stepfather, Luis Vega, take the child's body away bundled in a blanket. She never saw her sister or the blanket again.

Margarita knew that if she told anyone during her childhood, she would be in great danger. "The price for telling would be death, and I knew that," she said.

Margarita's mother, Anita Vega, who was fifty-two at the time of the trial, claimed her younger daughter had died naturally and that her body was buried secretly by Luis Vega because he was afraid he would be deported to Mexico.

No body was found, but investigators had proof of the child's existence in a birth certificate from Michigan, where Anna Marie was born, and a picture of her that was obtained from an aunt in Ohio.

Anita Vega was convicted of involuntary manslaughter, and faced up to ten years in prison.

Margarita's recurrent dreams, in which she saw "close-up shots of Anna Marie's face, pleading with me," were a torment. She lived with feelings of deep guilt, yet found it difficult to come forward because she had been told over and over from the time she was a child, "Don't tell." Finally, her nightmares drove her to overcome her fears and seek justice for her dead sister.

Appropriate Action to "Avenge My Murder" Messages

Although you are unlikely to have nightmares about the dead with the message "Avenge My Murder," you need to be aware that such dreams occur. Responding to these dreams when they arise can bring relief and resolution to the dreamer. Appropriate action may prevent further harm. Reporting such dreams to authorities is not necessarily advisable, as they have mistaken some descriptions of this type of dream for a confession. But action to uncover proof of a murder may be in order.

Notice that, unlike Hamlet's father's ghost, the dead person does not always speak the words "Revenge his foul and most unnatural murder." The message is delivered by means of a reenactment of the murder or a revelation of the location of the body, as well as by tears and an appeal by the victim for retribution.

Having explored how dreams may reveal the existence of a murder, how it happened, where it happened, and how the murdered person may call for justice, we turn to dreams in which the dead person grants the gift of life.

"I Give You Life"

....

Dream Message: "I Give You Life"
Deceased instills life into the dreamer.

Frequency: Extremely rare, but very important.

Response after Awake:
Dreamer feels certain he or she will live.

The Life Spark as Breath

Since ancient times people around the world have told myths and legends about the beginning of mankind that involve transferring the breath of God into the body of his creation.

The creation stories most familiar to Westerners are found in the first and second chapters of Genesis in the Bible. In the older account, given in the second chapter, God is depicted as more manlike, working as a potter might on his creations.

In this older version, "And the Lord God formed man of the dust of the ground, and breathed into his nostrils the breath of life; and man became a living soul," man is the first living creation after God has formed the heavens and earth. Next, trees and rivers were created, and beasts of the field and fowl of the air; lastly God fashioned a woman out of one of Adam's ribs, to relieve man's loneliness.

In the more recent version, given in the first chapter of Genesis, God spoke the word, and heavenly and earthly forms came forth. Only after all other forms existed were man and woman created, equally last.

Breathing into an inert form was the method of instilling life in many of the world's creation myths. Wind, too, was sometimes a symbol of the procreative force of the divine spirit. The very word "inspiration" means "filling with spirit." Among the life-instilling images in creation myths are: the breath of a god, breathed into the nostrils or blown upon an inert body; incantations uttered by a god; the wind in the air, a wind touching the lips of the lifeless form; and the breeze from flapping wings moving over it.

Today the "kiss of life," as the British call the administration of artificial respiration, is practiced to restore life to those who have stopped breathing. In a sense, the person breathing into a non-breathing person is like a god bringing the gift of life.

In dreams, wind, air, or breath can be an intermediary between the invisible life source, God, and the dreamer's awareness. We shall see how a similar image appeared in an astounding dream.

Claire Sylvia's Dead Donor Instills the Breath of Life

Claire Sylvia, in her middle fifties, is a dancer full of the joy of life.[7] She is also one of the longest-lived recipients of a double organ transplant. (Only about a thousand of these rare transplants have been performed; about fifty recipients remain alive.) When Claire was in her early forties, she developed a rare, progressive, fatal disease called primary pulmonary hypertension. She was unable to continue professional dancing or her work as a drama coach. Her condition worsened until she was barely able to walk, then she was confined to a wheelchair and the use of oxygen. Claire's physicians told her the only hope for survival was to undergo a complex heart-and-lung transplant. The chances were slim that both organs would become available: there was a long waiting list. To her astonishment, Claire soon received a call saying that organs had just become available that matched her exact requirements. At forty-nine, she received in a transplant the heart and lungs of an eighteen-year-old boy who had died in a motorcycle accident—that was all she knew about him.

Claire began to have other notions about her donor. After the transplant, Claire noticed some striking changes in herself, including cravings for green pepper, chicken nuggets, and beer—items she had formerly avoided. Eventually, Claire obtained contact with her donor's family, who corroborated many of Claire's changes in taste and behavior as being characteristic of the boy who had died.

Before her transplant, Claire had been avidly interested in her dreams. She continued to record them throughout the period after surgery when able to do so. On national television, she described the significant dream she'd had about six months after her transplant:

> It was of a young boy that I was in a relationship with, I was friendly with him. I saw him clearly. He was tall, thin, wiry, sandy-colored hair, and I knew his name was Tim Leighton. I called him Tim L. [a first name and initial that, like Claire's cravings, also proved to be accurate]. I was going to leave him to join some kind of performing group, and before I left, I turned around and walked back to him, and as we came together, we kissed. As we kissed, I inhaled him into me. I knew we'd be together forever.

When Claire awoke, she felt exhilarated. She felt that by "inhaling him into me" she had integrated the heart and lungs; she also felt certain this must be her donor. She said it was the biggest breath she'd ever taken, one that gave her energy to go on. Like the gods who breathed life into the forms of their creation, Claire's donor had instilled the breath of life with a kiss. Her donor—dead and yet not dead in all his parts—had said, "I give you life," with the gesture of a kiss. In her case, given the risks of organ rejection, the gift of life was literally real. To read more about Claire's fascinating experiences, watch for her forthcoming book.[8]

Implications

You may find this story intriguing but irrelevant to your dream life. Yet many dreamers will find themselves connecting with transplant patients in the near future, if not becoming a recipient. We have no idea how far this treatment modality may go.

In today's newspaper, there is talk of using body parts from baboons, as parts of pigs have already been used, to replace worn-out parts of human beings. Will some of the nature of the animal reside along with its body part? Does some of the nature of the donor person come along with the organ from him or her? As transplants become more common and less costly, we will need answers to some of the questions raised by unusual cases. The dream message "I Give You Life" takes us into a new frontier.

"I'll Always Love You" and "Hi! How Are You?"

"I'll Always Love You"

Dream Message: "I'll Always Love You"

Deceased assures the dreamer he or she is loved eternally. Love may be demonstrated by kisses, embraces, or gifts.

Frequency: Fairly common.

Response after Awake: Dreamer feels loved and deeply comforted.

Love Eternal

Romeo and Juliet, Orpheus and Eurydice, Dante and Beatrice, Tristan and Isolde, Demeter and Persephone, Héloïse and Abelard—the great dramas, myths, and romantic life stories celebrate the strength of love beyond death.

We find this same yearning in the dreams of modern men and women whose beloved has died. The theme is not limited to sweethearts; we find it in devoted parents and children, in siblings, and between close friends. We saw that this bond could take an ominous turn, by tempting the survivor to join the loved one in death. Here we see how the same love not only can have a sustaining influence but also can inspire the survivor to creative heights and spiritual or mystical unions. The literature of the East has often used the beloved as a symbol of the yearning for God. The beloved can also become the symbol of the greatest good, or the soul, leading the lover forward to supreme accomplishments. The message "I'll Always Love You" is for many dreamers the most precious of all. Perhaps it will be so for you.

Novalis's Chain of Sparkling Tears to His Dead Beloved

A striking example of the power of love to transcend death is seen in the experience of the eighteenth-century poet Novalis. Friedrich von Hardenberg, a young noble from Saxony, took the pseudonym Novalis for his poetry. He had been a frail child, who became a law student at the University of Jena, where he met the poet Schiller and other Romantics. After completing his studies at twenty-two, he fell in love with and became engaged to a twelve-year-old named Sophie von Kühn. Sadly the teenage girl died three years later, on March 19, 1797, from tuberculosis.

When Novalis visited Sophie's grave two months later, in May, he had a profound experience that changed the remainder of his short life. He expressed his grief in six exquisite prose poems entitled *Hymns to the Night*. In them, he celebrated Night, or Death, as an entry to a higher life in the presence of God. He looked forward to a mystical and loving union with Sophie, and with the whole universe, after he died.

The next few years were astonishingly creative for Novalis. In his works he attempted to unite poetry, philosophy, and science through allegory. He wrote a mythical romance set in the Middle Ages, telling the adventures and dreams of a young poet whose central image was a "Blue Flower"—which became a widely used symbol of longing among Romantics. It was tied to his dreams: "I do long to see that Blue Flower. I can't get it out of my mind, I have to think about it and make up stories. I seem to have had dreams about it before, or had got into another world in my sleep."[1]

Later, Novalis became engaged again, but he himself died of tuberculosis before he could marry, almost four years to the day after Sophie's death. As he lay dying in his parents' home on March 25, 1801, he asked his brother Karl to play the piano for him, as he often did, so that he died to the strains of music. He was twenty-eight.

The full revelation of Novalis's creative spirit emerged after the tragic death of Sophie. In his diary for May 19, 1797, Novalis wrote, "At the grave [of Sophie] it occurred to me that through my death I shall present to humanity an example of such faithfulness, even to death. I shall make such a love possible for mankind."[2]

In his third "Hymn to the Night," Novalis described being overcome at Sophie's graveside. "Once when I was shedding bitter tears, when dissolved in pain, my hope was melting away, and I stood alone by the barren hillock which in its narrow dark bosom hid the vanished form of my Life . . ." Then he appeared to faint:

The region gently upheaved itself, and over it hovered my unbound, newborn spirit. The hillock became a cloud of dust, and through the cloud I saw the glorified face of my beloved. In her eyes eternity reposed. I laid hold of her hands, and the tears became a sparkling chain that could not be broken. Into the distance swept by, like a tempest, thousands of years. On her neck I welcomed the new life with ecstatic tears. Never was such another dream; then first and ever since I hold fast an eternal, unchangeable faith in the heaven of the Night, and its sun, the Beloved.[3]

For Novalis, the dead Sophie became more than a muse. She developed into his guide to the invisible worlds opening within him. She was the archetype of the eternal feminine, leading him to the Divine Sophia, heavenly knowledge. The very name Sophia comes from the Greek word for "wise," *sophos*. To certain mystic groups, divine wisdom is personified as a goddess or spirit called Sophia.

Many of today's women and men yearn to love and be loved with a passion that will transcend time and death. Here's how that desire appeared in Joan's dream.

The Celestial Clock Tells Joan That Her Friend's Time Is Up

Joan had had a passionate love affair with Allan, her dance partner in a semi-professional group. Although the couple broke up after two and a half years, with Allan going on to other relationships and Joan marrying another man, the two retained a close friendship. Joan admired Allan's many talents and felt he would always be a part of her.

When Joan learned that Allan had been stricken with cancer and was dying of a brain tumor, she was devastated. All the unresolved aspects of their relationship arose again; she suffered as he deteriorated. His death was slow and agonizing, with much pain, then blindness, and eventual mental confusion. Joan and her musician husband, Roy, visited Allan several times, playing the songs he enjoyed. Later, when Allan moved home to a different state to be cared for by his parents, they kept in touch by telephone. Joan felt anguished about Allan's condition and her inability to affect it. Two weeks before he died, Joan had a powerful dream that expressed her mixed feelings—yet also brought comfort:

> I dream that I am talking with Allan. He looks just as he used to, though perhaps thinner. I have apparently been doing his laundry for him, because we are discussing when I should come over to do it next. I suggest next Tuesday, and he says, "I may not be alive then."
> We are standing in front of my parents' house. It is night. I tell him, "Allan, I've always loved you." I say many other things to him too, which were crystal-clear in the dream but have faded since. I tell him I have been furious at him, angry, upset, etc., but that I've always loved him. At the end of this long speech I say, "It isn't fair!" He

just looks at me and shakes his head. I hug him and begin to cry. In retrospect he seems taller in the dream than in real life, closer to my husband's height, because as I hug him my eyes are about the level of his collarbones and my tears fall on his chest. He begins to weep too, tears going silently down his face.

Suddenly something makes me step back and look up. In the night sky shines a full moon, surrounded by a spectacular ring which seems to fill the sky. It is absolutely breathtaking. Its brightness dims the stars, all but a few, about three very bright stars or planets, which intersect the ring at various points. I say to Allan, "I hope this doesn't sound odd, but . . . it looks like a clock." And then I wake up.

Joan felt the meaning of her dream was crystal-clear. "It's time. It's Allan's time, according to the clock of the universe. And oh, what a wonderful, beautiful clock . . ." She found herself suspecting he might die a few days later, when the moon would be full. In fact, his death at age thirty-nine was two weeks after this dream.

On one level, of course, her dream represented Joan's acceptance of the fact that it was time for her dear friend to die. On another level, however, she was expressing her enduring love for him, and felt his love in return. The imagery of doing Allan's laundry in the opening scene probably represents her "cleaning up" things between them.

Joan and Roy produced a special gift for Allan during his last few months, when he was totally blind and hearing remained his chief link to the world. They made a professionally recorded tape of the Ukrainian folk songs that Allan loved, with Joan singing the lyrics and Roy playing the bandura. Like Novalis listening to his brother Karl's piano music as he died, Allan was perhaps eased in passage by the beauty of his favorite music. Love can lead us to create unique gifts. Joan and Roy's brought pleasure to a dying friend.

Diana's Last Dance with Her Dead Lover

Diana also had an ex-boyfriend who died young, at thirty-four. Their passionate affair had lasted more than ten years. Andrew had been diabetic, and apparently died from an overdose of insulin. Although Diana usually remained friends with former boyfriends, her relationship with Andrew had been so fraught with "anguish, bitterness and massive miscommunication" that she had ceased speaking with him before she moved out of the country.

When Diana learned that Andrew had died, she was grieved. She bitterly regretted not having come to an understanding with him before they parted. The night she learned about his death, which was some months after he died, she determined to meet him in her dreams. She had this successful dream response:

Andrew comes to greet me. He looks much as he did in his early twenties, dark, mysterious, handsome, and aristocratic. Only now he looks healthy, happy, and serene. It is almost difficult to recognize him. He looks physically the same, but his attitude, mood, and demeanor are different. He was seldom, if ever, truly at peace. Now he is.

Andrew is dressed in white trousers and a pink shirt. He comes softly to me and immediately embraces me with such great love and gratitude. We are both immensely pleased and happy to see one another. In me there is some feeling of loss, which Andrew encourages me to drop, to be in this present moment and enjoy the love we have shared for so long.

Then we begin to dance together—a long, slow, graceful dance, perhaps a waltz. We are totally in sync with one another. Truly we are one; the yin and the yang, the male and the female sides, together at last. Andrew is so loving, gentle, sweet, and simple. Our hearts are wide open to one another. We float and glide in this bliss of unconditional love. It is a dance of love and surrender, the most peaceful moment of this lifetime—totally beautiful. We are reconciled and the past turmoil is so easily let go.

We are communicating on a very deep level. I know absolutely that we will be together again. It does not matter what the next meeting will be like. We will work out our karma, whatever that might be. For now there is the moment and eternity and bliss and love, and overall, peace.

Then Andrew must go. We embrace for one final moment. My heart is saddened, but again, Andrew assists me to let go and be in the present. This joy is forever; this love is eternal; this peace is real and absolute. Then Andrew is walking away, smiling, radiant, glowing. I awake so happy.

Diana declares that "I know absolutely that Andrew and I met, that this was not 'just a dream.' " She felt that his spirit was waiting for her to call him to her. She was overjoyed to see him so healthy and happy. She felt reconciled. "Andrew is my teacher, as I am his," she says. Diana feels sure they will always share a profound and abiding love. She found her dream of the last dance with Andrew healing, grateful for the love that flowed from it into her life.

Both Joan and Diana were able to find comfort about the deaths of their young former boyfriends in dreams that brought love and peace. For Melinda, it was love for and from her brother that found expression in a dream.

Melinda Sings with Her Dead Brother

Melinda's younger brother's death from an illness left her bereft. You may recall her dream of his rebirth, two years later (described in Chapter 9). More immediately, a dream a few weeks after his death brought needed respite:

I'm at a large family gathering about to attend a birthday party for my brother Jeff. I walk down the hallway of a luxurious hotel and go into a small theater area. There on the stage is my brother, opening gifts. He's sitting next to a beautiful birthday cake, surrounded by about twenty family members. As I walk toward him, I become aware of how well he looks compared to his condition before he died. He has his full weight back and is wearing dancer's clothes, a T-shirt, and excercise-like pants.

Suddenly Jeff's in the spotlight, and music begins—a blend of rock and Broadway-like music. It seems he's starring in a one-man show, a song-and-dance performance. He's doing very vigorous, almost acrobatic-like movements and I watch with great joy . . . his obvious good health, once again returned. He looks graceful and powerful and we all "ooh" and "ah" in astonishment. My cousin asks him how he's learned to dance like this. My brother answers that he's been studying dance for a number of weeks, which is actually longer than the time since he died. This throws me a moment for I am half aware that he's already passed on.

The next scene is in a music hall environment, with box seats all around. My parents, my older brother, and I are all there. We are getting ready for Jeff's next performance, which is to take place in an elevated Plexiglas side stage.

The production begins and the spotlight is on Jeff, who once again looks vital and well. He begins to sing along to a rhythmic beat, "Roll away, roll away the tomb." I'm looking up at him with great love and delight. Love is in my throat and in my eyes as I watch him full of life, doing what he loves, singing to the world. I have a poignant sense of the preciousness of this moment and its precarious feeling of being out of time. My older brother and I sway in our seats and sing along with him, "Roll away, roll away the tomb."

Notice the several dream messages conveyed in this dream. "I'm O.K." is easily seen in Melinda's brother's renewed vigor. "I'm Evolving" is also present, in the idea of her brother studying dance since, and even before, his death. The image of a birthday party with gifts symbolically represents her brother's new life on the other side. The lyrics of the song they share as siblings underscores the resurrection of her brother's spirit. "I'll Always Love You" is implied more than directly expressed, but the joyousness of the scene conveys it. Melinda and her brother honor their continued love and connection with song and dance. Would that each dreamer who has lost a loved one could join the celebration.

Melinda's Dead Brother Delivers Message of Love

The message of love was expressed even more directly for Melinda in a later dream she had about her deceased younger brother Jeff. Two years after his death, Melinda dreamed:

It's night, a beautiful, serene country night, and I walk outside onto a second-story porch, standing against a wooden railing, breathing in the sweet night air. All of a sudden my brother Jeff walks up and stands beside me to my right.

I catch my breath, realizing that in waking life he died, and how precious this dream moment now between us is. He picks up my right hand, and tenderly holds it, and tells me how much he loves me. It is a quiet, full, tender exchange and I'm so grateful for it, for the beauty of this moment.

Melinda awoke feeling "visited with love." This dream, she felt, "was his way of honoring a bond of loving nurtance between us." Melinda herself felt nurtured by the dream messenger.

Such a dream of love may be a long time coming, as it was for Susan, who received a Mother's Day gift.

Susan's Dead Grandmother Visits on Mother's Day

Susan's much-loved grandmother had been stricken with cancer and committed suicide. Some seven years later, on the eve of Mother's Day, Susan had a rare dream about her:

I see my grandmother coming out of a door to greet me. I know she is dead, and it is such a wonderful surprise to see her. We laugh and hug and tell each other how much we love one another. I know our time together is going to be short, and that only intensifies the feelings.

The next morning, Susan said, she felt great. "The feeling lasted all day long. I was so happy and filled with love. I felt as though I got a special Mother's Day gift from her by our visit. Months later, I still can bring up that wonderful feeling of love, joy, warmth, and security." Gifts of love from the dead nourish our lives.

Dave Shelters in the Rock of His Dead Brother's Love

Dave Jenneson's younger brother James died in a motorcycle accident. The twenty-four-year-old man had gone into what might have been a harmless slide off a country road, but his neck snapped in the fall. The family were heartsick at the needless death of the baby of their family.

In particular, Dave went into shock and became very depressed. He said, "I had become obsessed with finding him again. The idea of going back up to that country road and looking for him had become lodged in my mind, although I knew it was completely irrational. Yet I sensed that somehow I would have to find him if for nothing else than to tell my grieving and confused family he was all right after all. I sensed deeply that it was up to me."[4]

Two weeks after James's death, Dave had a dream about him that he sensed was different from his usual vivid dreams. It changed his life:

> I opened my eyes to a quiet Mexican street. It is narrow, shaded, and cool. I can't believe James is here. I am so happy to see him and am amazed that my little brother lives in such a beautiful place. I see the dappled shadows on the white walls, the rays of sun slanting down through broad, green leaves, and sense the wonderful casual air of the place. There is a breeze which is sweet. "James!" I say, and hold open my arms.
>
> He invites me into his room. It is just off the narrow street where I am standing; just a door. We go in and talk. I am so happy to be with him again. It is a small whitewashed room with a stereo set up on boards at one end. There are a few pictures and posters on the walls. It is enough for a young man. I am sitting in a chair while he relaxes on the floor. It is almost in suspended disbelief that I am actually seeing him again.
>
> He puts some music on and we talk for a while. This is his place. He locks his hands behind his head, leaning back and making himself comfortable. We talk for a good long time.
>
> Suddenly the ground is shifting beneath my feet, or the air is moving. Something is changing. I look at him and we both know what is happening. I am waking up. "James," I say, "I think I've got to go. What is this? How often does this happen? Can you come back anytime you want?"
>
> He pauses for a long moment. I can see he isn't thrilled about

being killed in a freak motorcycle accident at twenty-four, like a too-early retirement. The emotion he displays is incredibly subtle yet totally in character. He is miffed. He raises his eyebrows and nods with a slight smile. "Yep. Anytime I want."[5]

Dave awoke from his dream at six-thirty in the morning, sobbing and crying uncontrollably. He felt as if he were experiencing James's death all over again. He cried as he showered and dressed. He drove to work and as he pulled up in front of the office, saw his mother, father, another brother, Bob, and his son, who had come from out of town, waiting for him.

A few days later, Dave's brother Bob confided he had gone out onto the porch of his home, which overlooks the sea, and had spoken into the night air, asking their dead brother James to go contact Dave: "He really needs to see you." It was the same evening as Dave's vivid dream about James. Coincidence? Or contact?

Dave was able to confirm that he had seen James and that their dead brother was fine. The family accepted the dream as a visit from James. It relieved a burden for all of them. Dave said, "I dreamed that I saw him, but the sense of contact is far deeper than that. It was almost as if special permission had been given for him to briefly return and set things right. It literally put me at ease for the rest of my life. I know where he is—in a little room off a shady street with the music he loves. There is no doubt I will be with him again."[6] Dave's dream was reassuring, not only that his brother was all right after death, but that there is eternal life and eternal love.

It has been several years since James died. Dave says that because of his dream, "now there is simply no question in my mind that there is life after death. That knowledge is so deep it's in my bones. I guess you could say it changed my life because it changed the context in which I see my life—it's now not a beginning and an end, but simply part of a larger, ongoing process."

Although the message of this dream is primarily "I'm O.K.," its aftermath suggests "I'll Always Love You." After his momentous dream, Dave was able to write a song about his brother. He explains that "the shelter in the song is my brother's love for me and mine for him." Here are the first verse and the chorus:

Now that you're gone from my world,
The wind blows dust in empty swirls
Where the sun is breathing hot
Find the strength
If I can make it
I will lay down in the shadow
In the shadow of the rock.

Living in the shadow of the rock
Remembering the way you loved me
Living in the shadow
The shadow of the rock
Living in the shadow of the rock
Trying to stop the pain that never stops
I'm living in the shadow
The shadow of the rock.[7]

Dave's sadness and pain surely find expression here, but there is also a solace: the shelter of his brother's love. Maybe Dave's image of the rock, in addition to being a traditional symbol for shelter, speaks of the strength, the rock-solid love between these brothers. Out of pain can come beauty.

Dave says that he's had many subsequent dreams about his brother James in which they are having fun, laughing and joyriding, having a good time. None have the intensity of that spectacular early dream. Regarding the pain James's death caused the family, Dave says, "Nevertheless, I love him so much I'd forgive him a thousand times for that."

When we have loved and lost someone dear, there is still the bittersweet consolation of having truly loved.

Kody's Dead Husband Comforts Her

Kody, whose painful dream of her dead husband rolling out from underneath her bed to complain he was hungry and broke was mentioned in the "I'm Not Really Dead" chapter, had a more soothing dream about him some four years after his death. In it:

I am driving through Marin County and it is gray and foggy. I pull up in front of a house that has warm lights in the windows. I knock on the door and Michael answers. He is wearing a soft flannel shirt that he often wore, and his face shows very deep concern for me. He looks right into my eyes and somehow radiates warmth, love, and above all, concern.

I tell him that I like his house. It is filled with books, soft cushions, and Oriental carpets. He makes me something warm to drink and sits next to me on the cushions. I ask him why he left me. I want desperately to know why, but he cannot explain. He holds me tightly and I cry.

At the time of this dream, Kody still felt no resolution about her husband's death. She still wanted to know why, and felt the question would never be answered. However, this dream said to her that "even though he can't explain, he can love me; he can comfort me." At last, Kody was able to feel love and caring flowing in her direction, a big step toward healing.

Notice her movement in the dream from the gray, foggy atmosphere to the cozy house with warm lights, a warm drink, soft cushions and shirt to snuggle against. Such changes in dream surroundings suggest inner changes. Kody is able to take some comfort in the loving arms of the dream messenger.

Dante's Poems of Praise for His Dead Beloved

Dante's love for Beatrice (meaning "she who blesses") is legendary. The poet, who is considered one of the greatest in all literature, was nearly nine years old when he first saw the eight-year-old Beatrice.[8] She was wearing a delicate crimson gown, clasped with a girdle, and her complexion was "pearl-like." He thought she looked like an angel. Tradition places the date of their first meeting at May 1, 1274. Thereafter, throughout his childhood, Dante often sought her out and, watching, found her to be good and noble in every way.

One day, when he was almost eighteen and she seventeen, they passed on the street and she turned and greeted him directly. This time her gown was of purest white. The meeting overwhelmed Dante with such bliss he had to withdraw to his room, where he fell asleep thinking about her, and had a dream that transformed his life. In it, he saw Love personified as a lord, holding the sleeping Beatrice, naked but wrapped in a crimson mantle. In one hand, Love held Dante's burning heart. He wakened the woman and bade her eat the glowing heart, which she reluctantly did. Then Love wept and gathered Beatrice up and ascended to heaven.

Dante awoke and wrote his first sonnet praising his beloved, based on this dream of her consuming his heart. He wrote the history of his love for Beatrice, along with many more poems in honor of her, which appear in his collection called *La Vita Nuova* (*The New Life*). Like the later poet Novalis (whose chosen name also means "new"), Dante felt newborn by his love. "And so I decided to take as the theme of my writing whatever was praise of this most gracious being."

Although the identity of Beatrice is not absolutely certain, it is thought that she was the daughter of a prominent citizen of Florence, and that she married, and later died at only twenty-four.

Dante was grief-stricken by Beatrice's death. He had several visions of her, and dreams about her in paradise; these experiences, too, led to more poetry.

Finally, Dante had a "marvelous vision" of Beatrice that so affected him he decided "to write no more of this blessed one until I could do so more worthily. And to this end, I apply myself as much as I can, as she indeed knows. Thus if it shall please Him by whom all things live that my life continue for a few years, I hope to compose concerning her what has never been written in rhyme of any woman."[9] After that, Dante said, he was content to die and let his soul go to see "the glory of my lady, that is the blessed Beatrice." He kept his word.

Although Dante eventually married and, in a political struggle, was exiled from Florence, he continued his devotion to his early love. In 1321, Dante published the immortal *Divine Comedy,* with its three sections: *Inferno, Purgatorio,* and *Paradiso.* It was, indeed, worthy of her.

In this epic poem of one hundred cantos, Dante presents an allegory of the progress of the human soul toward God. In *Paradiso,* it is Beatrice who guides him to the place where he first hears the musical harmony of the heavenly spheres. Beatrice takes Dante through the nine concentric heavens, meeting blessed spirits. She answers his questions about good and evil. In the ninth heaven, Dante sees gardens of angels, in the center of which is God's court, pictured as a white rose whose petals hold angels and beatified souls glorifying God in unison. Here Beatrice resumes her place in the rose. Dante is allowed to gaze upon the supreme radiant light of the Trinity, and the poem ends. Much of the imagery in this final scene is thought to have come from Dante's "marvelous vision" of Beatrice.

Like Novalis after him, Dante found his spiritual guide in his dead beloved. She was first his muse during her life, then after death, an angelic spirit representing divine revelation. Love can lead us far.

We are scarcely likely to produce works on the scale of Dante or Novalis after the death of a loved one. But we have seen throughout this book how passion—for a dead parent, child, sibling, friend, or sweetheart—can transmute into fine expressions.

These productions may be lyrics and songs, as they were for Dave Jenneson; they may be poems, as they were for Alice Evans and Brenda Shaw; they may be books, as they were for Isabel Allende and others. However we express ourselves in song, dance, verse, or prose, we give form to our feelings, we touch and heal other people through our grief, and we honor our dead.

Honoring the Love That Endures

We have encountered dream gifts of love before. Perhaps you remember Colleen's dream of her father coming to say goodbye in a space suit, the very moment he died; before departing in the spaceship, he left her with a hug that she felt was a "soul union." Another woman dreamed of being with her dead father in a jewelry store, being offered a gift of jewelry and declining; he took her face in his hands and kissed her, leaving her feeling greatly loved. Arlene's dreams of her dead husband, Joe, were filled with his hugs and kisses; you may remember the special dream gift of a whole row of pink rosebushes he planted for her. My own dream about my dead father giving me an inheritance paper, holding me tenderly, and saying, "I love you, baby," was unique for me. Such dream gifts are literally precious. They are not material—although they may lead to material accomplishments, as they did for Novalis and for Dante—they are gifts of the spirit.

You will have noticed, most likely, that several of the dreams with the message "I'll Always Love You" have included music and dance. There is a celebratory aspect to many of these dreams. In them, the dreamer honors the genuine bond that has formed between the dreamer and the deceased. This bond does not die.

When you feel loved in a dream by someone who has died, accept that love as real. It is real. The love still exists. Cherish it.

"Hi! How Are You?"

> ### Dream Message: "Hi! How Are You?"
> Deceased casually contacts dreamer, as though to say hello or check in; he or she may wave while passing through.
>
> ### Frequency: Common after intense mourning period passes.
> Response after Awake: Dreamer feels pleased.

Once the intense mourning period for significant people in your life has passed, your dreams about them are likely to change. This period may vary from a few months to several years, depending upon the nature of your relationship and the manner of their death.

Early dreams about a person close to you who has died are likely to be vivid and painful. Gradually, the dreams about them may become soothing, and eventually inspirational. Finally, dreams about the dead seem to revert to casual encounters, except for times of personal crisis or at life milestones.

Dream messengers who deliver "Hi! How Are You?" often have the quality of a good friend who casually stops by to say hello, or check on how you are doing, when they are in the neighborhood. At other times, the deceased may simply be part of the background, while the main dream action centers on the dreamer's current problems.

These dreams often take place on significant dates. Don't be surprised if birthdays, wedding anniversaries, death anniversaries, or other special dates give rise to a dream about your loved person. New crises, too, may evoke them.

Carrie's Dead Cousin Stops By to See How She's Doing

Carrie dreamed about her cousin Dick—who had died in a small-airplane crash—on a special religious holiday she had paid no attention to in the waking state. After his death, Dick's mother gave away most of her son's clothing. Carrie received a beautiful leather jacket, which she wore almost daily. In her dream:

> I am sitting in a rocking chair on an outside porch of a small house that rests on a gentle hill. I'm wearing Dick's leather jacket, and am feeling very peaceful, rocking slowly back and forth.
>
> Suddenly, I notice my cousin Dick walking up the hill toward me. I'm very surprised, and am aware in the dream that Dick is dead.
>
> "Dickie!" I say, very excited and happy, calling him by his childhood nickname. "I can't believe this! I didn't think I'd ever see you again! You're dead!" Dick walks up to the porch. "I know," he says, smiling at me. "I just wanted to see how you're doing."
>
> "I'm doing great, Dickie!" I respond. "Your mom sent me your leather jacket and I wear it all the time." Dick looked me over wryly and laughed. "I can see. It looks good on you. I'm glad you've got it . . . Take it easy." I reach over and punch him lightly on his arm, smiling all the while.

Later that day, Carrie discovered her dream had been "eerily timed." She had been raised in a Jewish household, but had long since stopped observing customs and holidays, or attending to when they took place. The day after her dream about Dick, she was at work when someone asked her if she was planning to do anything special for Yom Kippur. This is the Jewish High Holy Day of Atonement, heavily connected with death, dying, and those who have died in the past or will die during the coming year.

Carrie replied she hadn't observed the holiday for years. When was it? The person looked at her curiously and said, "It started at sundown yesterday and will be over at sundown today!" Carrie's dream of Dick had taken place on the night of the High Holy Day of atonement and death, "yet I'd had no inkling till after the fact that it was Yom Kippur." This matching of a dream about the dead—the only dream she ever had about her cousin Dick—with the designated day of observance impressed Carrie.

Our dreaming minds seem to keep track of important markers for us, whether or not our waking minds remember.

Peggy's Dead Brother Stops By

Peggy, whose younger brother John had died in a motorcycle accident, had a dream about him approximately three years after his death:

> I am at a party that is taking place at "my home," although the surroundings are not familiar to me in my waking life. Sometime during the dream I open the front door to greet my grandmother, who had died five months before John did.
>
> There is a girl at the party with whom I had worked a few years ago, and just ran into recently. Next to her is her husband. I am talking to him when the girl asks me, "Who is the man sitting to your left?" I say, "This is my brother John. He's the one who died six months ago (although in reality it is over three years since he died). He comes for a visit with us every once in a while."

Peggy says that this dream "made me feel like John was trying to tell me that he is 'around' me every so often. Kind of like he's keeping tabs on how I am doing." Peggy still feels very close to her brother. Dreams like this one of a brief visit maintain the connection.

Why did Peggy state in the dream that her brother died only six months ago when it was actually over three years? Perhaps six months ago is when Peggy was able finally to accept John's death and move on with her life.

This does not mean that the loved dead person is forgotten. Far from it. But eventually his or her place in our lives shifts. The deceased are no longer central in our waking lives or in our dreams; they "come for a visit with us every once in a while."

Gil Waves to His Deceased Parents in Time of Trouble

Loved ones who have died are most likely to show up to say hello in our dreams at important anniversaries, or when we are in special need—or sometimes both.

A friend of the family, Gilbert Avery, who is a retired Episcopal priest, dreamed about his much-loved parents at a junction of crisis and anniversary. Gil's wife, Laura, had recently been diagnosed with liver cancer. She underwent extensive surgery to remove the tumor, as well as her gallbladder. Naturally, Gil and Laura were alarmed. Gil had had his own health crisis some years earlier. He told me that he had always expected to die first. The possibility that Laura could die before him was shocking. The immediate crisis for Laura had been weathered but her future was uncertain.

This was Gil's frame of mind when the third anniversary of his mother's death occurred. Gil dreamed:

> I'm in a church where a liturgical service is taking place. There is a full-blown orchestra with a conductor. They keep rehearsing. It may be an Easter service. Some kind of extravaganza. But the choir are all in red, as though in Santa Claus suits. What's going on? I'm in the back watching. The bell-ringers have finished. The choir turns. Now they seem to be in red outfits with beanie hats, like a college of cardinals.
>
> I have to leave, but Laura is going to remain. I notice Mother and Dad sitting in the audience. They're very close, maybe holding hands. I go up the aisle and see Mother and Dad. We wave to each other. I'm not supposed to take part in the service. It's appropriate that I not take part. I feel sad about it. I turn to leave. . . .

Then there is a scene outside the church. My nephew is there and his partner. He stands up. A woman on the sidewalk takes one look at him and says, "I want that man in my bed!" "I only have a few minutes," he replies. Laura and I are going to drive three thousand miles. My nephew is going to fly.

This dream is typical of "Hi! How Are You?" messages. The deceased person—a couple in this case—is present but not the focus of the action. They are acknowledged by a wave, a smile, or a brief exchange of words.

The bulk of the dream action revolves around other issues for the dreamer. Here, it is Gil's concern for Laura that is paramount. In his symbolic dream language, Gil describes being present at an important event whose nature is not quite clear (is it Easter? Christmas? A college of cardinals?). Yet he is excluded from participation and feels sad to be left out. His deceased parents, however, are attending. Will Laura be joining the congregation of the dead? The fact that the dream orchestra kept rehearsing suggests the recent crisis may have been practice for the actual event of death. Gil and Laura have taken part in bell-ringing services; in the dream the bell-ringers have finished.

What about the presence of so much red? A specific color in a dream always has significance. As a priest, Gil is aware that the red of cardinals' robes refers to the blood of Christ. It has the same meaning in Christmas symbols such as holly berries. Is this also his wife's lifeblood? Red has a multitude of meanings, and the dreamer must always consider individual associations, but in general, red suggests life energy, passion, or anger.

In the second scene, a time limit is specified. Although it is cast in the form of a joke, the nephew only having a few minutes to spend in another woman's bed, the notion of short time is underscored. Yet, in the paradoxical way of dreams, Laura is to accompany Gil on a long journey. Which is the immediate future? Will Laura stay behind in the church ceremony, or will she travel on by her husband's side? Gil agitates over these possibilities in his dream, while also remembering the loss of his parents.

Through all the threats and difficulties involved with the illness of a loved person, the fact that other loved people who have already

died may be waiting to welcome and guide the newly dead can help
sustain us.

My Dead Father's Valentine Hug

More than two years after my father died, I dreamed of his stopping
by to join a party:

*Our housekeeper is fixing a little Valentine's Day celebration.
There's something in the mail from my godmother. My father is there
and I give him a big hug. Do I have enough gifts? I'm putting white
candles into a flowerpot. I talk with my daughter, who is around six
in the dream (actually fourteen at the time) about her nice clothes.*

At this point, dreams about my father had become more "normal"
and less like a realistic "visitation." There was no great outburst of
sorrow or joy, just a happy acceptance of his presence. My still-
living godmother is another very special person to me, so receiving
a communication from her—in a dream or otherwise—is always
welcome. The relationship with my daughter was much more
peaceful at six, her age in the dream, than it was at fourteen. By
making her younger than she was at the time, I was making things
nicer between us. Putting candles in the flowerpot, rather than in a
cake, suggests my wanting the good feelings to "grow" as a plant
would. One "makes a wish" on candles. You can see that although
I'm very pleased to see my deceased father, he is not the focus of the
action or of my concern. I am concentrating on other issues in the
dream.

The dream took place about a month past Valentine's Day. At
the time of the dream, we were closing down our London flat and
preparing to take a five-month trip around the world; although
there was a lot of pressure from things to be done, I was feeling
loving and happy. I should mention, furthermore, that my husband's birthday is on Valentine's Day. By blending my father's "Hi!
How Are You?" dream visit with my husband's day of birth, I am
linking them in an emotional sense. Indeed, they share a spirit of
love and generosity.

You may want to keep alert for blendings of this sort in your own dreams, ones that link characteristics of the dead loved person with a living loved person.

Rae's Dead Husband Waves as He Walks Through

Dreams about a dead loved one stopping by to visit can emerge many years after the death. Rae was widowed when she was only thirty, leaving her with a two-year-old daughter. Almost four decades later, Rae, now in her late sixties, dreamed:

> I am in a hospital, huge in every dimension, with high ceilings and very large rooms. It is all white, including the floors. I am wanting to go home because I had left my daughter alone (although she would have been thirty then).
>
> I am alone, pondering how I can escape, and watching the only door in that very large room. Suddenly the door opens and my husband walks in, looking at me and smiling and waving to me as he walks across the full length of the room and just disappears!

This was the first time Rae had "seen" her deceased husband in a dream. She said, "I was not affected by the dream but felt quite happy to have seen him just as he was in 1938."

Rae did not provide any other associations to the dream, aside from saying how pleased she was to see her dead husband, but one can make some reasonable guesses.

At almost seventy, Rae probably would be contemplating what her future holds. In her dream, she found herself alone in an all-white, almost overwhelmingly large space, a place where people go when ill and, perhaps, dying. The imagery suggests a place of passage where she felt isolated and somewhat threatened. This is when her loved husband appeared, smiling and waving, before vanishing again.

Rae was likely to have been anticipating her own passage to the world beyond. Who better to lead the way than someone who cares for her who is already there?

Perhaps one of the functions of "Hi! How Are You?" dream

messages for the elderly or the ill is, in part, to help prepare the dreamer for his or her own demise.

Carl Jung has said that we dream about the dead to prepare ourselves to meet them again. Whatever the reason, we can welcome glimpses of them in our dreams, feel their concern and love for us, and listen to their messages.

Acknowledging the Brief Visit

If we honor enduring love and powerful dreams about the dead with our creations, how do we acknowledge the brief visits from the dead? You'll find suggestions in the last chapter. The answer also depends somewhat upon your age and condition.

If you are young and in good health, you may wish to think of these short appearances of the dead in our dreams as symbolic. They usually feel more representational than like real contacts or visitations.

If you are elderly, or in frail health, even brief visits from the dead in dreams may be helping prepare you to meet them again. If there is an afterlife, and those we have known are there to greet us, their faults are likely to be lessened, their virtues enhanced, and their physical limitations vanished.

Perhaps, in spirit, those who have gone first may truly lead us. Like Beatrice showing Dante the wonders of paradise, we may find, among the loved ones who have died before us, our personal spiritual guides. Following their shining figures, we join the ancestors, as we become dream messengers ourselves.

Nine Major Symbols in Dreams About the Dead

Throughout this book, we have considered dreams about the dead that involve the presence of the deceased. Naturally, you will have other dreams about your loss that do not directly picture the dead person. Even in dreams that do involve the deceased directly, there are often additional, puzzling, symbolic elements—strange birds or wounded dogs. These images usually symbolize either the person who has died or our feelings about the death. To understand these symbolic dreams and elements, you need to be aware of the most frequent types of dream symbols about the dead.

Although this topic could be an entire book in itself, here I will review the nine most common symbols in dreams about the dead. First, a quick reminder about the common origin of these symbols.

Basis of Nightmares About the Dead

Nightmares about the deceased person are founded on more than the trauma of a death, and our personal reactions of grief to it. Ancient beliefs that the ghosts of dead people are capable of harming the living still linger today. The Angel of Death; the Grim Reaper; Charon, the ferryman across the river Styx whom the soul must pay for the journey or remain lost; the emergence of the dead from graves at certain times of the year or night—all these and other mythological and folk underpinnings about death, dying, and mourning are important to be aware of because they influence our dreams about the dead. We examined some of these concepts in detail in Chapter 2, "I'm Suffering," and "I'm O.K.," in the section "Fear of the Dead." They vary from culture to culture, of course, but there are certain constants that we will consider here.

Basis of Comforting Dreams About the Dead

Likewise, dreams of guidance from the dead have their ancient counterparts in beliefs that the ancestors guard their descendants and warn them about danger. Our fairy tales retain this theme, as in the original version of "Cinderella," where she prayed at her mother's grave for a year, leading to the later appearance of her fairy godmother. We have seen how survivors are often comforted, advised, or guided by the images of the dead in dreams, much like the idea of a guardian angel. Myths, legend, folk and fairy tales, alongside religious concepts, all contribute to the modern dreamer's ideas about death and grief. Whether we "believe" them or not, these ancient ideas are still active in our dreams. This chapter will help you become more aware of related images that may surface in your dreams about the dead.

1. Lost and Found in Dreams About the Dead

Dream Image: Lost

Dreamer hunts desperately for the missing person.
He or she is rarely found.

Frequency: Fairly common.

Response after Awake: Dreamer feels lonely and
grieved anew.

When a significant person in our life dies, we are literally left with a "space" in our lives. "His death left a black hole," my friend Tommie said, after her father died.

In the literature of grief, the middle stage of mourning—after the numbness and shock have melted—often involves "searching" for the missing person. Remember how Dave Jenneson spoke of having a compulsion to go back to the country road where his brother died on a motorcycle, and search for him, although he knew it was hopeless? Survivors often speak of glimpsing someone on the street who resembles the lost love, being certain it is the person they miss, even following that person until a good look convinces them it is not the one they seek. Rather like Jimmy Stewart in Alfred Hitchcock's movie *Vertigo,* we may see a person so resembling the one we mourn that we painfully try to re-create that person. In his case, it was the actual woman (played by Kim Novak) whose death a conspirator had faked. Sadly, for us the loss is all too permanent. And, like Stewart at the end of the film, we lose the love all over again.

Traditional Symbolism of Something Missing

Dreams about hunting for the missing person force us to confront the reality of their absence once more. Thus, their ultimate impact is healing. The emptiness felt in the survivor's heart is depicted by the loved one being absent in a dream. The void becomes literal.

Lucas's Mother Dreams He Is Lost

Gordon Livingston, a psychiatrist and writer, gives a poignant account of grief in his book *Only Spring: On Mourning the Death of My Son*.[1] Lucas Livingston died of leukemia when he was only six years old, five months after his diagnosis, having just received a bone marrow transplant from his father. The child's death was agonizing for Livingston and his wife, Clare. About two months after Lucas died, his mother, Clare, had a "missing" type of dream. Livingston wrote:

> *Clare was moaning softly in her sleep this morning so I awakened her. She had been dreaming: we were late picking Lucas up at school. When we arrived, the fenced-in area in front of the kindergarten was filled with children, but look as we might, we could not find him. The dream left us weeping for a long time, holding on to each other. This place [Cape Cod], perhaps because of its beauty, has given us the chance to freely grieve together.*[2]

In a dream of Livingston's own, almost a year after the boy's death, Lucas was miraculously saved:

> *I dreamed about Lucas last night. We were again in the PICU [Pediatric Intensive Care Unit] and again he died. This time, however, in the way of dreams, we were somehow allowed to undo the bone marrow transplant and he was saved. When I awoke, he was not beside me.*[3]

Here, of course, Lucas is "found." How strenuously and how long we yearn to bring back the dead, to "undo" any action we regard as a mistake and restore our loss. Livingston suffered, in particular, for the decision to try the bone marrow transplant, which ultimately was rejected by Lucas's body, resulting in death.

Eventually, the Livingstons held a fund-raiser and established a fund in their son's name as a living memorial. Its income, along with individual contributions, pays for a suite in downtown Baltimore for the use of families whose children are hospitalized, as Lucas was, at the Johns Hopkins hospital. Many parents are unable to sustain the financial burden of medical care, including housing nearby so their ill child will not be alone. Livingston said, "I pray too that there will be those who, facing their own ordeals, will be lifted from despair by the knowledge that love, the truest energy in the universe, is never lost, not even in death."[4]

Whenever we take actions to better the lot of those who are suffering what we have suffered, we help ourselves as well as those to whom we give.

Russ's Son Is Missing

Russ's grown son was killed as a result of a freak accident in which he was struck on the head by a heavy branch falling from a tree. In one of his dreams about his son, Russ saw himself going back to a golf course where he was supposed to meet him. It was shrouded with heavy fog. He called and called, but could find no trace of his son. The emptiness left by such a loss is electric with currents of pain.

Mary Winslow's Gap

Mary Winslow, who dreamed about her son Greg, after his death from melanoma, coming back to "help you break up the ice in your heart," expressed several of her losses in a poem ending:

There are spaces—
Toothless gaps in ancient mouths
Eyes that stare at Lethe
Loved ones lost from my mind's camera
Empty boundaries in my heart
A half-empty bed.

There is no escape. I am bereft.[5]

At the time Mary wrote this aching piece, she was struggling with the serious illness and anticipated death of her second husband. Having lost a son, she dreaded watching the slow decline of her spouse from an affliction worsening for more than twelve years. She yearned for his release from suffering, while still valuing their moments together. Her position reminds me of the music of Gustav Holst in *The Planets,* in the movement "Saturn, the Bringer of Old Age." It was the composer's personal favorite of the seven movements. In it, the beat of the music grows louder and louder, mimicking the inevitable tread of time marching closer and closer to death, until at last the listener feels, "It's here!"

Yes, we all must face it—whether our own death or that of a loved one. Death is an essential part of the journey of life. But perhaps death is not the end of the journey. Following the climax of heavy marching time, Holst's music shifts to a lighter and higher register, with flutes and harps, and the suggestion of bells. Having depicted physical decay, the piece then shows a vision of fulfillment. Serene, soaring, ethereal, it reaches upward and rises, into the beyond.

Your Dreams About Something Missing

Any dreams you have about something missing or being lost while you are grieving are almost certain to be connected to the person who died. Keep in mind that eventually you will find something of value for that space.

2. The Journey of Life in Dreams About the Dead

Dream Image: A Journey

Dreamer is traveling or preparing to set out. Vehicles, departure points, problems en route are typical.

Frequency: Extremely common.

Response after Awake: Dreamer usually feels anxious or distressed.

We have seen how dreams about a journey frequently mark the passage of a significant person in our lives. Ships, trains, buses, airplanes, and other vehicles often appear in the dreams of people mourning a death. This imagery is so typical it probably echoes the long-held idea of life as a journey.

Traditional Symbolism of Journeys

Various cultures depict death as a "crossing over." The term has become a commonplace euphemism for dying. What deviates from culture to culture is the type of vehicle, the nature of what is crossed, and how the crossing is best accomplished.

The journey of life appears in folk and fairy tales, legends, and myths as a voyage across water, a pilgrimage along a road, a trip scaling a mountain, and other similar scenarios. We looked at this concept in detail in Chapter 3, "I'm Not Really Dead" and "Good-bye," in the section "Death as a Journey to the West."

Samples of Dreams with Water and Ships

When Dick dreamed, about nine months after his wife's death, that he was on a cruise ship like the "Love Boat'" in the television series, he was symbolically depicting his bereft condition. He described the boat as "looking fine on the upper decks, but when I started down the companionway, it was a rust bucket." He added that he himself felt like a "rust bucket," with his problems from arthritis. Past the chain separating the nice upper decks from the "companionway" (away from his wife) on the "Love Boat," life for the dreamer felt deteriorated. Don't forget that dream conditions—like life—can and do change.

When Wanda dreamed of meeting her dead cousin on a rowboat on a lake with fog all around, she was placing herself in a familiar setting, similar to the place where she and her cousin used to go fishing as children. For her, the fog suggested a sense of veiled mystery rather than foreboding. A happy dream, in which she was lucid, followed. She held hands with her cousin and they floated in the sky together, observing their childhood below. Before he left, Wanda promised her cousin that she would stay in touch with his parents.

If you can remember to do so, ask the dead you meet in your dreams, "What can I do for you?" The answer may bring comfort to others as well as yourself.

Keep in mind that trains and terminals, buses and bus stations, airplanes and airports, or spaceships, cars, and other vehicles may be the setting for journeys in your dreams. Question yourself in the manner below, about the vehicles, the settings, the quality of the journey, and your own personal associations to these.

Your Dreams About Journeys

When any imagery related to a journey appears in your dreams during mourning—vehicles, rivers, oceans, roads, borders, boundaries, visas, passports, and so forth—you can be fairly sure it relates to your feelings about the death that has taken place.

Notice what qualities characterize these images in your dreams. These qualities will reveal aspects of your feelings. Is the water dark and turbulent? Is it frozen solid? In the first image, the chaotic nature of the dreamer's feelings are being expressed. In the second image, it is the numbness, the coldness, the dreamer feels most. Understanding your feelings in your dreams about grief can help you make sense of them.

Your Dreams About Water and Ships

You are quite unlikely to dream directly of the river Styx or the ferryman Charon—unless you've studied the classics—but you can see their ancient reflections in modern dreams, drama, literature, and life.

When General Stonewall Jackson uttered his last words, "Let us cross over the river, and rest under the shade of the trees," he was completing his life's journey.[6] When D. H. Lawrence wrote his last poem, *The Ship of Death,* on his deathbed, he, too, was drawing on the universal connection between life and a journey, as his came to a close.

The ship or boat in your dreams about the dead is likely to symbolize either the life journey of the person who died, or your life journey. Here are some questions to guide your exploration of the ships, boats, and waters in your dreams about the dead:

- What is the boat/ship like? Describe it.

- Is the setting familiar? How?

- What characteristics of the ship are most emphasized?

- What feelings of yours correspond to the characteristics of the boat/ship? Do they match characteristics of the dead person?

- What is the crossing like? Smooth? Rough? Foggy?

- What is the water like? Describe it. Icy? Cold? Chaotic?

- Who are the passengers? Is there a crew?

- How do you feel during the journey?

Answering these questions will help you understand the meaning of the ships, boats, and bodies of water in your dreams. If your dream about the dead involved a different vehicle and mode of travel, make a substitution in the questions; for example, put the word "train" in place of the word "ship"; substitute "tracks" or "road," as appropriate, for "water."

3. The Tree of Life in Dreams About the Dead

Dream Image: A Tree

Dreamer watches something happen to a tree. The dreamer may or may not associate the tree with the person who died.

Frequency: Fairly common.

Response after Awake: Dreamer is usually distressed when a tree is destroyed and delighted when a tree regenerates.

Traditional Symbolism of the Tree of Life

A tree, like a journey, is one of the major representations of an individual life in folktales and myths. The growth of a tree parallels the growth of a person, whose life may be "cut down."

This symbolism extends to the images of ladders, steps, staircases, escalators, elevators, and other methods of moving upward.

Samples of Dreams with a Tree of Life

One bereaved daughter dreamed of a giant redwood being chopped down; another dreamed of all the shade trees in an old people's home being chopped up; another mourner saw a forest being destroyed by workers with a buzz saw.

Your Dreams About the Tree of Life

If you have a dream about something destroying a tree, you are almost certain to be symbolizing the death that has occurred. The type of tree involved, and what happened to it, is significant. Ask yourself:

- What type of tree or trees was in the dream?

- How would you describe this tree to a child?

- What is special about this kind of tree? What makes it different?

- Does this tree have aspects that relate to the person who died? If so, describe the correspondence.

If destruction of a tree depicts death, regeneration of one suggests ongoing life. Look for new growth, new shoots or saplings, blossoming trees, bushes, and plants as you begin to recover from your grief.

4. The Soul Animal in Dreams About the Dead

Dream Image: An Animal

Dreamer encounters or watches an animal associated with the person who died or who shares some characteristics with that person, including name.

Frequency: Fairly common.

Response after Awake: Dreamer may be intrigued or comforted.

A. Traditional Symbolism of Birds

The symbolism of birds is rather complex. In mythology, legend, and folktale, birds often symbolize the human soul. In ancient Egypt, birds with human heads were represented as leaving the mouths of dying persons. In ancient Sumer, the Babylonian tradition said that souls in the underworld wore garments made of bird feathers. Ordinary mortals were thought to become white birds, or butterflies or bees, while sun kings turned into eagles. The Slavs are said to believe that at death the soul turns into a bird.

On another level, birds often symbolize a divine messenger, as the eagle was said to bring messages from wandering heroes. In Christianity, the Holy Ghost is represented by the dove, a bringer of messages from God. By extension, birds have become symbols of thought, ideas, and the swift flight of imagination. Further symbolic meanings vary with the type of bird. A bird of prey has different implications from those of a songbird.

The absence of birds or butterflies is almost always regarded as unfavorable, as for example, when Greeks of olden times referred to the underworld as "the Birdless Land." A child in a concentration camp scratched on the wall, "There are no butterflies here."

Other birds, usually black, like ravens or night creatures such as the owl, have been associated with death. The call of these birds is said by certain tribes to precede a death.

Samples of Birds in Dreams About the Dead

Beth Witrogen McLeod and the Singing Cardinals

A San Francisco editor and writer, Beth Witrogen McLeod, gave a moving account of the death of her parents, in her feature series, "The Caregivers."[7] First her father died from a recurring sacral tumor, and then—only a few weeks later—her mother died from the crippling Lou Gehrig's disease and an Alzheimer's-like dementia.

McLeod, at forty-four, was exhausted and agonized by her beloved parents' long illnesses and painful deaths. Of her mother's death, she wrote, "Even though I was grateful for the mercy, losing her was even worse than losing my father. She was buried in the dead of winter as her coffin was lowered into three feet of ice water. Yet the knowledge that they were out of pain meant that my own healing could begin, a release from the despair and self-pity that were consuming me."

Six months later, McLeod held a ceremony to unveil the head-

stone at her parents' grave site, and then returned to their condo-
minium one last time. She heard an unfamiliar sound out on the
deck, and when she went to see what it was, found a pair of cardinals in full song. McLeod said that cardinals had always been her
parents' favorite birds, but she had never seen any of them around
the condo in fifteen years. She felt comforted, as if the birds were
there to let her know she was not alone.

A month later, about seven months after her mother's death,
McLeod dreamed:

> *I am sitting at a table with my parents, and my father keeps repeat-
> ing a phrase. Finally it registers: "The red cardinal only comes out in
> the winter." I jump up, exclaiming, "So it was you at the condo!" And
> as they rock back, laughing yes, yes, I run up to them and we hug
> until I wake up.*[8]

This dream, along with McLeod's journey through grief, inspired
her forthcoming book on caregiving and spirituality. Wherever
such good omens and dream messages come from, they are most
welcome. The singing birds in our dreams can awaken joy in our
hearts.

Liam Neeson and the Robins

Irish actor Liam Neeson, star of *Schindler's List* and many other
major films, says that a red bird, usually a robin redbreast, appears
whenever a Neeson dies.[9] The European robin is a much more
distinctively red bird than those seen in the United States. Here we
see the robin in the bird's role as divine messenger. The fact that
such appearances do occur has made the folk belief endure through
the centuries.

A related idea is that domestic birds and bees must be informed
of a death in the family, and a mourning ribbon hung on the cage
or hive. It's ironic that the wild birds are said to do the informing
about a death, while the domestic ones must be informed. The
bird's message relating a death or impending death may take place
during a dream, as it did for a famous novelist.

Isabel Allende's Daughter and the Birds in the Tower

In her recent book *Paula*, Isabel Allende gives a touching, true account of the death of her twenty-eight-year-old daughter from a rare hereditary disorder.[10] Porphyria (a defect in which iron and the protein globin are not properly metabolized) is not usually fatal if diagnosed correctly and if certain substances are avoided, including sedatives. However, things went wrong. Paula became gravely ill in December 1991, and was hospitalized in Madrid. After a possibly too-high dosage of sedatives was administered, she went into coma. She was placed on a respirator, and then, in a cruel twist of fate, the electrical power apparently was interrupted. The gap before emergency power came on was long enough to be critical; Paula's brain waves went flat. She languished, inert. After five months of waiting in the hospital for her daughter to awaken, Allende brought the comatose young woman home to California, to try every possible treatment to revive her. Nothing was effective. She remained in coma for several more months before dying on December 6, 1992, exactly one year after she had lost consciousness.

During the months Allende and her own mother kept vigil at her daughter's hospital bedside, or more often in the corridor of the intensive care unit where family members were asked to wait, she began to write the story of her family history for her unconscious daughter. Her agent, knowing that writing might help the distraught woman endure, had urged her to write, but at first Allende's reply was "I can't. Something inside me is broken." With the hope of someday sharing the story with her daughter, to help bring back her memory, Allende forced herself to begin. She told me that the writing was the only thing that kept her sane. This material became Allende's book *Paula*.

In it, Allende relates a vivid dream she had the night before her daughter's crisis and downward spiral:

I dreamed you were twelve years old, Paula. You were wearing a plaid coat; your hair was pulled back from your face with a white ribbon and the rest fell loose over your shoulders. You were standing in the center of a hollow tower, something like a grain silo filled with hundreds of fluttering doves. Memé's [her grandmother] voice was saying, Paula is dead. *You begin to rise off the ground. I ran to catch you by the belt of your coat but you pulled me with you, and we floated like feathers, circling upward.* I am going with you, take me, too, Paula, *I begged. Again my grandmother's voice echoed in the tower:* No one can go with her, she has drunk the potion of death. *We kept rising and rising; I was determined to hold you back, nothing would take you from me. Overhead was a small opening through which I could see a blue sky with one perfect white cloud, like a Magritte painting, and then I understood, horrified, that you would be able to pass through but that the aperture was too narrow for me. I tried to hold you back by your clothing; I called to you, but no sound came. For a few precious instants, I could see as you drifted higher and higher, and then I began to float back down through the turbulence of the doves.*[11]

Allende was totally distraught by this dream. She said she awoke crying her daughter's name. Rushing to the hospital in the middle of the night, she beat on the door to intensive care. A nurse assured her that Paula was fine, nothing had happened, but at last let Allende come in to see for herself. The machine still was pumping air into her daughter's lungs; she was not cold. After kissing her child on the forehead, she went out into the corridor to wait for morning.

Allende's mother arrived at daylight, bringing fresh coffee in a thermos and rolls warm from a bakery. They discussed her dream, with Allende's mother giving reassurances that it all applied to herself. When asked what the doves meant, her mother replied, "An agitated spirit, I suppose . . ."

With that response, Allende's mother was probably on the right track. In addition to sharing the general symbolism of a bird as a soul, the dove emphasizes an aspect of purity and innocence. When I talked directly to Allende about Paula, these qualities seemed foremost. In dreams, a large number—the hundreds of doves—often represents a superlative, "a lot of" whatever the singular symbolizes.

Allende's dream shows the presence of a great deal of soul, pure, innocent, fluttering, and departing. She said that she associated grain to nourishment and life; in her dream, that storage place for this essential was empty. She told me she now believes Paula's brain died the night of her dream.

Notice the usual boundary between the living and dying, in this case a narrow opening through which only the dying could pass.

Why was her daughter depicted as a twelve-year-old in the dream? Age in dreams is always relevant. I knew when I read the dream that some crisis must have arisen at that earlier age that led Allende to be extremely concerned about the well-being of her child then, as well as at the time of her dream. Later I learned that, in fact, when Paula was a teenager, Allende left her husband and children to accompany a lover to Spain. The young Paula, on the border of womanhood, was deeply distressed; she felt betrayed. It was Paula's misery, Allende told me, that led her to return to her unhappy marriage and care for her children until they were grown. Obviously, when her daughter was twelve was a time of great apprehension about her, as was the situation when the dream took place.

After all medical hope was abandoned, Paula, in her twilight zone, lived in Allende's house, where Allende tenderly cared for all her child's physical needs, still trying new therapies that might somehow help. The night before Paula died, Allende dreamed that her daughter came into her bedroom and said, "Listen, Mama, wake up. I don't want you to think you're dreaming. I've come to ask for your help . . . I want to die and I can't." She begged her mother to let her go and assured her of her love.

When the day of death came, Allende and her family members spent the day together with Paula, looking at family photographs and keepsakes, saying goodbye, and praying with lit candles. Allende slipped into bed beside her barely breathing daughter to hold her. She gradually felt the ghosts of her grandparents and other ancestral figures appear throughout the night.

At some point, Allende seemed to feel herself again in her dream of a tower filled with doves, but now her daughter was her present age. She had the sensation of rising with her, and this time the roof opened and she was able to ascend with her child, flying over valleys and hills to a redwood forest, where they descended. In a stream that Paula pointed to, Allende saw fresh roses, and she heard the music of thousands of voices whispering among the trees. She felt herself sinking into the cool water, dissolving, becoming part of her surroundings, being herself and her daughter, welcoming her daughter as spirit. Paula, who actually had been dressed in a white gown for her departure, was now herself like the spirit of the doves.

After I had written this material, I shared it with Allende to verify its accuracy. We both had a surprise. Reading this description, Allende realized for the first time that her nickname for Paula as a child was connected to the dream imagery. She told me that she often called her daughter "paloma," which means "dove" in Spanish, because she frequently sent the girl to deliver messages to her mother-in-law, who lived next door. "Mi paloma," a reference to "my messenger dove," was a favorite term of endearment she used for her daughter. The dream image of the agitated doves took on an even richer layer of meaning. We need to remember the possibility of plays on words as we work with dream images.

When I next spoke with Allende, some two and a half years after Paula's death, she said that after her daughter died, she had no dreams about her for months.[12] Then, the initial dreams were ones in which Paula was dead, just lying there with no movement. Later, she began to dream of Paula with her friends, talking. These dreams bring Allende such pleasure she sometimes tries to "invoke" them by picturing her daughter in a particular place before she falls asleep. The love survivors feel for cherished people who have died can keep us in touch with their spirits for a long time.

Your Dreams About Birds

If you, during a period of mourning or anticipated mourning, experience an intense dream about a bird, it probably relates to the death that's taken place, or one you expect.

The first thing to notice—if possible—is the kind of bird in your dream. Ask yourself:

- What kind of bird was it? Describe its unique qualities.

- What did it look like? Was there anything odd about its appearance?

- Was there anything unusual about its behavior? What did it do?

· Is there anything about the kind of bird or the name of the bird that resembles a pun on the name of the person who has died?

Always consider any personal associations you have to birds in general or to the type of bird in particular. For instance, when my husband, Zal, was grieving over the death of his ninety-one-year-old mother, he was impressed one morning by the presence of a bird as he took his daily jog. In an event that never happened before or since, a black bird circled him as he ran, and swooped low, almost touching his forehead. Usually, a bird colored black would be considered negative, but Zal, reflecting that his mother's maiden name was Blachman (pronounced Blackman), found the event oddly comforting. He is not often inclined to such thoughts, so I, too, was impressed.

Watch for any puns that may arise in your dreams about the dead with birds and other animals.

B. Traditional Symbolism of Mammals

Although the soul is more often depicted in the form of a bird or butterfly (see the preceding section), it sometimes appears in the shape of an animal in our dreams about the dead.

In general, animals in fairy tales, myths, and dreams depict our "animal nature." They mirror life energy. This energy can be acting against us, as in stories and dreams about threatening animals, or supporting us, as in stories and dreams with helpful animals. Further symbolism is very much dependent upon the individual type of animal, and the associations your culture and personal experience bring to it.

Dogs and certain other creatures are traditionally associated with death. The ancient Egyptians said that the souls of those whose hearts were heavier than a feather were eaten by a beast called Ammut, composed of a crocodile, a lioness, and a hippopotamus. The ancient Greeks said that the entrance to the underworld was guarded by a fierce many-headed dog named Cerberus. The home of the Tibetan Buddhist and Hindu god of death, Yama, is said to be protected by two wild dogs with four eyes. Certain dogs or packs of hounds are said to appear when a death occurs.

Since it is not possible to examine here all the symbolism associated with animals in dreams about the dead, you need to supply your own associations to specific animals that enter your dreams.

Samples of Mammals in Dreams About the Dead

Several dreamers mentioned dogs in their dreams about the dead. One woman dreamed of a wild dog trying to break into her car as she frantically tried to drive away; she associated the dog with her recently deceased father.

Keep in mind that other mammals may represent the deceased. Remember Paul Tholey's dream about his dead father as a tiger that needed to be confronted?

Dreamworker Joanne Rochon had two vivid dreams about her dead father in the form of a bear that was thought to be stuffed but was still alive, its paw moving and stretching.

Valerie lost her twin sons during a premature labor and delivery when she was only six months pregnant. It was her first pregnancy and she and her husband were shattered. For months, Valerie had dreams about dreadful things happening to the two family dogs. In one nightmare, she came home to find her two dogs in the backyard, shot to death. In another dream, she was hunting for two dogs she had owned in childhood (then dead) on a dark, rainy night, unable to find them; finally she located them trying to climb into a baby crib. In yet another nightmare, her family cat was drowning. Still other oppressive dreams dealt with her house being on fire, torched from the fireplace; this no doubt was associated with the physical sensation of burning in her womb, and her feelings about the destruction that had occurred.

Obviously, Valerie substituted her two dogs for her two lost sons in dreams. What may not be so apparent is that horrendous as such nightmares can be, they are less painful at the time than dreaming about damage to the lost children themselves. Many dreamers put animals into the role of being destroyed rather than picture their loved one suffering.

Even such devastation as Valerie's lessens over time. She eventually had a celestial-type dream about her dead sons. The last time I saw her, she was the mother of a robust boy, and with her husband, was blissfully enjoying their new family.

Your Dreams About Mammals

Your dreams about the dead may or may not include animals. If an animal appears in one of your dreams while you are in mourning, it is important to understand its meaning. Ask yourself these questions:

- What is this animal? Describe it as you would to a child who has never heard of it or seen it. Write your answer down and examine it for clues as to the animal's role in your dream. Is it a specific breed or color? What do you associate to these?

- Does this animal have any characteristics that you connect with the person who has died? What are they?

- Does the name or type of this animal connect with the name of any significant person in your life (deceased or not)? Specify them.

Pondering your answers to these questions and working with them will help you comprehend the animal's meaning in your dream.

C. Traditional Symbolism of Fish

Dreams about the dead that involve fish are less frequent than those with birds or mammals. However, because of the intensity of the dreams that do portray fish, you should be aware they, too, might occur.

Fish are treasures from the water; they provide food for the body and fascination for the mind. They sometimes have a sacred connotation, being associated with the soul in contrast to the body. In Christianity, the fish has spiritual associations. Fish in water may represent the ideas and feelings of our inner life. The element of a fish that is emphasized in dreams about the dead is being caught on a hook and dragged from the water to die.

Samples of Fish in Dreams About the Dead

One grieving woman, who had had a few dreadful dreams about her husband, began having nightmares about fish instead. Her young husband had died while at work, his chest crushed in an industrial accident. When I asked her to describe what a fish was, she replied, "A creature that can't breathe out of water." As she heard her answer, she gasped and began to weep. "That's the last thing my husband said to me before he died," she sobbed, " 'I can't breathe.' " Death, to this unhappy woman, was her husband caught on a hook. Once again, these awful nightmares are more tolerable to the dreamer at the moment than dreaming directly about the loved person suffering.

Another grieving woman dreamed about a fish being brutally hung from a hook.

Your Dreams About Fish

As with dreams of birds and of mammals, you will learn more about the meaning of a fish in your dreams if you question yourself. Ask:

- What is a fish? What makes it different from all other animals? What is unique about fish? Phrase your answers as if explaining to a child.

- What kind of fish appeared in your dream? What's special about this type of fish?

- What happened to the fish?

If during mourning you dream about a fish being caught, you are likely to be portraying the state of the person who died. In this sense, it is a variation of the dream message "I'm Suffering."

5. Black, White, and Color in Dreams About the Dead

Dream Image: Black, White, or Color

Dreamer is struck by the darkness or the lightness in a scene, or notices black, white, or a color associated with an image of the dead.

Frequency: Fairly common.

Response after Awake: Dreamer usually feels depressed by a preponderance of black, or uplifted by radiant white or some other color that the dreamer especially likes.

Death is the great unknown. Images of darkness in dreams often represent the confusion a person feels in the face of death. You may dream of struggling to find your way in the dark; recall the many darkened corridors and hallways that we saw appear in dreams about the dead. You may be tossed in a ship on a stormy sea at night, driving along a difficult road, fearful of falling into a black hole, or actually do so.

Traditional Symbolism of Black, White, and Color

In our society, in almost-twenty-first-century America, blackness is associated with death. In the dreams of white Americans, black people often are cast in fear-producing roles; they then represent a dangerous unknown. For African-Americans, white people may be put into the role of the more fearful dream characters; the white of ghosts may represent the dangerous unknown.

In general among Americans, black is the "color"—it is actually an absence of color, not a color in itself—for mourning. Although we have given up the elaborate Victorian code for mourning wear (dull black for three months after the death; black silk for the next three months; gold trim added at about eight months; then at about ten months, purple half-mourning for the remainder of the first year, before returning to the use of color), black is still considered appropriate dress for a funeral and may mark death announcements. Dreams in which the image of death appears almost always make reference to the black clothes of the figure, as did the woman who dreamed about a gaunt figure dressed in black, in a carriage, waiting.

There are wide cultural variations in colors associated with death. In India, the color of mourning is brown, the hue of withered leaves. In Syria, blue is associated strongly with heaven, so it is the color used for mourning there. In China, hope is associated with white; therefore, white is used for the color of mourning clothes and decorations. In some areas of Africa, bright scarlet is the color to be worn to funerals to indicate a "blood" (symbolized by the red) relative has died. Obviously, we need to consider the cultural background of the dreamer before making assumptions about the meaning of a dream color.

Samples of Black, White, and Color in Dreams About the Dead

You already have seen the presence of black in disturbing dreams about the dead—in clothing, settings, and spaces. Remember the dreams we encountered dealing with black holes and black space.

The images of white or lightness were amply evident in comforting dreams about the dead—the white garments, glowing faces, beaming moons and suns. Think about how many white gowns, full moons, gleaming heads of hair, shining eyes, and radiant faces illuminated the dreams of those who were enjoying happy exchanges with the dead.

Single colors tend to have more individual meanings. One dreamer was so struck by a particular shade of sky blue suffusing the atmosphere in a joyful dream about her dead mother that, afterward, she bought clothing and fabrics in that shade whenever possible. Shades of rose or gleaming gold were favored by other dreamers as they began to feel better.

Your Dreams About Black, White, and Color

If your traditions are in accord with the general American and European association of black with death and mourning, then your dreams about the dead are likely to display dark, gloomy conditions and clothing during the early phases of grief. These dismal qualities correspond to feelings of hopelessness and despair.

As you begin to move into a more healing space, your dreams will reflect this shift in attitude by the presence of warmer, softer colors, or glorious light. This luminosity represents not only the transfigured spirit of the dead person, but also the shift of feelings to a more hopeful, happier state.

You need to consider not only any cultural variant you may have about the meanings of certain colors, but also your own personal experience with colors; you are likely to be repelled by particular colors with negative associations for you, and attracted to other colors with positive ones. When a certain color appears in your dreams about the dead, ask yourself:

- How would I describe that color to a child?

- Is the color warm? Is it cold?

- Do I like the color or not? Why? Why not?

- Does that color have an association with a certain person or place? Is there any linkage between it and the dead person?

Make your answers simple and clear. They will contain part of the meaning that color has in your dream. Notice how the colors in your dreams change throughout the months or years of mourning.

6. Coldness and Warmth in Dreams About the Dead

....

Dream Image: Coldness or Warmth

Dreamer is struck by coldness in a person, object, or setting; or notices pleasant warmth in a person, object, or setting.

Frequency: Fairly common.

Response after Awake: Dreamer usually feels uncomfortable in the presence of cold, pleasant with warmth.

Traditional Symbolism of Cold, Ice, and Snow

Cold, ice, and snow are frequently mentioned in disturbing dreams about the dead. These images probably represent the dreamer's initial feelings of emotional numbness and loneliness. If you saw the film *Akira Kurosawa's Dreams,* you will remember the segment dealing with the death of a mountain climber during a snowstorm. As he lost consciousness, the image of death appeared to him as a beautiful snow goddess who was warming him with a blanket or veil. As he sank into death, the climber glimpsed the ugly-hag face of Death when she covered his face, suffocating him. White being the Asian color of mourning, to be covered in white snow is ominous. Those of you who have read Hans Christian Andersen's story "The Ice Queen" have memories of the icicle that was plunged into the heart of the boy hero, causing him to turn cruel and forget his love for his sister and his home. Only when the icicle was melted by his sister's tears could the boy come back to his normal life.

Fairy tales, legends, and myths are full of images associating coldness and death. On a physical level, of course, this is one of the facts of death—the body grows cold gradually from the feet upward, death supposedly occurring when the chill reaches the heart. But the cold in our dreams about the dead reflects more than the physical fact of death. It speaks of how "frozen" our emotions may feel without the person we lost, how alone we feel.

Samples of Cold and Warmth in Dreams About the Dead

Disturbing dreams about the dead often include images of cold. Mary Wollstonecraft Shelley—wife of the poet, and author of *Frankenstein*—recorded a dream in her diary about trying to warm her ice-cold baby (who had been stillborn) by the fire to bring her back to life. Elena, some of whose dreams were described earlier, dreamed the night after her sweetheart suddenly died about holding him as he gradually grew colder and died in her arms. Celeste, whose daughter died in a seizure, was put in the agonizing position of learning that the crematorium was temporarily backlogged so that her child's body had to be held in a freezer vault. "How can I leave my child's body in a freezer for a whole week?" she groaned. An answer came in a kind of vision/dream of herself pushing a canoe in which her dead daughter lay onto a beautiful frozen lake.

Pleasurable dreams about the dead often include sensations of warmth. Dreamers describe the happiness of feeling the warm flesh of the person who died, enjoying the lifelike clasp of a hug, the sweetness of a kiss.

Your Dreams About Cold and Warmth

You are likely to notice a change in the dimension of coldness and warmth in your dreams during mourning. Dreams about the dead in early stages of grief often refer to an icy coldness. Don't be surprised if your dreams about the dead involve the quality of coldness at first.

These icy images will recede from your dreams about the dead as you begin to recover. In later stages of mourning, you are likely to feel the warm flesh or lips of the dead person, or be enfolded in lov-

ing embraces. These changes depict the beginning of your own return to the warmth of living, while still longing for the person who
has died.

7. Hell and Death in Dreams About the Dead

Dream Image: Personification of Death or View of Dreadful Setting

Dreamer may encounter a mysterious stranger, or a dark, dismal scene.

Frequency: Fairly common.

Response after Awake: Dreamer usually feels alarmed by a mysterious stranger, and cast down by a gloomy setting.

Traditional Personifications of Death and Hell

In the original descriptions of the afterlife, the fire and brim-
stone we have come to associate with hell were not present. The
Judeo-Christian tradition of Sheol was a place of darkness and
shadows. For ancient Greeks, Hades was an underworld where the
spirits of the dead, referred to as "shades," wandered in the half-
gloom. It was several centuries before the idea of hellfire and tor-
ture entered the depictions of life after death.

The figure of Death, too, underwent significant changes. Although he usually is personified as a male in the Western tradition,
ancient cultures sometimes portrayed Death as a devouring goddess. Death was not pictured as Satan or the Devil in earlier times.
He was more often portrayed as a "destroyer," such as the ancient
god who mowed down the living with his scythe—the shadow re-

mains in our idea of the Grim Reaper and Father Time with his sickle. Among Tibetan Buddhists, the god of death is called Yama; he is an angry god with black skin, draped in necklaces of skulls. Skeletons or skulls and crossbones usually signify death; these still occasionally appear in the dreams of modern people.

Samples of Death and Hell in Dreams About the Dead

You remember, no doubt, the dark and gloomy corridors, the black holes and black spaces we traversed in frightening dreams about the dead. The contemporary dreamer is most likely to cast his or her hell-like settings in this form. Recall how often the figure of Death is robed in black in this culture. Dreamers whose loved person has died by violence may suffer more specific hells—replays of the brutal scenes of death while they watch helplessly. Catastrophic elements that were involved in the death, such as raging fires or hurricanes or flooding waters, may become part of the dreamer's personal hell.

Your Dreams About Death and Hell

Your dreams about death and hell are probably going to take the form of darkness and the dangerous unknown, rather than of a specific figure or a fiery place. You may not dream about either death or hell at all.

Watch, however, for the dark, threatening animal or male stranger. Notice the mysterious person in dark clothing. Some dreamers cast death in the form of an ugly old crone, as did the ill child in a hospital ward who, in a vision/dream saw her touch a bony finger to the forehead of those who later died.

You need only ask yourself:

· What would death and hell look like and feel like for me?

· Have you any portions of this image in your nightmares?

You'll have no difficulty recognizing the aspects that are "hell" for you in your dreams. Paradise is more veiled.

8. The Veil in Dreams About the Dead

Dream Image:

Concrete Image of the Veil between Life and Death

Frequency: Fairly common.

Response after Awake: Varies with nature of dream, but dreamer often feels assured of an afterlife.

Y ou have seen how often a boundary—such as doors, fences, hedges, sawhorses, and other obstacles—may separate the living and the dead in dreams. The barrier may be suspended for a moment—the door opens and the dead walk in—but it always returns, if not in the dream itself, then by the dreamer's waking up. In ancient times, this border was frequently symbolized as a veil or curtain separating the living and the dead.

Traditional Symbolism of the Veil

A veil hides something; it may be used to conceal or protect. In ancient times, the fertility goddesses were depicted in veils that represented their earthy, underground, hidden nature. The veil was an attribute of the Greek goddess of the hearth, Hestia (Vesta to the Romans). In the famous dance of the seven veils, the seven gates of the underworld may have been symbolized, suggesting it was originally a sacred dance. Night, as mother of all things, has been portrayed with a veil of stars, carrying her twin sons, Death (Thanatos) and Sleep (Hypnos), the first black and the second white. In the temple in Jerusalem, the tabernacle containing the holy of holies was blocked from view by a large veil or curtain. The general idea of a veil between a deity and a commoner was that the ordinary mortal needed to be protected from the dazzling radiance of the deity. The blazing brilliance of a god or goddess unveiled might slay the viewer. The Bible says that when Moses came down from Mount Sinai with the ten commandments, the skin on his face shone so brightly that he had to cover it with a veil while he spoke to the people because they were unable to tolerate its strong light.

The action of rending veils, or parting curtains, signifies a move toward penetration of a mystery. You will see how these ancient ideas live in the the dreams and actions of modern people. Women still wear veils at major transition points in life—the white veil at marriage or confirmation, the black veil at funeral services.

Elvis Presley's Blue Drapes

Today, in secular shrines as well as in orthodox ones, curtains are used with the same idea of separating the ordinary person from the nonordinary. At Graceland, Elvis Presley's embalmed body is hidden from visitors by heavy curtains beyond which only staff are permitted. Thousands of visitors each year make pilgrimages to their idol's home, kneel and pray in the garden of remembrance, to pay homage to the singer who seems to them like a wounded god.

Samples of the Veil in Dreams About the Dead

Patricia Maybruck's Dreamcatcher Curtain

Author, dreamworker, and dear colleague Patricia Maybruck died in 1994 from cancer. A little over two weeks before her death, Pat shared with me a special dream:

> I was in my bathroom, standing next to my whirlpool bath, which was covered by a ceiling-to-floor drapery. The fabric background was silver, woven with patterns of dreamcatchers in gold thread.
> I tried to open the curtain, but it wouldn't open. I felt very frustrated. All I could get were glimpses of water and a landscape be-

*yond. There was a light back there. The light shone through a face in
the middle of one of the dreamcatchers. The face turned into the
shape and radiance of a candle flame. This dreamcatcher was in the
middle of the curtain, like a brooch.*

*Then I realized it was a real dreamcatcher, not part of the pattern. I knew all I had to do was unfasten the dreamcatcher, then the
drapery would fall open, bathing me in the radiant light from beyond.*[13]

Although it was exhausting for her to talk, Maybruck was eager to
discuss her dream, so with the help of her caretaker of the moment,
she relayed that she had several dreamcatchers hanging all around
her bed. A dreamcatcher is a device originally made by Native Americans to hang above a child's cradleboard or sleeping place. It consists of a hoop with a net woven in the space. At the very center of the
weblike net is an opening. The opening is meant to allow good
dreams to pass through, while the surrounding web is intended to
catch any bad dreams, thus preventing nightmares from reaching
the sleeping child. Many dreamworkers, responding to the symbolism, have made or bought dreamcatchers for their own use.

Of course, Maybruck herself was a "catcher of dreams," probably the lifelike face in the middle of one of the dreamcatchers,
holding herself and her family together, like a brooch. She especially liked the gold in the pattern.

The light of a candle, like that in the middle of the dreamcatcher, has long been likened to an individual life; when it is
snuffed out, the life is ended. But Maybruck's dream assured her
there was something beyond. She could glimpse water, a landscape,
and light. By letting go of her body, unfastening the dreamcatcher,
allowing the drapery to fall open, she would die to this side. Eighteen days after this dream, she stepped through to the other side,
hopefully bathed "in the radiant light from beyond."

Your Dreams About the Veil

Veils or curtains or drapes may well appear in your dreams
about the dead, separating you from the great mystery. Do you
remember Joanne's dream about her friend teaching her how to

help people die? In it, the burgundy drapes were thrown open, allowing the dead to pass through. This imagery is a typical symbol of the moment of death. In drama and literature, it is the falling of the drapes that signifies the end, the "death" of the story.

If veils, curtains, or drapes appear in your dreams about the dead, ask yourself:

- What does the veil (curtain, drape) separate me from?

- Am I ready or willing to lift the veil (curtain, drape) aside?

- Do you have any special associations to the material or color?

Lifting aside the veil reveals the light. Luminous light is the paramount characteristic people mention in their dreams of paradise.

9. The Light of Paradise and Angels in Dreams About the Dead

Dream Image:

Dreamer Encounters Enchanting Images of Light and Sound, or a Being of Light.

Frequency: Fairly common.

Response after Awake: Dreamer almost always feels blessed.

Traditional Symbolism of Paradise

Images of heaven vary as much as the cultures they arise in. For those people who dwell in desert regions, paradise is a garden overflowing with fountains, leafy trees, singing birds, luscious fruit, and sometimes lovely maidens. There are the fields of Elysium for the ancient Greeks; the palaces of Valhalla for the ancient Teutonic races; the happy hunting ground of the Native Americans. For some Christians, heaven has streets paved with gold and angels who sing songs of praise and play upon their harps.

Traditional Personifications of Angelic Beings

In earliest times, birds were the beings who conveyed the spirit of the dead to the other world. These winged creatures were probably the origin of the concept of winged angels.

We have already noted that the word "angel" means "messenger of God," derived in part from the Greek word meaning messenger, and the suffix "el," meaning "the Lord" in Hebrew. In the Bible, angels play this role of messenger extensively. Later tradition added the idea that angels had special care of the soul after death, escorting it to the celestial realms.

The idea of angels has undergone a renaissance in current Western literature and television. Such resurgences of interest and beliefs lead to more dreaming about angelic beings.

Each dreamer, as each culture, will envision his or her own heaven and own angelic form. Modern dreamers echo traditional images, depending upon their beliefs and wishes.

Two elements so consistently appear in the depictions of paradise, regardless of culture or religion, that we may sense they have some substance: the radiant light and the heavenly music. Regardless of the form heaven takes in the myth or in the dream, you can be sure there will be light and melody.

Samples of Dreams About Paradise and Angels

You saw that dreams about celestial beings were not confined to ancient times, or Roman emperors who dreamed about Jupiter. Today's dreamers see themselves encountering similar heavenly figures. Remember the woman who saw her father in the form of God? And the woman whose path was blocked by a brilliant angel? Several dreamers mentioned hearing heavenly music, "the music of the spheres." Sometimes the dreamers themselves joined in the divine songs and dances.

Dreamers occasionally describe meeting beings composed of light in their dreams about the dead. These are not specifically identified as angels, but are obviously akin to them.

Paradise for some dreamers is a sunlit rose garden, grand sylvan parks, or golden fields. Valerie, whose twin sons died after premature labor, had a beautiful dream at about the time she would have given birth at full term. It was her only dream in which a child appeared. She saw a little blond-haired boy playing softball with her husband in a meadow up on a hill. It looked "almost like heaven," so happy and peaceful. Although she still wept at her loss when she awoke, Valerie's paradise dream was a far cry from the nightmares about dying dogs and a drowned cat. The memory of this dream brought bittersweet consolation.

Your Dreams About Angelic Beings and Paradise

You are very likely to dream about the dead person you miss in an improved and even transfigured condition. You may or may not encounter angelic beings of light or celestial figures, as well, in your dreams. This depends partly on your own beliefs, but not entirely. Some dreamers who think of themselves as nonreligous have been astonished to be greeted by beings of light in their dreams about the dead.

You may wish to ask yourself:

- What would heaven look like to me? How would it feel? Sound?

- Are there any aspects of this imagery in my dreams?

The light may come to you—instead of in the form of a specific figure—as an enveloping overall radiance, the one glimpsed on the other side of the veil.

If your early dreams of grief contain images of dark, dismal places, your later ones are likely to portray the light of paradise and celestial music. The candlelight that is snuffed out with a loved one's death may become a blazing, beneficent radiance of spirit.

You have seen how often happy dreams about the dead contain images of light surrounding the deceased or glowing from their faces, hair, or clothing. This splendor seems to reflect the soul or spirit of the deceased—the spark of life that went out with the person's death, rekindled in the still-living spirit. This transcendent light emanating from the dead gives dreamers hope that their person's spirit lives in peace. You are almost certain to encounter the bright light radiating from the dead.

Or, for you, the clear light and music of paradise may suffuse the entire dream setting. You may find yourself leaving the scenes of gloom behind and walking in flower-filled gardens or sun-drenched fields, or encountering spectacular vistas from cliffs overlooking sparkling waters.

However and whenever it comes, you, too, are likely to be enveloped in the comfort of this warm, healing light. May it bring you the blessing of peace.

13.

❧

Your Personal Dream

Journey

Your dreams after the death of a significant person are a kind of
journey through grief. Although at first you may feel you are
in too much pain to give attention to dreams, if you start a record of
your dreams you may find unexpected comfort. If dream recording
seems too much effort at the moment, read through the steps described here and remember any dreams you have for future use.

Whether or not you work with your dreams at this time, you
may find the following affirmations for easing grief helpful. These
are obviously suggestions; feel free to amend them.

Eight Affirmations for Easing Grief

1. Affirmation of Attention to Dreams

You may wish to start a journal of your dreams, if you do not
already record them. Any notebook will suffice, but it is pleasant to
have one made of material that feels good to hold and is of a size

and shape to carry conveniently. Bound blank books are easy to work with, although some dreamers prefer the flexibility of three-ring binders, as they are able to later add material to earlier entries. You may want to use the same journal to record excerpts of prose or poems that you find soothing. Many people find that keeping a journal helps them traverse difficult times.

Place your journal within easy reach of your sleeping place. Some people like to take notes or record key phrases during the night on standard notepads and then transfer them, expanding as needed, to the journal during the daytime; others want to write the dream directly into the journal.

Be sure to record the date of the death of your person into your journal. It may be engraved on your memory at the moment, but that recall lessens with the years.

Each night before retiring, take a few minutes to write the date and a brief paragraph or two summarizing the events of the day. Always indicate your emotional reactions to these events. Then, in the morning or whenever convenient the next day, describe any dream you recall. Note in particular the characters, the setting, objects, and actions. Underline or otherwise mark the presence of the person who died, if he or she is in the dream. Be sure to describe the appearance of any characters.

You may not dream for some time after a death, or you may be overwhelmed with troubling dreams. In any case, record what happened and patiently proceed.

The entries in your personal journal will help you make best use of the activities and affirmations that are set forth below. These roughly parallel the topics in the chapters of this book. You may want to use your dream journal to record your version of these activities and affirmations. Each set of affirmations is meant to be repeated to yourself.

Applying the Affirmation of Attention to Dreams

1. Today, I will remain open to my dreams. I will get ready to receive dreams by having a notepad or journal and a pen or pencil beside my bed before I go to sleep. I will record the date and the main events of the day before retiring.

2. Tonight, I will welcome any dreams that come to me, without rejection. I will lovingly receive whatever dreams emerge, knowing that even distressing dreams have a healing purpose, and that all dreams can teach me.

2. Affirmation of Peaceful Well-Being

We cannot be certain of the condition of the spirit of the person who died. If positive thoughts and prayers have an effect, our images and ideas about the person may help his or her spirit to achieve a peaceful rest.

You saw in Chapter 2, "I'm Suffering" and "I'm O.K.," how many survivors have tormenting dreams that the person who died is still suffering. We know that this kind of nightmare, if it occurs, is most likely soon after a death, especially one that has been painful, traumatic, or violent. It often leaves the dreamer feeling that the soul of the departed is not at peace.

If you should be troubled by such a dream there are things you can do, in addition to seeking emotional or spiritual support.

You can begin by visualizing the person who died as being happy and well in some other dimension. Find a photograph of the person from better times, or if this is unavailable, find some memento that feels connected to that person. Focus on the photograph or touch the memento. Close your eyes and for a few minutes see the person doing things he or she loved to do. See him or her having fun, joyful. Imagine the person vividly and sense his or her happiness.

Now surround your person with your love. Picture that he or she can feel your continued loving care. Let your love radiate and reach your person wherever he or she is. Send your person well-being and peace.

If you sense that the spirit of your person is uneasy, is there any reasonable action you could undertake that might bring comfort to his or her troubled soul?

Even doing something that seems silly can bring relief. One widow whose husband had had a severe drinking problem was distressed for the first nine days after his death by nightmares in which he demanded drink from her. Finally, feeling slightly foolish, she poured a glass of vodka, covered the top of it with a slice of bread, and left it on the kitchen counter. As the liquid evaporated, she added more. Her nightmares ceased, and at the end of the first year after her husband's death, she held a remembrance dinner during which she poured out the liquid permanently.

Most religions provide special prayers for the peace of the departed soul. Even if you do not follow the religious belief, you may find it comforting to locate such prayers, or express your version, and to light a candle for the person who is gone.

Applying the Affirmation of Peaceful Well-Being

1. Today, for at least five minutes, I will picture the person who died as being happy and well in some other dimension. I will vividly see my person doing what he or she loved to do, or would have loved to do. I will surround my person with loving thoughts and imagine him or her radiantly healthy, joyful, and able to sense my love. If appropriate, I will picture myself holding, rocking, soothing, and comforting my person.

2. I will find a poem, prayer, or piece of writing that makes me feel peaceful, reread it three times to myself, and record it in my journal. If I wish, I will read it aloud, with the realization that perhaps it may be heard by the spirit of my person.

3. I will compile a list of actions that would ease any troubled feelings of the person who died. I will consider whether I can reasonably undertake any of these actions—even simple ones—and if so, do them on behalf of my person.

3. Affirmation of Saying Goodbye

Saying goodbye to a loved one is difficult. Use this affirmation only when you feel ready.

Many people's grief is increased by a feeling of not having been able to say goodbye, especially in cases of sudden death. By using this affirmation, we allow ourselves to say the things we would have wished to say in person.

Think over all the unsaid things you want to communicate to the deceased. These may include the reasons you loved having him or her in your life, the things about the person you will miss. Depending on your relationship with the deceased, you may wish to express anger, resentment, or fear. Each unexpressed feeling needs to find form. You will want to include a statement of gratitude for having had the person in your life. Whether your attachment was deeply loving or fiercely ambivalent, the deceased played a pivotal role in who you are today. You learned from your relationship with him or her, and can offer thanks for that.

Applying the Affirmation of Saying Goodbye

1. Today, I will write a farewell letter to the person who died, just as if it were possible for him or her to receive it. I will convey my feelings of love or pain to my person. I will tell why he or she was important in my life, and what I will miss. I will thank the deceased for whatever I feel genuinely grateful for. I will express appreciation for learning from him or her. Having described all my feelings, I will wish the deceased well on his or her journey. I will say my goodbye, knowing that we—in spirit—may touch again.

2. I may prefer to have this exchange in an imaginary conversation. If so, I will prepare for this by making a list of the reasons I cared for the deceased, any grudges or fears I hold toward him or her, and what I have to be grateful for as a result of our relationship. Then, in my imagination, I will picture the deceased seated in a chair facing me, and I will communicate all my feelings about him or her. Finally, I will wish the deceased well. I may wish to embrace my person before ending this visualization, saying goodbye for now.

4. Affirmation of Accomplishing Desires

We grieve in part because there is nothing we can do to restore the lost life. Yet, by our willingness to act on behalf of the person who died, we impart continued vitality to his or her desires and wishes.

A death often leaves behind unfulfilled goals. You, as survivor, may be able to accomplish some of the dead person's goals. Although the deceased can no longer directly achieve them, by your actions you may indirectly achieve the goals for him or her.

One mother who was nearly destroyed by the suicide of her novelist son at age thirty-one made strenuous efforts to get his manuscript published and finally succeeded. Eventually, the novel was posthumously awarded the Pulitzer Prize.[1]

When we are steeped in grief, acting to further our own careers or to complete significant goals may seem worthless without the presence of the significant person who is no longer alive. Yet when we choose actions that are of value to our own work, we may not only ease our grief for a period of time but also make progress toward goals that would have brought satisfaction to the deceased had he or she lived.

Applying the Affirmation of Accomplishing Desires

I put the affirmation of *indirect* accomplishment into effect by deciding:

1. I will compile a list of at least three goals the deceased had that would have brought pleasure or pride had he or she lived.
2. Today, I will devote at least one half hour to actions that will further one of these goals.
3. At the end of my work period, I will spend five minutes picturing how the deceased would feel about progress on his or her goal. (The deceased's reaction will usually be positive.) I will see the deceased as aware of my efforts and pleased with them.

I put the affirmation of *direct* accomplishment into effect by deciding:

1. I will compile a list of my accomplishments since the death of my significant person. In the margin I will mark those that I loved achieving. These might include promotions,

prizes, success in career, relationships, development of skills, and the birth of new children or grandchildren. If there have been no goals completed since the person died, I will compile a list of those things I intend to work on that I love to do.

2. Today, I will focus for a certain period of time on my personal work. This does not mean that I forget the dead person, rather that I realize my work is for his or her benefit as well as my own.

3. At the end of my work period, I will allot at least five minutes to imagining how the dead person would react. This does not always mean that he or she would approve of or appreciate my work. I may need to show the dead person that I am capable of accomplishing things that he or she thought were impossible for me. If there is no appreciation to visualize, I may still be able to picture new respect from him or her. However, I may be able to imagine my person as very appreciative of my efforts.

5. Affirmation of Forgiveness

Being able to forgive those who have injured us is important for our health and well-being. Forgiveness can prevent damage to our bodies and emotions. Anger and resentment harm us more than the dead person we resent, making us irritable and wasting our energy. By forgiving, we free ourselves for the joy of life. We may still feel bitter over damage that he or she has done, but we can begin to release it by accepting that whatever happened is over and in this case cannot happen again.

If the person who died held anger or resentment toward us, we need to admit any wrongdoing on our part and forgive ourselves.

Applying the Affirmation of Forgiveness

I begin the process of forgiving by making these commitments:

1. I will spend five minutes having an imaginary conversation with the dead person against whom I hold some resentment.

I will explain what my complaints are, naming the resentments and fears. I recall when these took place, where, and what the behaviors were, as well as my responses. I recognize how my resentments and fears have affected my life. I will acknowledge to the deceased that I am thankful to him or her for having the chance to learn forgiveness.

2. In my imaginary exchange with the dead person I will tell him or her, "No matter how you hurt me, I will not continue to hurt myself because of you. I forgive you." I will remember that the person who injured me is not the same as the injury itself; his or her behavior might have been wrong, but the person was more than that behavior. I keep in mind that there may be a possibility for the spirit of the person to improve. I let go of the power this dead person has to make me suffer. I forgive.

I begin the process of asking forgiveness by these commitments:

1. I will make a list of at least three of my wrong actions toward the deceased. I make no excuses, alibis, or justifications. I am willing to make amends. I choose one of these misdeeds and plan how to make restitution, if possible, without hurting others. Gradually, I will make amends for each wrong action, if I can.

2. I will write a letter to the deceased, or have an imaginary conversation with him or her, in which I accept responsibility for what I did. I will tell the person, "I'm sorry I hurt you. I regret my actions. Please forgive me." I will forgive myself for the harm I did, restoring inner calm and peace.

6. Affirmation of Inheritance and Legacy

We always inherit something from the person who died. The inheritance may be traits or behaviors that we like or ones we detest. Consider what the three outstanding characteristics—positive and negative—of the deceased are.

Dreamers' answers about positive qualities often include being loving, tender, thoughtful, generous, reliable, artistic, talented, hardworking, intellectual, vigorous, or spiritual. Consider why you needed to contact any of these positive energies at this time. Are any of these qualities missing from your current life situation? Do you desire them now? If so, how can you bring more of the quality into your present life?

Dreamers' answers about negative qualities may include being angry, irrational, vulgar, frustrated, weak, domineering, impatient, cold, withholding, overemotional, moody, undeveloped, unreliable, or cruel. Are some of these negative characteristics present in your current life, and undesired? How can you reduce, eliminate, or transform them?

These very traits may be the ones we pass on as a legacy to our children and friends. Are they ones we want to leave others when our turn to die comes?

If there is an afterlife, and those we have known are there to greet us, their faults are likely to be lessened, their virtues enhanced, and their physical limitations vanished.

Applying the Affirmation of Inheritance and Legacy

1. I will make a list of the three most positive qualities of the deceased. I will consider whether any of these qualities are also characteristics of mine. If so, I will contemplate how I may support them in my life. If not, I will consider how to develop them.
2. I will write down the three most negative characteristics of the deceased. I will consider whether I retain any of these qualities. If so, I will consider how best to reduce them in my life. If not, I will guard myself against developing them.
3. I will make a list of all the gifts I received from the deceased, focusing on emotional and spiritual "gifts," things I have learned from the person. In an imaginary exchange with the deceased, I will express appreciation for all the good things he or she has brought into my life.
4. I will consider what of myself I want to leave as a legacy and will guide my behavior so as to make that possible. I will decide what parts of myself to toss into the pool of life.

7. Affirmation of Understanding Symbols

If you have been keeping a dream journal, you will have gathered several dream symbols that may be relevant to your grief. When you feel ready, the material in Chapter 12 will help you grasp the symbolism in your images. Meanwhile, it may be useful to work with this affirmation.

1. Today, I will attempt to understand the meaning of a specific image in my dreams. I will ask myself questions about it, defining it clearly, differentiating it from all other things that are similar. I will observe carefully my answers, and look for the parallel between my feelings and the dream image.
2. I will imagine the deceased in some other form. If the person were a tree, what kind of tree would he or she be? If the person were a bird, what kind of bird would he or she be? If the person were a mammal, what kind of mammal would he or she be? In each case I will consider why I chose that particular tree, bird, or mammal. I will notice whether any of my images resemble images in my dreams. I will be patient, knowing that understanding of my personal dream symbol language may come slowly.

8. Affirmation of Remembrance

Rituals of remembrance are important in every society, primitive and modern. You may choose to follow the rituals provided in your religious group, or you may wish to compose a personal ritual.

The main purpose of such rituals is to remember the dead and to honor them. Any way that feels right to you is acceptable. Some people like to perform rituals on birthdays or special anniversaries, such as wedding dates, date of death, or other significant times for the deceased. The ritual may be as simple as lighting a candle and telling a fond story about the deceased.

For some people, a formal memorial service is more meaningful. Survivors have made concrete gifts, such as donating a wing at a hospital, giving money to a charitable organization in honor of the person who died, or otherwise honoring his or her memory. Everything from planting a special bush to commissioning a portrait or statue may be done.

Many innovative methods of honoring the dead have emerged. Making a patchwork quilt from the dead person's clothes, the AIDS quilt, memorial groves in parks. The method and the expense are less important than the wish to remember and honor the deceased.

Applying the Affirmation of Remembrance

1. Today, I will set aside special time to remember the deceased. In any way that satisfies me, I will recall the person who died and dwell upon his or her being.
2. I will plan a way to more permanently honor the memory of my person.

These affirmations may be practiced for a period of thirty to forty days. Thereafter, they may be better used for special occasions and as needed.

We honor the dead in our dreams and in our deeds. We cherish their gifts to us, and try to live so as to give generously to those who follow. May we meet again.

Notes

CHAPTER 1: THE JOURNEY OF THE DREAM MESSENGER

1. Elisabeth Kübler-Ross, *Death: The Final Stage of Growth* (New York: Simon & Schuster, 1975).
2. See, for instance, Judy Tatelbaum, *The Courage to Grieve* (New York: Harper & Row, 1980); J. William Worden, *Grief Counseling and Grief Therapy* (New York: Springer, 1991).
3. Some exceptions are Verena Kast, *A Time to Mourn* (Stuttgart: Daimon Verlag, 1982); Alexandra Kennedy, *Losing a Parent* (San Francisco: HarperCollins, 1991); Marie-Louise von Franz, *On Dreams and Death* (Boston: Shambhala, 1986).
4. Descriptions of the phases of grief can be found in books by several authors, including John W. James and Frank Cherry, *The Grief Recovery Handbook* (New York: Harper & Row, 1988); Kübler-Ross, *Death*; Carol Staudacher, *Beyond Grief* (Oakland, Calif.: New Harbinger, 1987); Worden, *Grief Counseling*.
5. Worden, *Grief Counseling*.
6. Joseph Campbell, *The Hero with a Thousand Faces,* Princeton: Princeton University Press, 1968.
7. Deirdre Barrett, "Through a Glass Darkly: Images of the Dead in Dreams," *Omega: Journal of Death and Dying,* 24 (1992): 97–108.
8. D. Scott Rogo and R. Bayless, *Phone Calls from the Dead* (New York: Berkeley, 1979).
9. Patricia Garfield, *The Healing Power of Dreams* (New York: Simon & Schuster, 1991).
10. Sigmund Freud, *Mourning and Melancholia,* in *Sigmund Freud: Collected Papers,* edited by Joan Riviere, vol. 4 (New York: Basic Books, 1959).
11. Barrett, "Through a Glass Darkly."
12. Edgar Allan Poe, "Annabel Lee," in Hazel Felleman, ed., *The Best-Loved Poems of the American People* (New York: Garden City Publishing Co., 1936).

13. Kenneth Silverman, *Edgar A. Poe* (New York: Harper Perennial, 1991). Poe's young wife and cousin, Virginia Clemm, was only thirteen to his twenty-five when they wed in 1836. She became seriously ill in 1841. After her death in 1847, Poe was devastated, and his inclination toward morbidity grew worse.

CHAPTER 2: "I'M SUFFERING" AND "I'M O.K."

1. Described in Rosalind Cartwright and Lynne Lamberg, *Crisis Dreaming* (New York: Harper Perennial, 1993), pp. 83, 89.
2. Ibid, p. 83.
3. Kevin Fagan, "Lasting Pain for Victim's Families," *San Francisco Chronicle,* February 19, 1996, p. 1.
4. The Compassionate Friends is an organization that has helped many parents who have lost a child. This large self-help group with more than 650 local U.S. and Canadian chapters can be reached at P.O. Box 3696, Oak Brook, Ill. 69522; (708) 990–0010. They give national and regional conferences, have a newsletter, and offer books and tapes.
5. Aurelio Rojas, "Lingering Nightmare of 101 California," *San Francisco Chronicle,* September 24, 1993.
6. Ibid.
7. Ibid.
8. Anonymous poem from author's collection.
9. Alice Evans, originally published in *Fireweeed,* April 1990.
10. Definitions of Greek names come from Anthony S. Mercatante, *The Facts on File Encyclopedia of World Mythology and Legend* (New York: Facts on File, 1988).
11. Cartwright and Lamberg, *Crisis Dreaming,* p. 88.
12. Ibid, pp. 88–89.
13. Nancy's story was originally published in *Fate* 46, no. 5 (May 1993).
14. Brenda Shaw. Shaw's poem was first published in *Voices International* 26 (1991): no. 2.

CHAPTER 3: "I'M NOT REALLY DEAD" AND "GOODBYE"

1. Maggie Callanan and Patricia Kelley, *Final Gifts* (New York: Bantam, 1993).
2. Marie-Louise von Franz, *On Dreams and Death* (Boston: Shambhala, 1986).
3. Verena Kast, *A Time to Mourn: Growing Through the Grief Process* (Stuttgart: Daimon Verlag, 1982).

4. Kelly Bulkeley, *Spiritual Dreaming* (New York: Paulist Press, 1995), p. 113.
5. Von Franz, *On Dreams and Death,* pp. 111–12.

CHAPTER 4: "YOU FOOL!" AND "CONGRATULATIONS"

1. Kelly Bulkeley, *Spiritual Dreaming* (New York: Paulist Press, 1995), p. 9.
2. Joyce Brothers, *Widowed* (New York: Simon & Schuster, 1990), pp. 187–88.
3. Nigel Nicolson and Joanne Trautmann, eds., *The Letters of Virginia Woolf, Vol. 1, 1888–1912* (New York: Harvest/HBJ, 1975), p. 325.
4. Paul Tholey, "A Model for Lucidity Training as a Means of Self-Healing and Psychological Growth," in Jayne Gackenbach and Stephen LaBerge, eds., *Conscious Mind, Sleeping Brain* (New York, Plenum Press, 1988), p. 265.
5. Ibid, p. 265.
6. Ibid, pp. 265–75.
7. Ibid, p. 265.
8. Quoted in Robin Larsen, ed., *Emanuel Swedenborg: A Continuing Vision: A Pictorial Biography and Anthology of Essays and Poetry* (New York: Swedenborg Foundation, 1988), p. 35.
9. Quoted in Kelly Bulkeley, *Spiritual Dreaming,* p. 10.
10. Ibid., p. 7.

CHAPTER 5: "YOU'LL BE SORRY" AND "HERE'S A GIFT"

1. Madison Smartt Bell, "William T. Vollman," in *The New York Times Magazine,* February 6, 1994, page 20.
2. Ibid., p. 20.
3. Ibid., p. 21.
4. Ibid., p. 18.
5. Suetonius, *The Twelve Caesars,* translated by Robert Graves (Harmondsworth, Middlesex, England: Penguin Books, 1980), p. 205.
6. Ibid.
7. Ibid., p. 207.
8. A helpful resource is by Friends in Recovery, *The Twelve Steps: A Way Out* (San Diego: Recovery Publications, 1987).
9. Alice Evans, originally published in *Fireweed,* April 1990.
10. Ibid.
11. Ibid.
12. Ibid.

13. Paul Skenazy, "A Poet's Dreams of His Dead Father" (review of Li-Young Lee's *The Winged Seed* [New York: Simon & Schuster, 1995]), in *San Francisco Sunday Examiner & Chronicle,* March 5, 1995.

14. Isabel Allende, *Paula,* translated by Margaret Sayers Peden (New York: HarperCollins, 1995), p. 276.

15. Ibid.

16. Sam Whiting, "Listening to the Voices of Ghosts," article on Carol Edgarian in *San Francisco Chronicle,* April 25, 1994.

17. Dante, account from Dorothy Sayers's introduction to Dante's *Divine Comedy,* Penguin edition, as quoted in Carol Neiman and Emily Goldman, *Afterlife* (Harmondsworth, Middlesex, England: Viking Penguin, 1994), pp. 71–72.

Chapter 6: "Stop!" and "Go Ahead!"

1. Verena Kast, *A Time to Mourn: Growing Through the Grief Process* (Stuttgart: Daimon Verlag, 1982).

2. Alan Siegel, *Dreams That Can Change Your Life* (Los Angeles: Jeremy P. Tarcher, 1990), p. 5.

3. From author's collection, quoted in *Women's Bodies, Women's Dreams* (New York: Ballantine, 1988).

Chapter 7: "Join Me!" and "Your Turn Is Coming"

1. Michael Ryan, "It's Just Not Enough to Be a Survivor," *Parade* magazine, *The San Francisco Sunday Examiner & Chronicle,* December 4, 1994, pp. 4–5.

2. Marlo Thomas, as quoted by Michael Ryan, "It's Just Not Enough," p. 4.

3. Ibid., p. 5.

4. George L. Engel, "The Death of a Twin: Mourning and Anniversary Reactions; Fragments of 10 Years of Self-Analysis," *International Journal of Psycho-Analysis* 56 (1975): 23–40.

5. Quoted in Kelly Bulkeley, *Spiritual Dreaming* (New York: Paulist Press, 1995), p. 8. Matilde's dream was reported to anthropologist Lydia Dagarrod.

6. Described in author's book *The Healing Power of Dreams* (New York: Simon & Schuster, 1991), p. 299.

7. Sigmund Freud, *Mourning and Melancholia, Sigmund Freud: Collected Papers,* edited by Joan Riviere, vol. 4 (New York: Basic Books, 1959).

8. Stith Thompson, *The Folktale* (Berkeley: University of California Press, 1977), p. 256 (motif E215).

9. According to vital statistics reported in *The World Almanac and Book of Facts 1996,* Robert Famaghetti, ed. (Mahwah, N.J.: World Almanac Books, 1995), p. 974.

10. Karlis Osis and Erlendur Haraldsson, *At the Hour of Death* (New York: Avon, 1977).

11. Maggie Callanan and Patricia Kelley, *Final Gifts* (New York: Bantam, 1993).

12. Drawn from ibid., pp. 90–100.

13. Quoted in Brian Hill, compiler, *Such Stuff as Dreams* (London: Rupert Hart-Davis, 1967), pp. 15–16.

14. Brian Hill attributes the dream to Rev. John Coleridge (1719–1781).

15. Quoted in Brian Hill, *Such Stuff as Dreams,* pp. 23–24.

16. Ibid., pp. 28–29.

17. Suetonius, *The Twelve Caesars,* translated by Robert Graves. (Harmondsworth, Middlesex, England: Penguin Books, 1980), p. 42.

18. Ibid., p. 42.

19. Ibid., p. 158.

20. Jean Strouse, *Alice James: A Biography* (New York: Houghton Mifflin, 1980), p. 313. The two dead people in her dream were close women friends who died in the late 1880s.

21. As retold by Adrienne Quinn, in *Dreams of History That Came True* (Tacoma, Wash.: Dream Research, 1987), pp. 165–66.

CHAPTER 9: "I'M EVOLVING" AND "I'M BEING REBORN"

1. When the Fifth Ecumenical Council was convened in A.D. 553 by the Emperor Justinian, several earlier accepted teachings were ruled to be an "anathema," including all teachings that suggested the pre-existence of the soul in any form. Carol Neiman and Emily Goldman, *Afterlife* (Harmondsworth, Middlesex, England: Viking Penguin, 1994), p. 89.

2. Beverly Kedzierski, "The Representation of Death in My Dreams," *Lucidity Letter* 4 (1985): 20–30.

CHAPTER 10: "AVENGE MY MURDER" AND "I GIVE YOU LIFE"

1. The question of whether dreams are acceptable evidence in court is at issue. See Carol Ruppreht and Whitney Ruppreht, "Dreams and the Law," *ASD Newsletter* 12, Fall/Winter (1995): 13–15.

2. Based on the accounts given in Brian Hill, *Such Stuff as Dreams* (London: Rupert Hart-Davis, 1967), pp. 84–85, and retold by Adrienne

Quinn, *Dreams of History That Came True* (Tacoma, Wash.: Dream Research, 1987), pp. 206–11.

3. Quoted in ibid., p. 209.
4. Based on the account given in Quinn, *Dreams of History,* pp. 201–2.
5. Quoted in ibid., p. 201.
6. Based on account given by Anthony Jewell, "Why Daughter Turned Mom In," *San Francisco Chronicle,* August 5, 1994.
7. This account is based entirely on a presentation Claire Sylvia gave to the Association for the Study of Dreams, in Leiden, July 1994, and three television shows in which she and I appeared on the same program: NBC's *The Other Side,* aired November 17, 1994; ABC's *Good Morning America,* aired the week of February 1, 1995; and NBC's *The Secret World of Dreams,* aired May 12, 1995.
8. *Change of Heart,* to be published by Little, Brown in 1997.

CHAPTER 11: "I'LL ALWAYS LOVE YOU" AND "HI! HOW ARE YOU?"

1. Quoted in George MacDonald, trans., *Novalis: Hymns to the Night: Spiritual Songs,* Foreword by Sergei O. Prokofieff (London: Temple Lodge, 1992). Quotation in Afterword by William Webb, p. 56.
2. Quoted in ibid., p. 4.
3. Quoted in ibid., p. 12.
4. Dave Jenneson, "With My Brother Again," *Dream Network Bulletin,* January/February 1989, p. 11.
5. Ibid.
6. Ibid., p. 14.
7. David Jenneson and Alan Hovden, *The Shadow of the Rock,* registered with PROCAN, 1985.
8. This account of Dante's relationship with Beatrice and his dreams about her is based on Dante Alighieri, *La Vita Nuova,* Barbara Reynolds, translation and Introduction (Harmondsworth, Middlesex, England: Penguin Books, 1969).
9. Ibid., p. 99.

CHAPTER 12: NINE MAJOR SYMBOLS IN DREAMS ABOUT THE DEAD

1. Gordon Livingston, *Only Spring: On Mourning the Death of My Son* (San Francisco: HarperSan Francisco, 1995).
2. Ibid., p. 111.
3. Ibid., p. 151.
4. Ibid., p. 230.
5. Mary Winslow, personal communication, 1995.

6. Jackson's dying words are quoted in slight variation by different sources. Bergen Evans, in his *Dictionary of Quotations,* gives, "Let us cross the river and rest in the shade." Bartlett's *Fimiliar Quotations* gives, "Let us cross over the river, and rest under the trees."

7. Beth Witrogen McLeod, "The Caregivers," *San Francisco Sunday Examiner and Chronicle,* April 9, 1995.

8. Ibid., p. A-17.

9. Dinitia Smith, "It's . . . Liam Neeson," *The New York Times Magazine,* December 4, 1994, pp. 69–71.

10. Isabel Allende, *Paula,* translated by Margaret Sayers Peden (New York: HarperCollins, 1995).

11. Ibid., pp. 71–72.

12. Isabel Allende, personal communication, 1995.

13. Patricia Maybruck, personal communication, October 5, 1994. Maybruck was the author of *Pregnancy and Dreams* (Los Angeles: Jeremy P. Tarcher, 1989) and other works on dreams.

CHAPTER 13: YOUR PERSONAL DREAM JOURNEY

1. Edward Guthmann, "An Innocent Abroad," in *San Francisco Chronicle,* July 7, 1996. John Kennedy Toole was awarded a posthumous Pulitzer Prize in 1981 for his *A Confederacy of Dunces.* An earlier novel is *The Neon Bible.*

Bibliography

Allende, Isabel. *Paula*. Translated by Margaret Sayers Peden. New York: HarperCollins, 1995.

Barrett, Deirdre. "Through a Glass Darkly: Images of the Dead in Dreams." *Omega: Journal of Death and Dying* 24 (1991–1992): 97–101.

Bell, Madison Smartt. "William T. Vollman." *The New York Times Magazine,* February 6, 1994.

Brothers, Joyce. *Widowed.* New York: Simon & Schuster, 1990.

Bulkeley, Kelly. *Spiritual Dreaming.* New York: Paulist Press, 1995.

Callanan, Maggie, and Patricia Kelley. *Final Gifts.* New York: Bantam, 1993.

Campbell, Joseph. *The Hero with a Thousand Faces.* Princeton: Princeton University Press, 1968.

Cartwright, Rosalind, and Lynne Lamberg. *Crisis Dreaming.* New York: Harper Perennial, 1993.

Dante Alighieri. *La Vita Nuova.* Barbara Reynolds, translation and Introduction. Harmondsworth, Middlesex, England: Penguin Books, 1969. ·

Engel, George L. "The Death of a Twin: Mourning and Anniversary Reactions: Fragments of 10 Years of Self-Analysis." *International Journal of Psycho-Analysis* 56 (1975): 23–40.

Evans, Alice. "Grandfather Eagle." *Fireweed,* April, 1990.

Fagan, Kevin. "Lasting Pain for Victim's Families." *San Francisco Chronicle,* February 19, 1996, p. 1.

Famaghetti, Robert, ed. *The World Almanac and Book of Facts 1996.* Mahwah, N.J.: World Almanac Books, 1995.

Freud, Sigmund. *Mourning and Melancholia* (1917). In Joan Riviere, ed., *Sigmund Freud: Collected Papers,* vol. 4. New York: Basic Books, 1959.

Friends in Recovery. *The Twelve Steps: A Way Out.* San Diego: Recovery Publications, 1987.

Garfield, Patricia. *Women's Bodies, Women's Dreams.* New York: Ballantine, 1988.

Garfield, Patricia. *The Healing Power of Dreams.* New York: Simon & Schuster, 1991.

Garfield, Patricia. *Creative Dreaming.* New York: Simon & Schuster, 1995.

Guthmann, Edward. "An Innocent Abroad" (an article on work of John Kennedy Toole). *San Francisco Chronicle,* July 9, 1996.

Hill, Brian, compiler. *Such Stuff as Dreams.* London: Rupert Hart-Davis, 1967.

James, John W., and Frank Cherry. *The Grief Recovery Handbook.* New York: Harper & Row, 1988.

Jenneson, Dave. "With My Brother Again," *Dream Network Bulletin,* January/February 1989, p. 11.

Jewell, Anthony. "Why Daughter Turned Mom In." *San Francisco Chronicle,* August 5, 1994.

Kast, Verena. *A Time to Mourn: Growing Through the Grief Process.* Stuttgart: Daimon Verlag, 1982.

Kedzierski, Beverly. "The Representation of Death in My Dreams." *Lucidity Letter* 4 (1985): 28–30.

Kennedy, Alexandra. *Losing a Parent.* San Francisco: HarperCollins, 1991.

Kübler-Ross, Elisabeth. *Death: The Final Stage of Growth.* New York: Simon & Schuster, 1975.

Larsen, Robin, ed. *Emanuel Swedenborg: A Continuing Vision; a Pictorial Biography and Anthology of Essays and Poetry.* New York: Swedenborg Foundation, 1988.

Leach, Maria, ed. *Standard Dictionary of Folklore, Mythology, and Legend* (2 vols.). New York: Funk & Wagnalls, 1949.

Livingston, Gordon. *Only Spring: On Mourning the Death of My Son.* San Francisco: HarperSan Francisco, 1995.

MacDonald, George, trans. *Novalis: Hymns to the Night: Spiritual Songs.* Foreword by Sergei O. Prokofieff, Afterword by William Webb. London: Temple Lodge, 1992.

McLeod, Beth Witrogen. "The Caregivers." *San Francisco Sunday Examiner and Chronicle,* April 9, 1995.

Maybruck, Patricia. *Pregnancy and Dreams.* Los Angeles: Jeremy P. Tarcher, 1989.

Mercatante, Anthony S. *The Facts on File Encyclopedia of World Mythology and Legend.* New York: Facts on File, 1988.

Neiman, Carol, and Emily Goldman. *Afterlife.* Harmondsworth, Middlesex, England: Viking Penguin, 1994.

Nicolson, Nigel, and Joanne Trautmann, eds. *The Letters of Virginia Woolf, Vol. 1, 1888–1912.* New York: Harvest/HBJ, 1975.

Osis, Karlis, and Erlendur Haraldsson. *At the Hour of Death.* New York: Avon, 1977.

Poe, Edgar Allan. "Annabel Lee." In Hazel Felleman, ed., *The Best-Loved Poems of the American People.* New York: Garden City Publishing, 1936.

Quinn, Adrienne, reteller. *Dreams of History That Came True.* Tacoma, Wash.: Dream Research, 1987.

Rogo, D. Scott, and R. Bayless. *Phone Calls from the Dead.* New York: Berkeley Books, 1979.

Rojas, Aurelio. "Lingering Nightmare of 101 California." *San Francisco Chronicle,* September 24, 1993.

Rupprecht, Carol, and Whitney Rupprecht. "Dreams and the Law." Association for the Study of Dreams Newsletter 12, Fall/Winter (1995): 13–15.

Ryan, Michael. "It's Just Not Enough to Be a Survivor." *Parade* magazine, *The San Francisco Sunday Examiner & Chronicle,* December 4, 1994, pp. 4–5.

Shaw, Brenda. Poem. *Voices International* 26 (1991): no. 2.

Siegel, Alan. *Dreams That Can Change Your Life.* Los Angeles: Jeremy P. Tarcher, 1990.

Silverman, Kenneth. *Edgar A. Poe.* New York: HarperPerennial, 1991.

Skenazy, Paul. "A Poet's Dreams of His Dead Father" (review of Li-Young Lee's *The Winged Seed* [New York: Simon & Schuster, 1995]). *San Francisco Sunday Examiner & Chronicle,* March 5, 1995.

Smith, Dinitia. "It's . . . Liam Neeson." *The New York Times Magazine,* December 4, 1994, pp. 69–71.

Staudacher, Carol. *Beyond Grief.* Oakland, Calif.: New Harbinger, 1987.

Strouse, Jean. *Alice James.* Boston: Houghton Mifflin, 1980.

Suetonius. *The Twelve Caesars,* translated by Robert Graves. Harmondsworth, Middlesex, England: Penguin Books, 1980.

Tatelbaum, Judy. *The Courage to Grieve.* New York: Harper & Row, 1980.

Tholey, Paul. "A Model for Lucidity Training as a Means of Self-Healing and Psychological Growth." In Jayne Gackenbach and Stephen LaBerge, eds., *Conscious Mind, Sleeping Brain*. New York: Plenum Press, 1988.

Thompson, Stith. *The Folktale*. Berkeley: University of California Press, 1977.

von Franz, Marie-Louise. *On Dreams and Death*. Boston: Shambhala, 1986.

Whiting, Sam. "Listening to the Voices of Ghosts" (article on Carol Edgarian). *San Francisco Chronicle,* April 25, 1994.

Worden, J. William. *Grief Counseling and Grief Therapy*. New York: Springer, 1991.

Index

About the Author

Patricia Garfield, Ph.D., is a worldwide authority on dreams. A clinical psychologist who graduated summa cum laude from Temple University, in Philadelphia, she has been studying dreams professionally for more than twenty-five years.

Dr. Garfield's *Creative Dreaming* is considered a classic in the field. A bestseller when it was first published, in 1974, it has been in print continuously ever since and has appeared in eleven foreign languages.

The author and illustrator of *Pathway to Ecstasy: The Way of the Dream Mandala*, Dr. Garfield also wrote *Your Child's Dreams; Women's Bodies, Women's Dreams;* and *The Healing Power of Dreams.*

Dr. Garfield lectures and teaches around the world and frequently appears on radio and television. Her work has also been described in major magazines, including *People, Harper's Magazine, Woman's Day, Reader's Digest, Psychology Today, Family Circle, Parents, Shape,* and *New Age.*

She has served as a dream consultant for national corporations and publications and was one of the founders of the international organization the Association for the Study of Dreams.

Dr. Garfield lives with her husband, a psychotherapist, in San Francisco.